# Hustlers, Escorts, And Porn Stars

The Insider's Guide
To Male Prostitution
In America

Matt Adams
Insider's Guide

First Printing August, 1998
Second Printing December 1998 with corrections and modest changes.
Second Edition June 1999 Re-edited and revised

Credits:
Front Cover Model: Joey Hart
Cover Photo: Copyright © 1998 Captured by Code Studios
http://www.caturedbycode.com
Cover designed by Mirage Studios, Inc.  http://www.miragestudios.com
Back Cover Model: Matt Adams  Photographer: Carlo Roncancio

**Publisher's Cataloging-in-Publication**

Adams, Matt, 1958-
      Hustlers, escorts and porn stars: the insider's guide to male
prostitution in America / Matt Adams – 2nd ed.

      p. cm.
      ISBN 0-9665796-2-3
      1.    Male prostitution--United States.  2. Gay men--Sexual Behavior.
      I. Title.

HQ144.A33  1999                              306.74'3'0973
                                             LCCN: 99-61505

Dedicated to
Ben,
Orson, Patches, and Sophia
Until death did we part.


And


Rob,
The dogs, the cats, the birds, and the fish
Who make each day wonderful.

# Table of Contents

How Elite Escorts Choose Sponsors•The Life of An Elite
Escort•Developing a Relationship with an Elite Escort•The Cost
of an Elite Escort

Getting Discovered•Class Structure•Industry Leaders•Scum•The
Escort and the Adult Industry•Working in the Industry
•Difficulties on Set•Porn Stars as Escorts

The Bisexual Market•Male Escorts for Women•Bodybuilders
•Transgender•Tandems•S&M

How to Identify a Top Quality Escort•Marketing and
Advertising•Professionalism•How the Top Escorts Screen Their
Clients•Business Practices of the Top Escorts•How the Top
Escorts Run Their Personal Lives

Types of Clients•Client Expectations•How an Escort Screens
Clients•Things a Prospective Client Should Not Say•The Use of
an Agency•The Use of Search Services•What a Client Can
Expect to Pay

Public Policy•Public Safety and Public Policy•High Risk
Activities•Legal Penalties•Legalization of Prostitution

## Foreword

I decided to write this book because I realized there was not a book that comprehensively described the male prostitution market. The book started as a series of interviews with many of the top male escorts. As the book progressed, I realized the market for male prostitution was far more complicated than I had imagined. There are many market niches that interact in many ways. Male prostitution is a very complicated market where the participants range from the very unscrupulous to the very professional.

**Hustlers, Escorts, and Porn Stars** has wide appeal for individuals with an interest in the male prostitution market. It is a detailed overview of an underground culture. The book deals extensively with issues of sexuality, why individuals become male prostitutes, and why clients use male prostitutes. This book would be of interest to psychologists, social science teachers, and makers of public policy.

This book exposes the inner workings of the male prostitution market in the United States. This book provides an inside glimpse into the business practices of escorts, and how clients find escorts. This book is the reference manual for anyone who studies male prostitution in the United States.

This is the third printing and second edition for Hustlers, Escorts, and Porn Stars. I have taken into consideration all of the helpful comments made by readers of the first two printings. The improvements to this edition include re-editing, a significant reduction in repetitive material, increased use of comments provided by readers, updating of all of the listings, and about fifty pages of new information.

I would like to thank a number of people who have helped with this project. First, there was my partner Rob that had to put up with my moodiness while writing this book. He made sure I ate and took care of myself during the intense periods of writing.

It would be impossible to list all of the people who contributed to this book. Many of them are anonymous. The individuals who reviewed the book before publication were very helpful. The reviewers include Raul, Jay, and Peter Scott. Raul who manages the local gay and lesbian bookstore Get Booked is extremely helpful to the small community of first time authors in Las Vegas.

I would also like to thank McNaughton & Gunn, whose staff was extremely helpful, professional, and courteous. They are one of the top book printers for small publishers. Also, I would like to thank Bert Hermann at Alamo Square and Ron Handy at Bookazine who support first time authors. I would also like to thank amazon.com. Amazon.com is amazing in its support of first time authors, and was instrumental in the sell out of the first printing. These individuals and companies are supportive of first time authors, and self-published works.

The standard in the adult industry is to use a stage name. I learned my lesson very early on that a stage name is necessary in order to maintain a certain amount of privacy. As such, I have used the same stage name I used when I was involved in gay adult films.

Matt Adams
Insider's Guide
4640 Paradise Rd.
Suite 15-123
Las Vegas, NV  89109

e-mail:  BestofVGS@aol.com

# Introduction

There is a misperception about the sex industry that people exchange sex for money because they have no other choices. Likewise, there is the misperception that clients are sexual abusers. In many cases prostitutes choose to be in the business and are entrepreneurs. Clients oftentimes choose to use escorts to fulfill their sexual fantasies or do not have the time to invest in long-term relationships.

This book is written to give a clearer idea of how the male prostitution market operates in the United States. It is written with the escort, client and casual observer in mind. This book is written to be a comprehensive observation of the male prostitution market in the United States.

This book is not written for the sexual voyeur. You will not find any juicy gossip. You will not find any juicy stories. You will find a lot of advice and a lot of resources so you can observe the workings of male escorts.

It should be noted prostitution is illegal in all fifty states. This book is not to be used as a guide for breaking any laws. It is written for educational and scientific purposes only. Stop reading this book now if your intentions are otherwise.

### Sex in America

The state of sex in America is confusing at best. We are bombarded by the news media every day about sexual issues. The majority of the public believes sex is a private matter. The interest of the media in sexual issues is over analytical and at best unhealthy voyeurism. In reality, the sensationalism created by the media has been very disruptive to anyone wanting to explore sexual relations with anyone.

Examples of the unhealthy voyeurism of the media are:

- The scrutiny by the military and the media on adultery.

- The scrutiny of the media on sex lives of public officials.
- The insistence of some groups to preach only abstinence to young adults instead of educating individuals on safe and responsible sex.
- The inability of our society to reach a consensus on what constitutes reasonability on issues of sexual harassment, date rape, and other sexual relations that may, in fact, be consensual.
- The media's need to expose the sexual imbroglios of otherwise private individuals.

The media could report on sexual issues from the standpoint of respect, tolerance, and rights of privacy. However, much of today's reporting gives far too much credence to the arguments of the far right. Unfortunately, there are many instances where the media undermines the dignity and rights to privacy all individuals should enjoy.

In part due to media reporting, there is a pervasive fear about engaging in sex. There is extreme concern about disease, mistrust in sexual partners, and mistrust in anyone who might have any knowledge of a person's sexual past.

These issues are as important as the civil rights issues of the sixties. These are defining issues in terms of fundamental limits and boundaries for all individuals. Unfortunately, in the process of arriving at a consensus many people are being financially, emotionally, and professionally ruined.

Given, this climate of sexual intolerance it may well be cheaper and less cumbersome to seek out a professional when it comes to exploring sexual desires.

Exploring sexual fantasies is natural and healthy. Most sexual curiosities that were once labeled as psychological disorders are now only considered sexual disorders if the sexual behavior results in material detriment to a person's occupation or other personal relationships.

When I am told I should not expect my cake and eat it too, I naturally reply there is little sense in having cake if you cannot eat it. Sometimes it is less expensive to buy cake than it is to make cake from scratch.   If living your sexual fantasies is healthy, it is no less healthy to pay for sex.

## *How to Use This Book*

There are many ways to read this book.  I suggest you read the book the way I wrote the book.

I came up with a number of topics and wrote an outline first.   After I wrote the outline I worked on each section depending on my mood.  The order also depended on the time sensitivity of the information, and whether I had collected enough information to write the section.

I suggest you read the chapters that interest you most. There are many database listings.  There is also a lot of good advice.

I cannot guarantee everything in this edition is true and factual.  It is true and factual, as I know it.  To paraphrase the immortal words of the British economist, John Maynard Keynes, when my information changes, so do my conclusions.

Likewise, although much of the book is objective, I am also very opinionated.  Many of the issues addressed in this book are very complicated.   I have strong views against underage prostitution, but I also realize the issue is more complicated than just saying it is an abomination.  I have strong views on street hustling, but am also very intrigued by its dynamics.  In short, I have ambivalent personal feelings about nearly every aspect of escort work.  Much of this book is written objectively, but I admit I have, at best, thinly masked my personal opinions.

Many issues concerning escorts are very complicated.   I share Mark Twain's philosophy on the spelling of words; "A person can't be very bright if they can only spell a word one way."  A corollary to this rule: a person cannot be very bright unless that person can have multiple views on a single subject with no individual view representing the pure and holy.  Views and opinions come in black, white and every color of the rainbow.

There are many generalizations in this book. For each generalization there are numerous exceptions. My hope was to describe behaviors that fall within one or two standard deviations of expected behavior. The exceptions to the generalizations in the male prostitution business are also described and clearly identified.

## Nomenclature

This book contains a lot of slang and subtle use of words used in the field of male prostitution. For example, hustlers have customers and escorts have clients. I have attempted to use the preferred terms in the business and have avoided the use of terms such as "hooker", "john", "trick" and even "prostitute". These terms have a slightly offensive connotation in the business.

The male prostitution market is 97% comprised of men having sex with men. As such, I rarely use feminine terms. However, when I describe a segment of the market that involves women I use appropriate terms.

## Your Opinion Counts

Issues on sexuality are very controversial. Very simply, sex sells on television, in movies, and in newspapers simply because it satisfies our voyeuristic tendencies. If you have a view or views which differ from the ones in this book, just write me and I will probably include those views in the next edition.

Contact information is provided at the back of this book. Please feel free to write or e-mail me with your thoughts. This book has been written with information from thousands of sources, and it will continue to grow based on information provided from hundreds of other sources.

## Summary of the Contents

*Section I* describes the various types of male prostitutes by market segment. There is a misperception one type of whore is a better class of whore than another class of whore. I have found that quality varies in every category of male prostitutes. There are reasons why people choose to work in one market niche rather than another. Likewise, many clients have distinct preferences for male prostitutes who market themselves in a particular manner.

The seven chapters in this section describes hustlers, massage therapists, escorts, agencies, top models and bodybuilders, porn stars, and specialty escorts. Everyone works the market segments that are most effective. Many prostitutes choose to work in only one or two of the market niches. Each market niche requires different skills in order to succeed.

*Section II* describes the business aspects of the escort market.

*Chapter 8* discusses the qualities of the top escorts. After more than a decade of business books written on quality, it seems appropriate the issue needs to be addressed in the world's oldest profession. It may be another decade before politicians address quality in their profession.

*Chapter 9* describes the qualities of top clients. There is the misperception by many clients that the top escorts actually want their business. In reality, the top escorts generate 80% of their income from repeat business and are very selective on who they will take as a new client. This chapter describes the behavior of the top clients and exposes a lot of myths.

Chapters 10 through 13 describe the risks in the escort market. There are chapters on the legal risks, sexually transmitted diseases, mental health issues and the various scams committed by escorts and clients. It would be irresponsible for us to ignore these issues. Then again, sex is not about being responsible; it is about human urges. I cannot guarantee protection by reading this section, but it will not hurt anyone to read these sections.

*Section III* is a series of appendixes that provide additional information on the male escort market and references to other sources. The purposes of this section are to provide supporting material for the size of the male prostitution market, the diversity of the male prostitution market, and the depth of the male prostitution market.

*Chapter 14* is a market analysis of the largest geographical markets in the United States. I have researched each of these markets, but your feedback would be greatly appreciated to expand this section in the next edition.

*Chapter 15* is a listing of locations that have strippers. Although not all strippers are escorts, many of them are available as escorts. Many clubs with strippers also attract hustlers.

*Chapter 16* is a listing of places where sexual activity can be found. Oftentimes hustlers hang out in these places.

*Chapter 17* is a listing of gay publications. Many of these publications list male escorts.

*Chapter 18* is a listing of escort agencies with male escorts.

*Chapter 19* is a listing of Internet addresses with information on male escorts.

*Chapter 20* is a listing of the most respected escorts in the United States. This list is derived from public sources. These escorts were selected for special mention due to their reputation for exceptional professionalism. I am sure there are many more have not been included. I hope to expand on this list in future editions.

*Chapter 21* provides contact information for reader feedback. I am certain the next edition will include many reader comments. I appreciate your help in the evolution of this guide.

# Types of Male Prostitutes

P eople often ask how someone gets into the business of being a male prostitute. There is a certain mystique to being a male prostitute. Although the market is very limited for male prostitutes who cater exclusively to women, there are many heterosexual males who fantasize about being a male prostitute for women. In reality, it is not uncommon for people to fantasize about becoming prostitute. In fact, it would surprise most people that they probably know someone who has worked as a prostitute at one time or another. It is estimated three million people a year engage in prostitution at one time or another during the course of a year.

A large number of the three million engage in prostitution once or twice during the year. This type of person engages in prostitution for a number of reasons. First, the individual is given the opportunity when someone approaches them and asks if the individual will exchange money for sex. Second, the individual either has an immediate need for money, or they see the opportunity as easy money. Third, the individual does not see anything wrong with making a few dollars doing what they enjoy doing. For many, it is a fantasy fulfilled. The individual engages in prostitution once or twice, fulfill their fantasy, and retire from the profession.

There is a second group of male prostitutes who work on a part time basis. They work the bars, advertise, and have a few regular clients. These types of escorts engage in prostitution for the extra income while in school or to supplement their income. These types of male prostitutes may be found in bars, at strip clubs, advertised in the paper or sitting in a chat room on the Internet.

A third type of male prostitute works full time as a male prostitute. They advertise regularly and have a large following of regular clients. These types of male prostitutes are called escorts. In some publications, they advertise as models or male adult entertainers.

A fourth type is also a professional escort, but limits themselves to between one and five regular clients who may provide them with housing expense, transportation, and a monthly stipend. These are the elite male prostitutes.

The term prostitute is used in this book when describing all male prostitutes. The term hustler describes a male prostitute who typically markets to a customer face to face. The term escort is used when describing male prostitutes who work for an agency or advertise in publications for clients. Customers of escorts are generally referred to as clients in the industry.

### Underage Prostitutes

The group of prostitutes who are true victims are those that work the streets and are underage. I have encountered a number of individuals who had to leave home at an early age because their parents were either abusive or unable to care for them. A fourteen-year-old child does not have many choices, and is not prepared for the real world without a family.

These children do not have many choices. Society does not offer a very good support system for near adults who do not have the care of a parent. Many of these children have serious psychological problems from years of mental, physical, and sexual abuse. Many of these children have drug or alcohol dependencies. Many of these children also have psychopathic tendencies where they do not base their decisions on a system of right and wrong.

Likewise, the customers of these children are also sexual abusers. There are instances where someone takes the child into their home, ensures the child receives an education, and may have a long-term relationship with them. Generally, however, the people who look for underage prostitutes simply use them to meet their sexual needs, then turn them out onto the street again.

The criminal justice system is ineffective in raising adolescents. Child labor laws and other laws prevent children from raising themselves. These laws merely add to the problem. The child may have very few choices but to engage in prostitution. In cases where the child has not engaged in prostitution the child has had a sponsor who may or may not of had sexual relations with them and provided a stable home environment.

There are various organizations in large cities that are addressing the issues of disposable children. These organizations help get these children off the streets. Organizations such as the Larkin Street Youth Center in San Francisco are very important in working with young prostitutes and giving them a chance to engage in a life where they can make choices about what they want to do in life. There are also programs being instituted by local police departments and corrections departments to help these children.

Law enforcement and the judicial system are beginning to realize children who engage in prostitution are more often than not victims. New programs are being implemented to teach these children skills so they can live useful and productive lives. Likewise, there are many children who cannot be reached by the time they are caught engaging in prostitution and will continue to live antisocial lives that include theft, prostitution, drugs, and violence towards others.

I have a very strong bias against underage prostitution and their customers. As such, I choose not to write about this area of the market. Likewise, I advise young readers, if any, to find alternatives to escort work.

Likewise, I sincerely hope government organizations continue to find ways to teach children on how to protect themselves from sexual abuse, teach children how to be sexually responsible, and provide programs to give children a means to survive when they do not have a family support system.

### *Types of Escorts*

The vast majority of male prostitutes work very sporadically. This type of prostitute generally has chance encounters with a client, has a friend who is an escort and teaches them how to work as an escort, or hangs out in a place where there are customers. This type of escort may work two or three times a year to get a little extra money.

Another type of prostitute works part-time. Oftentimes they have full time jobs or go to school. They may hustle bars from time to time, work for agencies, or run an advertisement in local gay papers. Generally, they establish a few good clients, and see escort work as a short-term occupation.

There is an even smaller group of professional escorts. These escorts choose to make a career of escort work. Many of these escorts are older, fairly secure, relatively debt free and well established in their communities. The average professional escort earns two to three thousand dollars a month. Many other escorts consistently earn over $50,000 a year. There is even a smaller group of escorts who earn over $100,000 a year.

There is still another group of escorts. These are individuals who are so good-looking they are constantly asked if they do escort work. These individuals may maintain only a few clients who may pay them very large monthly stipend provide housing and other forms of remuneration. These are the elite escorts.

# Chapter One

# Hustlers

H ustlers are a very distinct part of the market for male prostitutes. A hustler is thought of as an individual who stands on a street corner waiting for a car to drive up. The hustler goes up to the car, negotiates the services, negotiates the fee, hops in the car and returns back to his corner in fifteen to thirty minutes. We also have the impression of a hustler as being on drugs, homeless, dirty, and basically someone who is described in the vernacular as poor white trash.

Admittedly, poor white trash is a derogatory term. In the world of hustling it is a term that reflects a very real fantasy by many clients. It is the fantasy of the poor boy right off the farm coming into town on the bus to make a better life. He comes with little education, no money, and no friends. There is generally a big difference between reality and the fantasies of clients. However, it is this fantasy that drives the desires of all types of individuals to pick up hitchhikers, to search the bus terminals, and drive by the local hangouts for the latest bit of meat to hit town.

In reality, there are many types of hustlers. The differences between hustlers and other types of escorts are; they do not advertise, do not work for agencies, typically do not have regular clients, and do not typically treat their work as an ongoing business.

Hustlers are the nomads of the escort world. They are here today and oftentimes gone later in the day. They are oftentimes breezing through town, they may have just been released from prison, they may have come to town to pick up a little extra money, or they are looking for funds for their next drug buy.

Most hustlers, for one reason or another do not last long. They live for the moment. Once they have the money to leave town, they leave town. Once they have the rent money, they go back to their regular jobs. Once they have experienced the thrill, they move on to other things. Once they find someone to support them, they give up working the streets.

Hustlers who continue to work the bars and streets tend to get arrested. Typically, hustlers working the streets will eventually get arrested for drugs, disorderly conduct, theft, or soliciting prostitution.

On a recent trip to San Francisco I once again spent time observing hustler life on Polk Street. I was told by a number of individuals there was no longer much of a hustler market on Polk Street. Over several days I observed dozens of hustlers on Polk Street. Street prostitution exists in most cities because the neighbors and businesses in the area have little influence with the police or politicians. Also, there is denial by most people as to the significance of the problem. Finally, there are few, if any, social services available to help street prostitutes find alternative methods to survive.

The typical hustler on Polk Street spends hours on the street waiting for a customer. The typical hustler was looking to make enough money for food, a place to sleep, and a drug buy. Several hustlers made eye contact with me, asked me what I was up to, and asked whether I was looking for company.

Brian was one such hustler. He was tall, slender, blond, and blue eyed. He told me he was twenty-one and had only been hustling for a few weeks. He told me his rate was $40 or $45, but wondered if I would give him a tip if he was extra good.

I took Brian to a nice place in order to spend time with him and find out his real story. He was walking with some difficulty and told me he had been in a fight.

As we got to know each other it became apparent he had been hustling in San Francisco for three weeks, but started hustling in Seattle when he was fourteen. He had been addicted to heroin for six months. He had had a number of sponsors who threw him out of their houses when he misbehaved. He had numerous staph infections due to intravenous drug use, and from cuts he had received when a customer had shaved off his pubic hair. He had been arrested three times in three weeks, and was afraid of being arrested again.

After my interview with him I gave him sixty dollars. Enough for some drugs and a place to sleep. Brian, the attractive all-American boy was certainly a lost cause who would require a large investment to save from his own actions and the streets. Brian was just one of twenty to thirty guys working Polk Street that Sunday afternoon. So much for the glamour of being a street hustler.

Individuals without a home, friends, or family are often involved in drugs, stealing, or even violence. There are a few types of hustlers who do not fall into this category. However, anybody who succeeds as a hustler also has the characteristics of a con artist. As such, someone who establishes a long-term relationship with a hustler has a good chance of being burned.

A good example of this situation involved Representative Barney Frank from Massachusetts. Representative Frank had engaged a male hustler, and befriended him. He provided the hustler with a job in his office and financial support. The hustler returned the favor by engaging in behavior that caused embarrassment and an ethics investigation for the congressman. Fortunately, the congressman was able to weather the storm, but the situation illustrates:

- No one is immune to the possibility of embarrassment by having a long-term relationship with a hustler.

- A long-term relationship with a hustler will almost certainly involve financial loss.
- The chance of "saving" a hustler from a life on the streets and use of drugs is remote.
- It is possible for anyone to be attracted to the charm of a hustler.
- The risk of physical violence is very high in a relationship with a hustler.

I differentiate the types of hustlers by where they market themselves. Hustlers may succeed at marketing themselves in one venue and fail miserably in another venue. There are several factors involved in being successful at hustling. To be successful at being a hustler involves location, appearance, energy, negotiating skills, flexibility, and opportunity.

### Location Defines a Hustler

Hustlers work at a location. Customers look for hustlers at specific locations. There are many locations where hustlers can be found. Many of these locations may discourage hustlers from their establishments. Some locations encourage hustlers, but keep a close eye on their activities.

### Street Hustlers

In some cities there are places where street hustlers can be regularly found. Typically, a customer will drive along the area, drive up to the hustler, have the hustler get inside the car, negotiate the transaction, and all is done in fifteen to thirty minutes.

Many street hustlers are underage, don't have any money, need money for drugs, do not have a home and may be unhealthy. With street hustling usually goes drug dealing.

Businesses and residents of areas where street hustling occurs do not feel safe, do not like the litter, and do not like cars cruising the area. Many cities have adopted very strict programs to curb street hustling. First, the police departments make regular patrols of these areas both in marked and unmarked cars. The police also use uniformed and undercover patrols. Second, the police make every effort to entrap street hustlers. Third, the police may employ decoys to catch customers soliciting for sex.

Many cities have become equally creative in the types of penalties for customers caught soliciting prostitution. Generally, for a first time offense a customer will be cited with a ticket and let go. A second offense may be considered a felony, and if convicted a customer may be required to register in their hometown as a sex offender. Other programs include public embarrassment by having the customer's name in the paper. There is a growing movement to post pictures of individuals engaged in prostitution in newspapers and on the Internet. Many local and state governments are implementing plans to list sexual offenders on the Internet.

A very expensive penalty for a customer is to have their car seized. This means an individual who solicits a prostitute using a vehicle may have it seized and auctioned off by the police. This is very similar to the drug seizure laws. Many cities have begun to institute this program to stop street prostitution. It is a very extreme measure that has been upheld by the United States Supreme Court.

If the possible judicial risks and penalties do not cause fear with prospective customers then they should also consider street hustling is very dangerous for customers and hustlers. First, there is the risk of physical violence. Second, there is the risk of theft. Third, there is the risk of disease. These are risks occur with any type of prostitute, but are most likely to occur with street hustlers.

### The Fantasy of the Street Hustler

Despite all of these issues, the street hustler is the object of many people's fantasies.

I believe most street hustlers see their position as degrading. Generally, they work the street out of an immediate necessity and not out of choice. Typically street hustling has the worst pay, the worst customers, and the most risk.

There are very few street hustlers who will try to attract customers by looking them in the eye. They are very evasive about the transaction. Most have shown up to "work" to get their next drug fix, pay the rent, or get enough money for a meal. Many are homeless and need a place to shower and a bed to sleep in.

I have talked to many individuals who engaged in street hustling because they had become homeless. In many cases, these individuals had just moved to a town, and had underestimated the amount of money needed to get settled into their new home or had not been able to immediately gain employment. In these cases, the individuals would agree to spend the night with someone for as little as $100. These individuals saw these times as being among the low points in their life, yet did not regret their actions because they were taken in order to survive.

The reason why street hustling is so dangerous is because street hustlers definitely feel no one respects their limits and boundaries. This means, for the most part, they do not feel any need to respect the limits and boundaries of anyone else including their customers. Street hustlers have a lot of anger and resentment over their situation, and at best they see their customers as a short-term means to make their situation better.

There are exceptions. There are the hustlers who have just come to town and are trying to get a few dollars so they can get an apartment. There are hustlers who go to school, and see this as a way to pick up some extra money. There are hustlers who do it for the thrill. These examples are the exception and not the rule.

For the most part, it is the customer who has the fantasy of the street hustler.

There are a number of reasons why a client seeks out street hustlers:

*Underage Sex.* Many street hustlers are underage. Underage hustlers tend to fall into several categories:

- A large percentage of underage street hustlers are runaways or are children whose parents have given up on them.
- There seems to be an increasing number of children who have discovered their sexuality at a very young age, and are very sexually active. These children learn they can make money by having sex with others and learn from friends how to hustle.
- There is another group of underage hustlers who hustle through a network of adult friends and acquaintances.

Street hustlers tend to be young, but many of them look much older than their age due to poor health, drugs, or alcohol dependencies.

Underage street hustlers tend to congregate in areas near bars that cater to hustlers. In some cities there are well known streets where hustlers hang out. In other cities hustlers hang out at the bus terminals.

*Anonymous Sex.* Since street hustlers are relatively transient, sex with a street hustler can be relatively anonymous. This is especially true when the customer and street hustler have sex in a rental car.

*Quick Sex.* Typically, a street hustler will know all of the secluded areas near the pick up spot. The customer will drive to that spot, they will have sex, and then the client drives the street hustler back to his pick up spot. The entire time involved is generally less than thirty minutes.

*Cheap Sex.* Sex with street hustlers will cost $40 to $50 at best. There are even stories where it costs much less. Usually, it just involves oral sex. Customers should not expect the best quality, since if the hustler is on drugs or has had a busy night their performance will not be very exciting.

*Sex for Drugs.* I have very strong feelings against the use of drugs. However, there are many street hustlers who will exchange sex for drugs.

Customers are fascinated by street hustlers because of their survival skills and many street hustlers are very charming (remember, most street hustlers are also con artists in some degree). Many customers have a sincere desire to make a street hustler's life easier if only for the evening. If the customer has a sincere desire to help a hustler it is best to offer the hustler a meal and pay for a room for the hustler for the night. Tips are also appreciated.

### Adult Bookstore Hustlers

Adult bookstore hustlers are perhaps the lowest on the totem pole when it comes to hustlers. They are also perhaps the riskiest.

Adult bookstores pose many risks. In many cities adult bookstores are targets of undercover police operations. If the police catch a customer with their pants down in an adult bookstore the customer is likely to be cited for lewd and indecent exposure. In some localities this is considered a sex crime and if convicted the customer may be required to register in their community as a sex offender.

Some newspapers feel it is their responsibility to print the names of individuals who are caught having public sex. Typically, this form of public embarrassment serves no constructive purpose in deterring public sex in the long run. However, many suicides have resulted from this sort of news coverage. Many of these same newspapers do not report on heterosexual activities, but only arrests involving homosexual activities.

Adult bookstores tend to attract hustlers who are desperate for the money. These hustlers tend to be homeless, broke and possible intravenous drug users. They are high risk for contracting lice and other diseases. Actually, given adult bookstores tend to be the alternative to sexual addiction counseling, anyone would run a fairly high risk of contracting a sexual transmitted disease when having sex with someone in an adult bookstore.

There are cases when the bookstore hustler will come up to a customer and offer them the best oral sex the prospective customer has ever had for twenty dollars. Other bookstore hustlers tend to wait in their video booth waiting for customers to come to them. Sometimes a hustler will ask for the money right away and sometimes the hustler will tease a customer first and then ask for money. Generally, the offer is to perform oral sex on the customer.

Typically, the fee runs from five dollars to twenty dollars although a request for forty dollars would not be uncommon. Of course, in this case a person gets what they pay for. Many bookstore hustlers are looking to fund their next drug fix. Generally, their performance is poor.

Another risk with the adult bookstore hustler is the high probability of theft. Many hustlers will go after a customer's wallet or money clip while the customer is enjoying their services.

Customers who search for adult bookstore hustlers look for bookstores with video booths that have locking doors to ensure privacy. Customers also look for a bookstore that is gay friendly. In many areas, the bookstores get busy when the bars close although hustlers can be found there many times during the day. Sometimes the clerk at the bookstore will direct customers to a hustler or warn customers of hustlers who may be dangerous.

Hustlers are not appreciated or tolerated at many adult bookstores since they tend to harass the customers, do not spend money in the store, and have a tendency to pick pockets. Most adult bookstores attract a regular clientele who enjoy cruising the arcade for possible sexual partners and having quick sex. Customers of adult bookstores do not particularly want to pay to have sex, and the biggest challenge to the video store attendant is to ensure all patrons are continuously spending money in the video arcade.

There are instances where the store clerks at adult video arcades make themselves available to customers for a price. Also, there are hustlers who are also given permission by adult video stores to unofficially work in the store provided they adhere to set standards of conduct.

The vast majority of adult bookstores do not tolerate hustlers or sexual activities. Many localities have very strict laws on prostitution, public sex, and loitering.  Many localities require adult bookstores discourage sexual activity in their video arcades through the following means:

- Video surveillance.
- Regular employee surveillance.
- Removal of doors from the video booth or installation of glass doors.
- Discouragement of loitering.

Some adult bookstores will call the police if a customer is caught having sex on premises.  Undercover police also routinely monitor the activities that occur in adult bookstores.  Adult bookstores have been known to attract individuals seeking to commit hate crimes including murder against gays.

### Bathhouse Hustlers

Bathhouse hustlers are more difficult to find.  Most do not actively solicit for customers.  In the case of procuring a hustler in a bathhouse chances are the prospective customer would need to approach the person and make a tactful offer.  There are, however, cases where a hustler will openly approach prospective customers.

The nice thing about bathhouses is they provide showers, steam rooms, and a Jacuzzi.  This means the hustlers are generally clean.  Bathhouses also provide rooms and some of them are quite luxurious.

The other advantage of a bathhouse is even if someone is unable to find a hustler there are a lot of other options.  Usually a bathhouse will have adult videos running.  Usually a bathhouse will have orgy rooms with some activity.  These rooms oftentimes include such amenities as mazes and glory holes.  The steam room is always a good hang out.  At the very least someone will be able to witness some enjoyable spontaneous entertainment.

Bathhouses are also good places to take hustlers a customer meets somewhere else.  Expect to pay about $40 admission for two for a convenient and clean place to play. Many bathhouses are located near to places where hustlers congregate.

The risk of a police raid is small these days, although raids are not unheard of. Typically, however, the purpose of the raid is more directed at the management and is used to intimidate the customers. In cases where customers have been cited the charges are usually dismissed. Most jurisdictions allow bathhouses to operate because it reduces the incidence of sexual behavior in public places such as public restrooms and public parks.

The risk of theft and disease is also high in bathhouses. Most bathhouses provide safe deposit boxes for valuables. It is best to use them. As far as disease, most diseases can be prevented through safe sex. Lice and scabies can be contracted by skin contact or contact with surfaces used by someone with the parasites.

Hustlers are more frequently seen in some bathhouses than other bathhouses. Bathhouses, like adult bookstores, are not the best venue for hustlers because there is generally an abundance of free sex available in a bathhouse. The motivation is generally similar to hustlers found in bookstores - raising money for drugs. Bathhouse hustlers typically charge $50 for their services although the price can vary considerably if the hustler is featured as a stripper at the club.

There is a list of bathhouses towards the end of the book.

### Bar Hustlers

A hustler can be found in almost any bar. Any attractive male who sits or stands alone checking out the surroundings is generally fair game. Sometimes a bartender or doorman will point them out. When dealing with hustlers the word of mouth recommendation of a bartender or doorman should be seriously considered.

When approaching a hustler, it is best to strike up a pleasant conversation. A good hustler will have already done a thorough inventory of a prospective customer's clothing and jewelry. A hustler will generally say their line of work is sales, marketing, or a student. Some hustlers will say they just came into town. A number of hustlers will head right to the nearest gay bar to try to raise funds for their stay or to travel to their next destination.

Some hustlers will live near by and do in-calls. If there is a bathhouse nearby that is another good spot to go. It is always best for a customer and hustler to agree on money and agree on services before going anywhere. Again, there is always the risk of possible theft so it is best to lock the valuables in the glove compartment of the car.

It is not unusual for a bar hustler to evade questions about price and sexual activities. Many hustlers play the game of charming customers and not bringing up the subject of money until they have arrived at the customer's location. This generally puts the customer in an awkward position.

Prices vary considerably depending on the bar, the quality of the hustler, and geography. The prices range from forty dollars to three hundred dollars.

### Hustler Bars

There are some bars that market themselves as hustler bars. These types of bars range from very seedy to very classy expensive restaurants and bars. Bars that cater to hustlers and their clients have a flea market atmosphere to them. There are buyers, sellers and customers who come to watch the show. The transactional environment is as open as the New York Stock Exchange.

A potential customer will enter the bar, sit down, eye over the merchandise, and then go up to the merchant to negotiate a deal over drinks. Negotiations can take some time, so be prepared to buy a drink or two for the merchant.

There are many types of hustler bars. Some bars cater to the street crowd that hangs around the bar. Hustlers who do not spend money in the bar do not get to sit in the bar. However, these hustlers may be allowed to periodically take a quick tour of the bar and use the bathroom. Other bars discourage street traffic, and monitor the hustlers very carefully.

## *Numbers*

A hustler bar worth mentioning in detail is Numbers in Los Angeles on Santa Monica Boulevard (Numbers moved in early 1998 from their location on Sunset). Numbers is a very high quality restaurant and bar with one of the best T-bone steak specials around. It is a hangout for every type of hustler imaginable and some very important customers.

Numbers has a number of dining booths across from the bar. In many cases patrons will invite a hustler to have dinner with them. The food is very good and dinner will cost $70 to $80 for two.

Hustlers at Numbers charge anywhere from $150 to $300 with most at between $150 and $200. With their new location near West Hollywood their tends to be a good selection with more sellers than buyers on many nights.

## *Small Towns*

Small town gay bars tend to be a virtual Peyton Place where everyone knows everyone else, and everyone else's business. Hustling is not encouraged in small town bars, but it occurs with some frequency. There is always a young and attractive gentleman who is in need of funds to meet the monthly payments on something.

Typically, the bartenders will know who is available, or be able to refer a customer to someone who knows someone. In small towns many of the guys who hustle live with their families or have just started living on their own. Hustling is a source of extra funds, and many of the guys who hustle will have a few regular local customers who help them in many ways. Some of these customers provide apartments, jobs, and small loans.

The dynamics of hustlers in small towns are a special type of situation. First, they typically have low paying jobs and need to supplement their income. Second, since they are in small towns where everyone knows each other, they tend to be fairly honest individuals, although there are many exceptions. Third, they tend to come from low-income families.  Fourth, they tend to have a need for father figures in their lives.

The dynamics of sex in lower income individuals is very unique.  First, persons from low-income families in many cases see sex as opportunistic.  This occurs in many ways.  A person who is basically heterosexual is more likely to engage in a homosexual relationship if a woman is not available (I believe bisexuality is generally very understated, and I maintain the opinion many men will fuck mud if deprived of any other outlet of sexual expression).  A person from a low-income environment is less resistant to exchanging sex for the opportunity of getting a job or promotion.  Someone from a low-income environment is more likely to favorably view the idea of exchanging sex for money or something of value.  In most cases these sexual relationships are consensual to some degree.

These types of relationships occur in all communities regardless of the size of the town, but they are more observable in a small town where everyone knows everyone else.  These relationships can go on for many years.

There was a time when I absolutely could not believe these sorts of relationships existed.  In fact, I was very dismayed with a boyfriend of mine.  He came from a small town in Illinois and was a graduate from an Ivy League law school.  He could not find a job until he had sex with an attorney.  He was then hired into the firm.

This attorney provided Stephen with a job and provided him with a monthly salary many years later when he was too ill to work.  This relationship continued until Stephen died.

In some fields such as modeling, dancing, bodybuilding, and acting these relationships are known as "sponsors".  Many people in these fields work for very little money.  They may have moved from a small town and do not have a very good support network in the large city.  A sponsor provides important emotional and financial support.  The support of a sponsor allows the individual the financial ability to work in an artistic field they love, but is low paying.

In small towns the sponsors tend to be small business owners who provide young guys with jobs in exchange for an ongoing sexual relationship.    In other cases the guys are employed as houseboys who handle cleaning or gardening.

Hustlers exist in most small towns, but many of them stick to a sponsor.  If hustlers are available, they will be known at the local bars.  In fact, many may be working at the local bar as a bar back or bartender.  Hustlers in small towns may be less obvious than in larger cities.  Given everyone talks in a small town, it is best to be discrete when approaching a potential hustler.

With the advent of the Internet there is now another way to find hustlers in small towns.  Customers search the user profiles for male and the geographic location.    Customers look for usernames that have some sense of suggestiveness.    Then the customer looks in the profile for descriptions such as young, student, gay, and needs money.  The customer then develops rapport on-line and then makes an offer.

These small town relationships, however, have risk. Typically, there is a significant physical and emotional age difference between the customer and the hustler.  The customer is typically driven by a need to control and be loved.  The hustler is driven by the need to get as much as possible out of the relationship and then get out of the relationship.  In many cases, the object of the customer's desire may be heterosexual.

Sexual abuse, drug use, domestic violence, and the occasional murder of the customer or hustler often characterize these relationships.  In many cases the hustler will get as much money, property, and possibly a vehicle before breaking off the relationship.    Generally, the relationships get strained very quickly, and terminate after a period of intense infatuation by the customer.  During this period, love is blind to the reality money does not buy love.

### Dance Clubs

Dance clubs are not the easiest place to find a hustler.  The reason why hustlers are available in dance clubs is that a lot of escorts go out to clubs with some frequency.

Gay dance clubs attract a wide variety of potential escorts. Gay dance clubs not only attract the top escorts they also attract transvestites and transsexuals.

Most people are having a good time at a dance club. With the liquor, music, and energy of a dance club most prospects would react favorably to a proposition even if they were not favorably inclined to exchange sex for money.

When escorts are out on the town, they are not generally available for work. Soliciting someone in a nightclub is very hit or miss. Although some hustlers may be actively seeking customers in a nightclub, generally most people are out to just have a good time.

A common pick up line in a nightclub is offering to give someone a hundred dollars to perform oral sex on the prospective hustler. Most people I know are generally very flattered by the offer even if they decline the offer.

### Strip Clubs

Strip clubs vary in the availability of hustlers.

First, not all strippers are involved in hustling. Second, a lot of strippers are straight and would not feel comfortable having sex with a man. Third, a lot of establishments with strippers keep a very watchful eye over prostitution, and a stripper caught accepting a customer's offer may get fired. Fourth, undercover police monitor many strip clubs.

Customers should have a lot of dollar bills if they are interested in soliciting a stripper. A good tipper is more likely to attract the stripper's attention and the stripper will be more receptive to solicitation.

Strippers make a good amount of their money off of regular clients. Strippers who have good audience interaction make the most money. The strippers who make the most money are the strippers who are not afraid to touch a customer and allow customers to touch them. Most clubs have very strict rules on what a stripper can and cannot do while performing. Most good strippers are very good at tactfully letting customers know the rules when they go too far in touching.

A customer should be sure to follow the rules, since a stripper will generally be suspended or fired for breaking the house rules.  The strictness on enforcing the house rules depends on the local laws, and degree to which these laws are enforced. Many clubs have lost their liquor licenses or have had their licenses suspended for breaking the local laws.

Some strippers actively escort when they are not stripping. A good stripper may give a customer their beeper number for contact during off-hours.  If a stripper does not do escort work they may be willing to refer a customer to other strippers who work as escorts.  In many clubs, however, strippers keep word of their escort work very quiet and they may be very selective on who they will take as customers.

Stripping is a very unique segment of the adult industry. There are many people who make very good livings just stripping.  These strippers work for a club and build up a loyal following of fans.  There are some geographic areas that are saturated with strippers including the New York City area, Florida, and Texas.  These areas have a large appetite for strippers who cater to both men and women.

Getting hired at a club is not always easy for someone who wants to become a stripper.  These are some of the issues a stripper encounters:

- Some clubs require an act.  Among the most popular acts are cowboy, construction worker, James Bond, sailor, Indian, Batman, Superman, and almost any other current macho character.  If an act is required the stripper must have costumes, a selection of songs, and some dance choreography.  Working a club with an act may reduce audience interaction and may reduce the ability to get tips.
- Some clubs have amateur night auditions.  These audition nights are good for individuals who want to strip as part of a fantasy.  Usually the top performer receives a prize and possibly a job offer.
- Owners of clubs have preferences.  The preferences of the owner are sometimes a major frustration in getting

hired in a club. Some owners have very specific
preferences in terms of skin color, hair color, muscle,
and other physical characteristics. Clubs that have
strippers representing all types tend to be more
successful. The most important characteristic for a
successful stripper is to be able to interact with a crowd
and build up a regular following of customers.

- Local groups of strippers. There are local groups of
  strippers in many areas. These groups have a routine
  and develop regional followings of fans.
- Performance rules vary depending on geography.
  Different clubs have different performance standards
  that vary based on local laws; some clubs require
  strippers to masturbate and ejaculate, some clubs allow
  translucent g-strings, some clubs permit nude dancing,
  and some clubs require the buttocks to be covered.

The best preparation for someone who wants to become a
stripper is to spend a lot of time watching other strippers. A
stripper in training should study the local requirements for
stripping and spend a month or so in preparation for an audition.
In areas that cater to men and women, someone who wants to be
a stripper should study how the performers operate in both
settings. The most successful strippers are those who can
successfully interact with both male and female patrons.

Strippers are typically paid $50 to perform at a club. There
are a number of exceptions to this rule:

- Some clubs require strippers to pay the house a fee to
  dance in the club. This is common in clubs where
  strippers are allowed to solicit private dances or lap
  dances.
- Some porn stars and models command fees of between
  $500 and $2000 to perform at a club. These
  performances are usually arranged through agents.
- Strippers who are trying out will typically work for tips.

The easiest method to get a job as a stripper is to approach the owner or manager of a club that has strippers.  There are many individuals who travel throughout the country and work as strippers to pay for their travels.

Strip clubs also attract hustlers who are not strippers.  A sharp eye might identify some interesting hustlers who are not performing.

There is a listing of clubs that offers strippers in the appendixes.  Some clubs only offer strippers infrequently or they change their programs frequently.  Some clubs only offer strippers for special events.  It is always best to call the club for the availability of strippers.

Here is a letter I received from a typical good customer of strippers:

*I fit the mold you highlight.  I'm a good tipper and do not fondle the dancer.  I clear with him as to what is permitted and what is not permitted.  If the stripper allows some liberties I tip appropriately.  I am respectful of the fact these guys need to work the room and make money.  At an opportune moment I will ask if they escort.  In most cases they do.  If they say no, I thank them for their time and either stay to watch or I leave.*

One exceptional club is the Nob Hill Club in San Francisco.  The Nob Hill has performances every half-hour and has facilities for private performances downstairs.  The entrance fee is $30, and there are also private video booths in the basement.

The Nob Hill hires a variety of dancers to suit nearly every taste, and also features the top porn stars as headliners.  The attitude of the Nob Hill is to hire a wide variety of dancers who are attractive and friendly.

Private dances run between $50 and $100, however I suspect most customers make counteroffers.  My experience is the dancers do not ordinarily initiate lower offers to ensure a sale.

The Nob Hill is very clean, recently refurbished, and has a friendly atmosphere.  It is well worth a visit when in San Francisco.

### Internet Hustlers

The Internet is rapidly becoming the media of choice for many clients and escorts. The Internet is where many of the top escorts and agencies in the country can now be located. I deal with the top escorts and agencies later in this book. There are, however, thousands of individuals who use the Internet to hustle for clients.

The difference between hustlers on the Internet and the top escorts has to do with their permanence in the market and how they conduct their business. In other words, a hustler on the Internet is more fly by night. The top escorts will have a permanent web page, e-mail address, and will oftentimes provide a phone number.

A hustler on the Internet will typically sit in a chat room on the Internet and either solicit customers or create a profile that makes themselves available to customers. Professionalism is what differentiates a hustler from a more established escort on the Internet.

The emerging technology on the Internet is the ability to videoconference. The cost of a video camera that connects to the computer is less than $100. Most computers currently have microphone attachments.

A new group of Internet hustler is emerging. This hustler uses the videoconferencing ability to sign up in less than two minutes with a service that allows the hustler to perform live sex shows through the Internet. The service handles all of the billing and accounting, and sends the hustler a check every week. Viewers have several options for communicating with the on line hustler. The model can also remotely control sex toys in the viewer's home.

There are multiple ways to handle the new videoconferencing technology. Already, there are a number of companies who provide teleconferencing software at low cost or free. With the videoconferencing technology the high tech hustler can make home movies, take current photographs, give live performances, and demonstrate the truth of their advertising.

Tomorrow's hustler may never need to leave home.

## *Characteristics of an on-line Internet Hustler*

On-line Internet hustlers sit in the chat room and either actively solicit customers or have profiles that makes it clear they are available for escort work.

On-line Internet hustlers typically do not have a web pages. They are typically in the business of hustling on an intermittent basis or do not want people to know they do escort work.

An on-line Internet hustler may or may not have a picture available. Again, many hustlers either do not understand the business or are very afraid someone will find out about them. There is a very real threat of exposure to friends and employers on the Internet because of the number of people who use the Internet.

On-line Internet hustler can be somewhat nomadic. They travel from town to town and use hustling as a way to pay their travel expenses. There has been a dramatic increase in the number of periodic on-line hustlers. These individuals are typically in a severe financial situation and decide to try to make some money quickly. Many of the on-line hustles are between jobs, or in need of a quick cash infusion.

An on-line Internet hustler generally will not have a pager number. Again, many on-line hustlers do not understand the business and simply rely on clients at the moment. As such, timing is everything. Hustlers who are on-line want to work then and there.

There is a subgroup of Internet hustler who sits in the chat room but is not looking for customers. Many people who describe themselves as students, dancers, or models may be available for escort work. If they are not interested they will generally say no when asked about their availability. Another method to attract an on-line hustler is to type into the main chat room a line such as "Are there any escorts in the room?" There is oftentimes someone in the room who would not ordinarily do escort work, but could use an extra hundred dollars.

There have been increasing reports law enforcement is actively monitoring the Internet for prostitution. Although these activities have been limited to escort agencies and escorts who have web pages, it can be expected it will only be a matter of time when there will be widespread police sting operations.

There has been one reported case where a police officer posed as an escort and entrapped a customer. In this case, the police officer lured the unsuspected customer to a neutral place to make the arrest. It is unlikely police would arrest a person at their home or hotel rooms since the privacy protections afforded by these locations are greater than those provided by a neutral site.

### *Other Chance Places*

There are hundreds of stories that relate where hustlers have been found. Here is a partial listing of where customers have reported finding hustlers:

Beaches (especially life guards)
Cocktail Parties
In the office
Parks
Phone sex lines
Personal ads
Public Bathrooms
Restaurant waiters
Ice cream shops
Convenience store clerks
Classrooms (especially driver rehabilitation)
Repairmen
Landscapers
Pool cleaners
Maids
Truck stops
Shopping malls
Bus Stations
Train Stations

There is no shortage of places to find someone willing to exchange sex for money. The key ingredients for a successful transaction seem to be:

1. The customer finds someone who attracts interest.
2. The customer finds someone in need of money (hence a lot of the places mentioned are low paying).
3. The customer strikes up a conversation with the target.
4. The customer discretely brings up the subject of exchanging money for sex.
5. A deal is struck, and the transaction is consummated.

There is by no means 100% certainty this will work. I suspect the customers who employ these methods get rejected more often than their offer is accepted. However, in many cases the offer may be rejected because the amount offered is too little.

Customers that pursue this method get a thrill out of the pursuit. It may be driven by the need to have power over another individual. It may simply be driven by lust. The primary thrill to the customer is in the hunt and the conquest.

I received a letter from one customer of hustlers who describes his methods:

*Most of us strongly prefer a fresh face, not a tired full-time professional. Your stress on quality of escorts differs with most of our views. The johns strongly prefer a fresh young face, preferably a college student seeking extra money. The regular hustlers were not in demand by the regular johns. Only tourists hired the full-time hustlers.*

*I have been successful in having guys visit me without compensation. These have been really terrific looking college graduate students. We simply work out a swap of room and board for an hour of sex or massage once a day. Most of us could never afford to pay the high day rates of most escorts.*

**The Chance Hustler**

The chance hustler is someone who does not seek out work as an escort. The chance hustler is someone who is given the opportunity to hustle, and on occasion may accept an offer. In many cases, the chance hustler will accept an offer because the money is easy or they want to fulfill a fantasy. There are many individuals who see hustling as a way to earn money during college breaks, when they are between relationships, or when they are between jobs.

I have heard any number of stories where a customer has solicited someone based on a gut feeling the individual would be receptive to an offer. The customer can be someone the chance hustler knows or someone the chance hustler does not know. It can occur in any environment. Generally, the approach is not terribly overt. A common line is when the potential customer asks to assist with their light bill.

Most people that are approached tend to get scared and politely say no. Quite frankly, that is the approach I took. However, if I had been in a better psychological state of mind when I was offered money for sex I probably would have accepted. I believe a person that is curious about the opportunities in the world will at least think it over. Someone who sees the world as very threatening will tend to reject the offer.

The most common overt line is to offer someone $100 to give them oral sex. People I have talked to are either flattered and decline, or give it a second thought and accept.

There are dangers to this approach. There are a number of people who have become victims of violence by soliciting the wrong person. Some potential clients have been murdered using this approach. This can occur when a potential client solicits someone who identifies as heterosexual and is insecure with sexual identity. It is best to develop rapport with a person first, and if the individual declines the offer, to back off quickly.

The most frequently reported problems involve customers picking up hitchhikers. Typically, the customer will pick up a hitchhiker and use the opportunity of control to initiate sex with the hitchhiker. In many cases the hitchhiker may be sexually insecure or heterosexual. This can oftentimes result in violence toward the customer, theft, or even murder.

There are seven fundamental factors that lead directly or indirectly to the successful consummation of a contract with a hustler:

*Appearance.* Hustlers dress to stand out in a crowd. There is no particular uniform for a hustler, but there are several types of looks that a hustler will use to draw attention.

- The most obvious would be tight and short pants. This effeminate look certainly will certainly draw attention.
- The muscle look is also a good way to attract attention. Tight jeans and a muscle shirt.
- The poor white trash look. Dirty clothes and a down and out look.
- The college prep boy look. The chino pants and dress shirt.

The difference between hustlers wearing these clothes and others wearing the same types of clothes is they stand out in a crowd.

*Energy.* Many hustlers have a personal energy that attracts customers to them. The most successful hustlers I have encountered never seem to have a problem attracting customers. They are very attractive, they are very careful with their personal appearance, and they dress very well, but they also have an energy that attracts customers to them.

Many hustlers have a naturally distinctive look. They have a very sexy look that sets themselves apart from other people. Hustlers are also good at getting through someone's defense systems very rapidly. Typically, a hustler will be able to evoke sympathy, and sell a customer on the pleasure the customer will receive by using their services.

These same factors are also very common with con artists. Many hustlers are con artists. As such, someone who feels the pleasant energy of a hustler pulling them into their orbit might want to check for their wallet.

*Flexibility.* The success of a hustler depends on their flexibility in terms of doing business. Since, the objective of a hustler is to make a quick buck; the hustler does not give much thought to the basic business infrastructure needed in order to consummate a transaction.

Many businesses fail because the operators feel all they need to do is hang out a shingle and the world will beat a path to their door. Oftentimes, when a good prospective customer comes to their door a new business operator has no clue as to what is needed to do to consummate a sale.

A good hustler has thought through the basics. The hustler has established some flexibility in terms of location, transportation, sexually activities offered and communications systems. Most hustlers have given little or no thought to these issues when they start hustling and learn through trial and error.

*Location.* A typical customer of a hustler generally does not have a place to take a hustler. The customer is either married, do not want a hustler in the house, or are visiting from out of town. Many hustlers either live at home or live with roommates. As such, many hustlers operate in alleys or back streets where they can perform their services in the front seat of the car or at a secluded outdoor area. Some hustlers will live by themselves in a nearby weekly rental place. It is generally best for a customer to think through the issue of location before engaging a hustler. There are bathhouses, nearby motels, or even spa's that have private rooms with Jacuzzi's.

*Transportation.* Many hustlers do not have cars. Hustlers may be hustling just for a place to stay the night. In fact, there are many guys who will exchange sex simply for a place to sleep. The customer who engages the services of a hustler should have intentions of consummating the transaction somewhere close to where the hustler was picked up.

*Sexual Activity.* All hustlers and high quality escorts have sexual limits. It is always to best to be up front with expectations in the areas of kissing, oral sex, rimming, and anal intercourse. These are the most common requests. Interests in other sexual activities such as water sports, sadomasochism, bondage, spanking, or any other form of activity should be discussed up front.

*Communications.* Hustlers do not tend to go after repeat business. As such, they do not give much thought on how they can be reached. Any good hustler will have a beeper where a customer can leave a numeric or voice message.

*Negotiating Skills.* There are several issues that need to be negotiated before a transaction with a hustler can be consummated. However, before the negotiations can take place a customer will need to get through the hustler's defense system and develop trust.

Generally, it is better to go with a hustler that has thought out their business. The reason for this is that a hustler that lives in the neighborhood has transportation, and some form of communications is less likely to steal from a customer or cause physical harm to a customer. A hustler who is working in an attempt to make their life better is more likely to have respect for themselves and consequently more respect for their customers.

The hustler's primary concern is that a prospective customer does not work for law enforcement. Likewise, a customer may very well have the same concern. Being entrapped in a sting operation is a very real risk for both the hustler and the customer. It is a common myth police officers must answer truthfully if they are asked if they work for law enforcement. In fact, police officers do not need to answer the question truthfully. There is no sure way to avoid this risk. Chapter 10 discusses legal issues in great detail.

In some cases, hustlers are very good at conversation and direct in solicitation. This tends to be the exception rather than the rule. Generally, a customer must control the conversation and carefully choose their words when negotiating with a hustler.

First, it is important for a customer to develop trust as quickly as possible. Generally, this means exploring mutual interests. After exchanging pleasantries there are several lines that can be used:

- Are you interested in making some money?
- What do you like to do sexually?

- I would be interested in some company tonight.
- Are you working this evening?

A hustler who is actively looking for customers may use the following lines:

- I'm working tonight.
- Are you looking for a date?
- I could really use some money.
- You know that this will cost you.
- Would you buy me a drink?

It is best to negotiate location, amount of time, sexual activity and price before leaving the place of meeting.

A hustler will generally not take very long to decide if a potential customer is serious about a transaction. Some potential customers are just looking for companionship for several hours while they sit in a bar. Or worse, have the expectation that they will be able to pick up a hustler without having to pay. Typically, if the transaction is not negotiated by the time the first drink is completed or within a few minutes in the case of a street hustler, the hustler will make an excuse and move on to more fertile fields.

*Opportunity.* Successful hustlers rely on various means to create opportunity. These are the signs to look for in a good hustler:

- *Good hustlers have good body language.* Good hustlers try to establish eye contact, keep an open posture, and try to smile at potential customers. It is the rare hustler that has good body language. This may have to do with the fact that many of them are on drugs and in their own little worlds. In general, it is best to avoid hustlers who have blood shot eyes or have any other indication of drug use. The behavior of hustlers can be very erratic, and the sexual performance will generally be poor.
- *Good hustlers are open to conversation.* A good hustler will be able to survey a crowd and know exactly who will make

a good customer.  A good hustler will look for body language, clothing, jewelry, and what type of car a prospective customer is driving.  If a hustler feels someone has the potential to be a good customer, the hustler will welcome a prospective customer's advances or may even approach the prospective customer.

• *Good hustlers have good attitudes.*  A good hustler will be able to hold a pleasant conversation.  A good hustler will make good eye contact, be attentive, and appear businesslike.  If the conversation carries on too long without reaching agreement on a transaction the hustler will move on to another table or bar.

• *Good hustlers are respectful and expect respect.*  All good relationships begin and end with respect.  If a hustler feels that the potential customer is being demeaning or degrading during the conversation the hustler will terminate the conversation and move on.  It should be remembered that most hustlers have complicated defense systems, and may take what would ordinarily harmless statement to be threatening.  It is best to tread lightly in terms of conversation.

• *Good hustlers make themselves physically available.*  A good hustler will stand or sit in a place that is visible and provides a good observation point.  A hustler will tend to be alone since customers are less likely to approach the hustler if surrounded by a group.  A good hustler will also approach potential customers in a discrete manner.

*What a customer can expect to pay.*  Customers of escorts and hustlers make a serious mistake when their first question is price.  The first rule of sales in **any** profession is that a potential customer who asks the price first is not a serious customer.  A hustler will generally never discuss price if it is the first question, but will ask, "What are you looking for?"  If the customer is only interested in price, the hustler may decline the customer simply because 90% of the time price shoppers do not make good customers.

A serious customer explores needs and logistics before talking about price.  A serious customer will develop rapport, explore mutual interests, and establish that there is a suitable location to consummate the transaction. Price should always be the last thing discussed.

Prices range anywhere from twenty dollars for oral sex in an adult bookstore (and five or ten dollars is not unheard of) to three hundred dollars (or more) for hustlers who have outstanding looks. The higher priced hustlers are very particular about the types of customers they accept.

In general, a customer can expect to pay the following amounts:

- **Bookstores.** Twenty to forty dollars.
- **Street Hustlers.** Forty to fifty dollars.
- **Bars.** Normally, fifty to one hundred dollars. For top of the line hustlers a customer can expect to pay $125 to $200. A customer should expect to pay at least $100 for any hustler of any quality.

Tips are always appreciated and generally expected. However, the price is negotiated up front, most hustlers will not be disappointed if a customer does not tip and will be appreciative if the customer does tip.

Hustlers are very well aware of the various con games customers will play. It is best for customers to avoid the following behaviors that could lead to a confrontation:

- **Do not negotiate for one set of services with the expectation of another set of services.** Most hustlers are very good at setting their limits, and if the hustler senses a customer has been dishonest with them, the hustler may attempt to rectify the situation physically, verbally, or through theft.
- **If the price quoted is too high for the customer's budget, the customer should make a counteroffer.** Many hustlers quote an artificially high price. In general, hustlers who quote an artificially high price will end up being a disappointment. However, there are cases where a hustler quotes an artificially high price because they expect to be negotiated down to the market price.

- **Pay the agreed amount.** A number of customers attempt to short change hustlers. This is one reason why most hustlers ask for the money up front. Of course, the risk to a customer is the money will be paid and the hustler will then disappear with the money without performing any services. However, a customer that shortchanges a hustler can expect trouble.

Customers need to keep in mind that dealing with hustlers have several dangers. There are many customers that have been physically harmed by hustlers or have been robbed by hustlers. In most instances where a customer has been physically hurt it has been because the customer did something to instigate the violence.

There is a common thread to encounters with hustlers that lead to violence. First, the customer is typically someone who has a great deal of experience in picking up hustlers, and the customer has a sense of security based on past experience. Second, the customer attempts to con the hustler into providing services without payment. The customer may use several ruses such as representing themselves to being wealthy, being a talent scout, or by making an offer to provide something of value at a later date.

The hustler may be taken in by the con and will go back to the customer's home or hotel room. When the hustler discovers that the con of providing services without remuneration the hustler may resort to theft or violence to get their payment.

There are also many hustlers who consider theft as part of their routine of providing services to a client. The hustler may go after a customer's wallet or steal jewelry or other valuables. When the customer discovers the theft this will generally result in a confrontation with the hustler. This confrontation may lead to violence.

The vast majority of these incidents do not get reported to police. However, most large communities will have at least one or two reported murders a year due to hustling activity.

In the case of theft it is best for the customer to secure their valuables and only have enough money with which to pay the hustler and pay a tip.

In dealing with hustlers it is important for the customer to realize a hustler does not get a lot of respect in life. Most people are far more willing to part with their money than to offer their respect to another individual. The respect a customer shows towards a hustler has far more meaning than the money the hustler is paid. Likewise, if a hustler feels the customer is simply another person who is attempting to abuse them or exploit them the customer becomes a likely target for violence or theft.

# Chapter Two

# Massage/Body Rubs

---

assage is how many people get their start in the escort business. Most massage therapists have no interest of becoming an escort. Essentially, many massage therapists get propositioned so many times they finally give in and decide to do escort work.

There are some individuals who have worked all aspects of the male prostitution market. In some respects they see changes in the job as a promotion of sorts. I received this letter from an escort in New York:

*I have explored many aspects of the male prostitution market for the last ten years. I started hustling at Rounds in New York City about ten years ago, but I didn't like the idea of picking up someone with out knowing at least something about them.*

*I then started doing massage work or bodywork. I worked out of my house for many successful years. I built up a large list of clients who mostly lived a straight life.*

*I am now working as an escort.  I am listed on a number of web-sites.  I have built up a nice list of regular clients who I see on a weekly basis.*

Many clients look for massage therapists because they are looking for sex at a fraction of the price of an escort.  While most escorts charge between $100 and $250 for an hour, many massage therapists charge $40 to $100 for an hour.  Even at those prices many clients will ask for a half-hour price.  Most of the top massage therapists will not offer a half-hour price.

The difference between someone who advertises for massage and body rubs has to do with a number of factors.  Good massage work generally requires training.  A person who advertises body rubs will typically not have any formal massage training.  In some localities a person must be licensed to legally use the term massage in their advertising.  An advertiser is typically required to provide a copy of their license to a publication in order to use the term massage.

A prospective client who calls someone for a massage or body rub should inquire about the therapist's training in massage.  Massage therapists will either state the number of training hours earned or tell the prospective client what types of massage they have received training.  Although a massage therapist must receive 500 hours of training to be nationally certified, it is usually sufficient for someone to have completed a course in massage and a course in anatomy and physiology to be competent to give a massage.

Many massage therapists who are trained in erotic massage receive their training from the Body Electric.  The Body Electric offers a number of classes around the country in the art of sensual massage.  They have classes for both men and women.

The Body Electric offers a number of interesting programs including:

- Various classes in erotic massage at all levels with classes held in Atlanta, Boston, Los Angeles, and San Francisco, Washington, D.C. and most major cities.

- They offer various intensive classes around the country on a number of topics.
- They offer a number of retreats to resorts such as Hawaii.
- They offer a number of special workshops on sexuality.

The Body Electric's web-site offers a full description of the classes offered. The web-site is **http://www.bodyelectric.org**. This school is excellent for body workers or any individual interested in erotic massage or alternative healing methods. The variety of their programs and locations where they offer their programs make for a convenient get away for anyone.

I would not suggest getting a massage from someone without at least have basic training. The reasons for this are:

- Massage therapists with training will generally have a routine that will result in a pleasant massage.
- Massage therapists with training will be familiar with contraindications to massage and will adjust their massage techniques to avoid harming a client.
- Massage therapists with training will be able to treat problems such as a bad back, pulled muscles, edema, headaches, and other neuromuscular problems without aggravating the condition.

Although injury or death is uncommon when receiving a massage, it does happen. These are some of the contraindications for massage work:

- A client being treated for cancer should not get a massage. If the cancer is terminal, light massage is generally acceptable with a doctor's approval. Keep in mind massage can hasten death in a client with a terminal illness. Massage therapy activates the lymphatic system. Cancer spreads through the lymphatic system.
- Clients with high blood pressure should receive a massage where the hand movements are directed away from the heart.

- Clients with diabetes should avoid deep pressure as it can result in bruising.
- A client with an extreme mental disorder can experience unintended emotional effects.
- A client with neuromuscular injuries should be certain the massage therapist selected has training on these problems.
- Areas affected by varicose veins should not be massaged. Varicose veins are a condition where the valves of the veins are not working properly. Massage of this area can worsen the condition and cause pain.
- Clients with a history of blood clots in the legs should avoid massage.

If someone advertises for body rubs and does not have formal training in massage there is little likelihood the individual will use any massage techniques that will result in injury to a relatively healthy client. Common mistakes made by persons unfamiliar with massage techniques include too much pressure on the spine, too much pressure on the kidneys, too much pressure on joints or hyperextension of the joints, and massaging the stomach with a counter-clockwise motion. There are even experienced massage therapists who make these mistakes. The client should always alert the massage therapist if the pressure is to great or of any feelings of pain.

Many escorts advertise in the massage and escort sections of their local papers. Clients realize the prices quoted for massage are considerably lower than the prices quoted for escort work. Generally, an escort who advertises for massage is only willing to do a massage in the nude and masturbate the client (referred to in the business as "stress release", "complete body massage" or "massage to completion").

There are also many massage therapists who will not do escort work or perform any types of sexual acts. Unfortunately, many clients are not up front about their expectations. There are also many clients who are dishonest about their expectations. This leads to some friction between the massage therapist and the client. Generally, a massage therapist who does not do sexual release or other sexual acts will clearly state in their advertising and on the phone that only non-sexual massages are offered. However, many of these same massage therapists will perform release or sexual acts with their regular clients.

When looking for a massage therapist I recommend that a prospective client cover a number of issues in their initial conversation.

*Types of massage practiced.* There are several common types of massage. The most commonly advertised forms of massage are sensual massage, Swedish massage, deep tissue massage, accupressure (sometimes called Shiatsu, a form of accupressure), and sports massage.

It is not uncommon for a client to call a massage therapist and ask what types of massage are offered. Unfortunately, most clients who ask this question do not have the slightest clue of the differences in massage techniques. Here is a brief description of the most common forms of massage offered:

- **Sensual Massage.** The purpose of sensual massage is to be erotic and relaxing. There is an expectation the massage will end in masturbation and ejaculation. There is also an expectation the massage will be performed in the nude. There are reputable schools that teach sensual massage techniques. However, many people who advertise sensual massage may not have any training in massage.
- **Swedish Massage.** Swedish massage is a form of massage therapy that employs certain types of movements. The signature movement of Swedish massage is the long sweeping movements of the hands over the body. Sensual massage usually employs the techniques of Swedish massage.
- **Deep Tissue Massage.** Deep tissue massage is a form of massage that is therapeutic in nature. It should not be confused with Swedish or sensual massage since it can be a painful form of massage. Generally, it is the best form of massage to treat back problems and sciatica (a painful condition caused when a muscle in the buttocks compresses the sciatic nerve and causes pain down the back of the legs).

A person who uses deep tissue techniques will have good knowledge of muscles, and how to treat neuromuscular problems. For the client with a bad back, this is their best bet.

- **Accupressure, Pressure Point, or Shiatsu.** These are forms of the same type of massage technique. Essentially, this type of massage involves the working of various pressure points in the body to improve the flow of energy through the body. This technique originates in China and has been shown to be effective in treating a number of conditions. There are various methods used, and some can be painful.
- **Sports Massage.** This form of massage is a combination of many massage techniques geared towards the individual who is physically active. Typically a massage therapist trained in sports massage is very knowledgeable of muscles and how the muscles work.

*Whether the massage therapist uses a table and oils.* A client interested in getting a massage should ask whether the massage therapist has a table and what type of oil is used. Even if the client wants to have the massage done on the bed, the client may ask if the massage therapist has a table. This is an indication the person has training in massage. The top massage therapists use Biotone cream. This massage cream is relatively expensive, but has several advantages over oil. This cream is good for moisturizing the skin, and it soaks into the skin. Oil is not good for moisturizing the skin, and can block the pores of the skin.

*Whether the massage therapist performs the massage in the nude.* It is best to ask a massage therapist if the massage is performed in the nude. If the massage therapist does not do massage in the nude this is a good indication the client will receive a legitimate massage. If this is the massage therapist's policy it is better to respect this policy and to go to someone else. It can be uncomfortable for both the client and the massage therapist if the subject comes up during the massage.

*Whether there is a release at the end of the massage.* This basically means the massage therapist will masturbate a client to climax at the end of the massage. In many cultures this is considered a very acceptable part of a massage. In the United States this is considered prostitution and is illegal. Most people who advertise for massage will limit their sexual activity to masturbating a client. There are, of course, exceptions, but clients should not expect any additional sexual activities unless they have negotiated it before going for their massage appointment.

*In or Out-Calls.* Massage therapists are likely to offer services in their home or at the client's home or hotel. Prices for out-calls are generally about $20 more than in-calls. Some massage therapists only do in-calls and some massage therapists only do out-calls.

*Price.* A client can expect to pay from $40 to $100 for a massage. A good massage therapist will not negotiate price or offer a half-hour rate. An experienced massage therapist maintains price integrity, and seeks clients who will be repeat clients at the normal rates. However, a good massage therapist will refer the client to other massage therapists who charge lower prices. These massage therapists may be just starting their practice. Typically the top massage therapists have a system of referrals to accommodate clients.

Massage therapists differ in many respects from people who advertise as escorts. The most obvious is massage therapists charge less, but their services are also different. Also, massage therapists tend to have a large repeat clientele. The top escorts also rely heavily on a repeat clientele, but many of the individuals who advertise as escorts do not have as large a repeat clientele as massage therapists.

The average massage therapist is probably older than most escorts, and may or may not have the muscles or body of an escort. Another difference with massage therapists is the hours that they keep. Massage therapists are generally available during the day and many of them do not work past 11p.m.

There are some very good reasons why massage therapists do not take calls late at night. First, massage therapists see themselves as professionals and not as someone who can be called at the last minute for an appointment. Second, the quality of clients diminishes greatly after midnight. Many clients after midnight are drunk or on drugs. Also, many clients after midnight are only looking for sex. Massage therapists do not see these types as clients as being very high quality. These types of clients are impulse buyers who do not make very good repeat clients for a massage therapist.

On the whole, massage therapists probably make more money than escorts because they have more clients, their business is steadier, and they see more people during the day.

Although most professional massage therapists will see anyone, there are many massage ads that target specific markets. Generally, these massage therapist's charge lower rates. These massage therapists see massage as a way to live out their sexual fantasies. Examples of these restrictive advertisements are:

- Leather daddy
- Senior Dude
- Experienced guy to other in-shape guys
- Grandson for hire
- All Asians
- For men over 40
- First timers that are under 35 and have tight bodies
- Real bear

A client looking for a legitimate massage should look for certain words in an advertisement:

- Certified
- Trained
- Type of massage (Swedish, Deep Tissue, Sports Massage, Accupressure are the most common)
- Table
- CMT (Certified Massage Therapist)

A client looking for sex should look for the following words in an advertisement:

- Any mention of penis size.
- Get naked and I will do the rest.
- Prostate massage
- Dominant top
- Verbal top
- Bottom

Massage therapists tend to do very well with repeat clientele, and tend to be leery of new clients. Here are several things to keep in mind:

- Most massage therapists will not discuss penis size.
- Most massage therapists seek clients who are interested in their skills and not their appearance. Even massage therapists who are very attractive will be hesitant to take a client who is overly concerned about appearance.
- Many massage therapists will be hesitant to accept a client more concerned about sexual activities than their massage skills. Some massage therapists run advertisements for escort work. If a client calls on their massage advertisement and asks for sex, the client will either be quoted the escort rate or declined as a client.
- Massage therapists do not like to be asked their age. In the world of massage age is just a number and many massage therapists prefer to keep it unlisted.

As a general rule of thumb, if the advertisement does not mention age, penis size or description then the prospective client should be careful and polite when asking these questions. If the advertisement is non-sexual it is better for the client to express their sexual expectations than to ask the massage therapist about what the massage therapist will do sexually. Again, clients should be careful and polite.

Many massage therapists run multiple advertisements in the larger markets. These ads may use different names or even different phone numbers. There are several reasons to run multiple advertisements. The primary reason for running multiple advertisements is to market to different types of services. Typically, five to seven advertisements in competitive markets will provide sufficient saturation. The various types of advertisements placed in publications are:

- A generic advertisement that describes professional massage therapy.
- Separate advertisements for different types of massage such as erotic massage, deep tissue massage, sports massage, and Swedish massage. Typically different forms of massage attract different types of clients and the most successful advertisements are limited to marketing one form of massage.
- Advertising for tandem massage. Two people perform a tandem massage. The top of the line massage client oftentimes likes tandem massages. Also, it is a good service to offer regular clients.
- If a massage therapist does one-hour massages or 90-minute massages, the two should not be mentioned in the same advertisement. Typically a client will always try to hedge their bets. The client will say that they will try the one-hour, and then decide on whether or not to go for a ninety-minute massage. This wreaks havoc with scheduling. It is better to negotiate the amount of time up front.
- Advertisements can also focus on physical appearance. Oftentimes a person can be described in several different ways, and each description attracts a different type of client.
- A massage therapist may also want to run an experimental advertisement that targets different markets.

There are several other reasons for running multiple advertisements:

- Different advertisements attract different types of clientele. When things are busy it is easy to tell the quality of the potential new client by which advertisement caught the client's eye.
- During slow periods, the advertisements bring in a diverse type of clientele helps to alleviate income swings.
- Multiple advertisements allow the massage therapist a way to experiment with pricing.

The potential client should keep in mind several points when considering what type of person to employ:

- Massage therapists represent the best value for the money. Massage therapists are generally less expensive than escorts, and offer similar if less broad services. Many escorts also advertise for massage and have training in massage.
- Many massage therapists offer in-calls. Most escorts do not offer in-call service.
- Massage therapists are very keenly aware of the words a client in a conversation. Prospective clients should be careful about what they ask and how they ask it.
- Massage therapists are the lowest risk for theft and physical violence. A massage therapist heavily relies on repeat clients for their income.

## Licensing

Licensing is not necessarily an indication of quality. Licensing processes tend to be based on bureaucracy and are perfunctory in measuring the knowledge and skills of a massage therapist.

A potential client should ask the type of training the massage therapist possesses and the number of hours of training. The potential client should not ask these questions in a manner that is condescending or judgmental. A well-trained massage therapist will not accept a client that is condescending or judgmental during a conversation. A potential client who exhibits the need to control does not tend to make a desirable client.

In some areas there are distinctive advertising categories for licensed massage therapists and for body rubs (essentially a category for those massage therapists who are not licensed). Licensed massage therapists are generally expected to state their license number in their ad. Typically, a licensed massage therapist will generally not offer sexual services, and if the massage therapist does provide sexual services it is only with repeat clients. A massage therapist who advertises body rubs may very well have the same training and experience offered by licensed massage therapists.

A client receiving a massage should keep in mind the following points before and during a massage:

- A client should disclose all relevant medical information. A trained massage therapist will adjust their massage techniques for relevant medical conditions.
- A client with a bad back can either request to have it worked on therapeutically or the client can specify a lighter touch. Massage therapists are concerned about a client's well being. If the client has a bad back and does not want therapeutic work on their back then it says to the massage therapist that the client does not want to get better. Massage clients who prefer to live with a bad back than have treatment for the bad back do not make very good clients.
- A client should give feedback during the massage on the level of pressure and feelings of pain. If there is an area of the body that is tender it is generally an area that needs additional work.
- It is very natural for a client to become erect during a massage. Massage activates the parasympathetic nervous system that activates sensual arousal. Touch by nature is very erotic and results in the erotic senses. Also, it is very natural to fall asleep during a massage. If the client starts dreaming a penile erection will naturally occur.

- It is very natural to have the need to urinate during a massage. Massage stimulates the lymphatic and circulatory systems, and this can result in an increased need to urinate.

### The Health Benefits of Massage

There are a number of health benefits to massage.

- Massage is relaxing, and very good therapy for stress.
- Massage activates the lymphatic system and promotes removal of toxins from muscle cells.
- Massage is good for the removal of excess fluid build up in the legs and arms if there are no other medical problems such as high blood pressure or the potential for blood clots.
- Massage can be used to treat headaches.
- Massage will speed recovery from muscle pulls and other muscle damage.
- Massage will speed recovery from surgery.
- Massage will promote blood flow through the muscles.
- Massage will increase the sense of well being.

A massage therapist appreciates clients who have respect for the healing aspects of their training.

There are several types of clients who go to massage therapists in an attempt to live out their sexual fantasies. The reason massage therapists attract certain types of sexual fantasy seekers is because they are less expensive than most escorts and massage is an activity that fits into many people's sexual fantasies.

Massage therapists attract the following types of clients seeking to live a sexual fantasy:

- *Couples.* Heterosexual couples who are willing to pay for sex generally seek out massage therapists. Typically the male has the fantasy of having their female partner massaged and then having the massage therapist engage in sexual activity with the female. In many cases this is because the male has an impotence problem. Problems generally arise when the male partner has not told the female partner of the fantasy. Likewise, there are many massage therapists who are gay and have no interest in having sexual relations with a female. These types of clients are not typically repeating clients and are typically price sensitive.

- *First timers.* There are many clients who have never had sex with a man. These clients tend to see massage therapists as less threatening than escorts because they get time to develop a comfort level with the massage therapist before engaging in a sexual relationship.
- *Straight men.* For some reason, men who see themselves as heterosexual feel they can continue to deny their homosexual tendencies by seeing a massage therapist. These individuals are typically referred to as "trade". Trade is a term that denotes a heterosexual male who likes to have sex with men without reciprocation. A massage therapist is more likely to attract trade than an escort. The reason for this is because it is easier for a heterosexual male to rationalize it is the massage therapist making the sexual overture. There are in fact many massage therapists who advertise in straight magazines simply to attract such clients.

Massage therapists attract a more varied type of clientele than escorts. Massage therapists attract a younger and more attractive group of clients than most escorts. The reason for this is the therapeutic benefits of massage and the fact massage is less expensive then hiring an escort. Also, clients can justify in their minds that massage is not cheating on a spouse and does not adversely affect their heterosexual status.

There are many massage therapists who will only give a professional and non-sexual massage. There are many clients who do not want a sexual massage. The services advertised in the gay magazines (and many straight publications) are generally perceived by prospective clients to be in part sexual.

Most massage therapists do not enter the profession of massage expecting to have sex with their clients. A client generally initiates sex with a massage therapist. If a massage therapist states the massage will be non-sexual it is best to not try to initiate sex with the massage therapist.

There are obvious logic problems with the idea that sex between a client and a massage therapist does not constitute sex. For many clients, however, that is their story, and they are sticking to it. Many of these same clients read Playboy for the interviews.

# Chapter Three

# Escorts

T here are many types of escorts who advertise. In some markets such as New York, Los Angeles and Miami the prospective client can choose from a broad assortment of escorts. In other markets there may only be a few available escorts, or the market may be controlled by an agency. In some markets the only option is the chance availability of a hustler.

Many escorts who advertise only do escort work part-time and are either students or have full time employment. A prospective client who calls the advertisements will find great diversity in terms of availability, physical characteristics, and types of services offered.

### Reading the Advertisements

There are a few things to keep in mind when reading the advertisements. First, in many markets the bulk of the classified advertising is controlled by escort agencies. The advertising is written in a way to make it look like an individual is advertising when in fact it is an agency advertisement. This is not necessarily a bad thing, but it is something a prospective client should know when calling an advertisement.

Second, many escorts advertise under different names and run multiple classified advertisements. There are many reasons for doing this:

- Many publications have several pages of escort advertising. It makes sense to have advertising on as many pages as possible.
- In order for an individual escort to compete effectively against the agency advertising, they need to run numerous advertisements.
- The escort may want to market several distinctive services. From a marketing perspective it is best to keep each advertisement to one type of service.
- Multiple advertisements allow escorts to be alerted to potential clients that are shopping around for prices, potential clients calling advertisements for phone sex, and uncovers clients who are making bogus appointments.
- Multiple advertisements allow for test marketing of wording, services and diversification into new markets.

A potential client should consider several things before calling an advertisement. These issues include desired appearance, personality, sexual activity, penis size, communications, location, and budget.

### *Appearance*

Generally, the appearance of an escort is important to the client. As a general rule, an escort prefers clients that have broad tastes in appearance rather than clients who have narrow tastes in appearance. Typically, a client with very narrow tastes is very difficult to please and is not typically a repeat client. Clients who have broad tastes are generally more interested in the personality of an escort than their physical appearance.

When a client is overly concerned about an escort's appearance the client is generally looking for reasons to reject the escort. When a client's first question to an escort is "What do you look like?" when an adequate description appears in the advertisement, it is a clear sign the client is looking for reasons to exclude the escort from consideration.

One agency, that represents many models who have appeared on magazine covers, in magazine centerfolds, and on gay porn box covers is amazed how many times their models are rejected by some clients. This agency has a policy of not accepting shoppers as clients. Shoppers are clients who like to call multiple advertisements. These clients may make up the majority of potential clients, but they tend not to be loyal clients. Loyal clients may make up about 20% of the prospective client base, but they also represent about 80% of the income for an established escort or escort agency.

Appearance is a very subjective matter. There is clearly a market for every imaginable type of escort. There is even a report that one client's favorite escort is in his sixties and he uses him because he is a fabulous kisser. In fact, there are several escorts and massage therapists in the United States who are over sixty years of age.

There is always the risk of misrepresentation in an advertisement. It is safer to call picture advertisements than advertisements with no picture. If it is a picture advertisement, it is safer to call an advertisement that displays the face, than one that is cropped. Most magazines check whether the picture belongs to the escort. If the magazine requires a release to publish a picture then the client can be certain it is a picture of the person in question. It is legitimate to ask an escort the age of the picture, since some escorts use pictures up to a decade old in their advertising. Some agency advertisements do not use actual pictures of their models, although many of them do use actual pictures. It depends on the market and the agency.

The characteristics a client should consider when reading the advertisements include; the age, height/weight, hair color, body hair, and race.

## *Age*

This is an area where most advertisements are deceiving. There are some escorts who shave as many as twenty years off their age. Generally, however, the age shaving is in the range of five to seven years. Many escorts do not lie about their age or will give a range. There are also many escorts who regard age as just another number, and it is a number that is unlisted.

The most popular age group is 18-21. In reality, there are very few individuals who are 18-21 and have the ability to operate as an independent escort. There are several reasons for this:

- Younger escorts do not have the business sense to operate their own business.
- Younger escorts oftentimes live with friends or family and does not have the ability to work discretely as an escort.
- Younger escorts oftentimes lack the communications or transportation to conduct a business.
- Younger escorts are not emotionally prepared for the business.

Younger escorts typically work as hustlers or for agencies. Some hustlers may develop enough stability to advertise on their own, and some escorts who work for escort agencies will develop enough business sense to work on their own. These are the exceptions, rather than the rule.

Typically someone in the 18 to 21 age range who works as an independent escort will have learned how to run their business from a friend or from their experiences working with an agency. These escorts are typically pretty intelligent if they are able to run a business at such an early age, and may be using their earnings to work through college.

The vast majority of independent escorts are in the age range of 24 to 30 even if they market themselves as 18 to 21. This is typically an age when a person can develop some muscle due to changes in their metabolism, have become independent from their family, have developed business skills, and have developed the financial means to maintain a business.

Many clients and new escorts believe the only requirement for escorts to run a successful business is to place an advertisement in a local publication. Establishing an escort business does not require a lot of capital in comparison to other businesses, but it does require some capital and business skills. Many of the things we may take for granted in terms of operating a business are hurdles for most escorts who start in the business. There are many assets and business skills that come with age. This is the reason why older escorts are generally more successful than younger escorts.

Many of the most successful escorts are well over thirty or even forty years of age.

Typically, escorts who are over thirty have been in the business for many years and have an established list of clients. These escorts treat their work as a business, and enjoy their work. Escorts may continue to market themselves as if they are in their twenties, but in reality they are generally blessed with good genetics, disciplined training, disciplined diet, good business skills and a good plastic surgeon.

Older escorts tend to have a more established clientele and rely heavily on repeat business. Younger escorts tend to move around quite a bit or do not stay in the business very long. Also, clients who seek out younger escorts do not generally stay loyal to an escort. Older escorts tend to be more emotionally stable and attract clients who are attracted to emotional stability. Younger escorts tend to be less emotionally stable and attract clients who are attracted to emotional instability. This can be very draining on a client, so the client who uses younger escorts tends to use many escorts rather than staying loyal to any particular escort.

Older escorts are becoming more popular in many markets. This can be explained because the majority of clients are baby boomers who are forty to fifty years of age. These clients typically prefer escorts with some emotional and physical maturity. Many of these clients prefer escorts who are slightly younger, but not markedly younger.

## *Height/Weight*

The most popular type of escort is 21 years old, 6 foot and 200 pounds. There are very few individuals who meet this description in the real world.

The generic ways escorts advertise themselves are slender, tight swimmer's build, muscular swimmer's build, muscular, beefy, ripped, and bodybuilder. Here is a method to interpret these descriptions:

*Slender.* This refers to someone who is below or near the minimum standard weight for someone's height and has very little muscle definition. For example, someone who is 5'9" and 135 pounds is slender.

*Tight Swimmer's Body.* This describes someone who is from the low point to the mid-point of the standard weight scale and has some muscular definition. For example, someone who is 5'9" and 140 to 155 pounds would have a tight swimmer's body.

*Muscular Swimmer's Build.* A muscular swimmer's build is someone with good definition and between the mid-point and the upper end of the standard weight charts. Someone who is at 5'9" and between 160 and 170 pounds would be considered to have a muscular swimmer's build or gymnast's build.

*Muscular.* Someone who is muscular is over the high end of the standard weight charts but below the weight level for to be considered a bodybuilder. This individual would typically weigh between 190 and 200 pounds.

*Ripped.* This describes someone who has superior muscle definition regardless of weight. It is indicative of body fat below 6%. Some escorts will cite their body fat in their advertising.

*Beefy.* Although the ideal escort for most clients is muscular, many of the top escorts are beefy. Beefy escorts have muscle, but also have higher body fat and may have a bit of a tummy. There is a growing trend towards "real" men types of escorts. These types of escorts are rarely in demand by agencies, but many of them have a very loyal clientele who look for an older more masculine look.

*Bodybuilder.* Typically, a bodybuilder is someone between 200 and 300 pounds and is incredibly muscular. These escorts typically train for body building competitions and may be on steroids to gain muscle mass. There are many natural bodybuilders who use natural supplements; however, because the use of steroids is a felony in some states very few bodybuilders will admit to the use of steroids.

The 21 year-old, 6 foot, 200-pound ideal escort is very rare. Someone who is 6 foot and 200 pounds is typically lying about their age if they advertise as twenty-one. Most people do not have the metabolism to have this sort of body at a young age.

It is important for prospective clients to have realistic expectations. Many escorts fall into the slender and lean swimmers build categories. Very few escorts have bodybuilder bodies.

### Hair Color/Body Hair

Hair color and body hair are very important to most potential clients. There are very few choices in this area, but these attributes are important to the client.

Hair color tends to come in blonde, light or dark brunette, black, and red. Blondes are the most sought after type of escort, though there are many clients who do not like blondes. Most clients will take a brunette if there are no available blondes, but there are many clients who will only take blondes. Red is the least desired hair color, but fortunately many of these escorts can market themselves as blondes, though they may have difficulty getting a tan.

Most clients do not like overly bleached blondes. An escort who dyes their hair blonde should have it done professionally, and it should look as natural as possible.

Body hair is also very important to clients. The most popular type is smooth. Many escorts shave their body hair to give a smooth appearance. An increasing number of clients prefer a masculine and natural look. This means body hair is desirable to many potential clients. There are very few escorts with body hair, and these escorts tend to have a very loyal following.

There are many things an escort should not do with their body hair.

- Eighty percent of clients do not like facial hair or long sideburns. Most clients prefer a clean-cut look.
- There are some clients who like long hair and will only go with escorts with long hair. Most clients want short hair.
- Clients who like smooth bodies generally do not like shaved pubic hair.
- Clients do not like extreme hair colors. The unnaturally dyed blonde should go for a more natural look.

Good hustlers are very aware of the optimum manner in which to keep their hair, while many advertised escorts do not see it as important. This is because the hustler knows what attributes attract customers. Hustlers tend to learn from the trial and error experiences derived from working the streets and the bars. Many escorts who advertise underestimate the fact that spending time on hair is very important in terms of marketing themselves.

### Race/Skin Color

Race is a very important physical characteristic for many potential clients. In some markets there is very little or limited demand for escorts of color, but in the larger markets there is significant demand for escorts of all colors.

Most advertisements will state the race or nationality of an escort. Some escorts of color will run advertisements that state their color and advertisements that do not state their color. Oftentimes escorts with mixed parentage or light skin may advertise with different descriptions such as "exotic", "half-breed", or "half-this and half-that".

Since many clients have a preference for Caucasian escorts, many escorts with mixed parentage or light skin may advertise themselves as white.   Likewise, clients have varying fantasies about escorts of color.   These are the most common fantasies:

**African American.**   There are many clients who will only see African American escorts.   The typical view of African American escorts is they have large penises, are muscular, and tend to be tops.   A difficulty for African American escorts is many of their potential clients want a specific shade of skin color.

**Latino.**   Many clients prefer Caucasian or Latino escorts. Just as many clients have different preferences for the shade of color in African American escorts, clients tend to have specific geographical preferences for Latino escorts.   Typically a Latino escort will market themselves as from Puerto Rico, Central America, South America, or Spain.

**Asian.**   Asian escorts are also very popular and some client's only hire Asian escorts.   Like the Latino escort, many clients hire based on geographic origin.   Asian escorts oftentimes market themselves as being from Thailand, China, Japan, the Philippines, or as Asian American.

***Other Popular Nationalities.***   There are certain clients who have personal tastes for exotic looks (or are exotic by American standards).   In competitive markets it is always best to advertise in a way to stand out in the market.   The types of nationalities that have some appeal from an advertising point of view are: Indian, American Indian, Pacific Islander, Hawaiian, Persian, Egyptian, Eastern European, German, British, French, Greek, Australian, and nearly any other nationality that evokes a favorable physical image.

As in most fields it is harder for a person of color to succeed due to discrimination.   However, clients tend to be very loyal to an escort with the racial characteristics they seek.   This means, once escorts of color have developed a stable clientele they are as likely to make as much money as other escorts.   It just takes longer to establish a repeat clientele.

*Appearance and Selection of an Escort*

By now it should be clear there are a number of variables that make an escort desirable to a client.

If a client has five essential physical attributes desired in an escort, and the client is uncompromising on all of these attributes, then a field of one hundred or more escorts can easily be narrowed down to two or three escorts who meet their stated standards. If a client has multiple stated standards, it is probable the remaining two or three will be disqualified on unstated standards.

This goes back to a previous question: how many magazine covers does an escort need to appear on in order to be considered attractive. The truth of the matter is, everyone is attracted to someone for very personal and individualistic reasons. People attracted to others based on very broad criteria tend to be emotionally healthier than people who are attracted to others based on very narrow criteria.

For the escort who does not meet a potential client's stated physical criteria, it is best for the escort to decline the client and realize he would not be in the business if there were not people who found him attractive. The potential client with precise requirements should stick to advertisements that clearly state their desired physical characteristics.

## *Personality*

After physical appearance, personality is probably the most important factor to a client. Client's who place almost their entire selection criteria on appearance report the highest degree of dissatisfaction with escorts. These clients are also the clients who are most likely to be robbed or involved in physical violence with an escort. Client's who think with both heads when choosing an escort report the highest degree of satisfaction.

There are several clues in an advertisement as to the personality of an escort. Types of phrases used to indicate a good match are:

Warm and easy going personality

Eager to please
Over 80% repeat
Affectionate
Friendly and fun
Nice guy
No attitude

There are also a number of clues as to whether an escort will have a difficult personality:

No mention of personality
Body worship only
Oversell of physical looks
Only mention of price is "expensive"
Spoiled boy
Priced from
Overemphasis on penis size

There are no guarantees with these clues. There are many professional escorts who are very good at knowing what a client wants to hear. These escorts are also very good at making a warm and friendly personality come out over the phone. Once the escort is in the client's room, the escort turns into a pure hustler. The only clue to this sort of behavior is the escort will state the price as "starting from". This is a sure sign that the attitude will change when the client is in the room with the escort.

Personality is also an area that can best be screened by word of mouth referrals. It is always best to get a referral from another escort or a client who has seen the escort before.

### Sexual Activity

There are many variations on the types of sexual activities an escort will provide. Some escorts will provide very limited activities and others will be very willing to do just about anything.

Many escorts are unwilling to talk about what they will and will not do over the phone. Very few will openly volunteer this information. It is best that potential clients bring up the subject of specific sexual activities.

Most escorts are willing to do some sexual activities with some clients and limit their sexual activities with other clients. This generally has to do with the degree of sexual attraction. Some escorts have problems with getting erections, may be having an off day, or may be unable to ejaculate. This problem also occurs when the escort is on drugs. As such, it is best for a potential client to state their expectations. There is no guarantee an escort will not lie about their ability to perform, but there are many escorts who are honest.

Here are some of the most common requests for sexual activity:

*Kissing.* There is a misperception most escorts will not kiss. This is generally true with hustlers, but many escorts will kiss and show affection.

*Oral.* Most escorts will give and receive oral sex. Some escorts may require condoms to be used. Most escorts will not allow ejaculation into their mouths, although many escorts will not have a problem ejaculating into someone else's mouth.

*Anal.* This refers to the being anally penetrated by someone's penis. Most people prefer either top or bottom positions. Top position is when the escort anally penetrates the client. Bottom position is when the client anally penetrates the escort. Versatile is when the escort will perform either as a bottom or a top. Some escorts charge more to take on the bottom role.

*Rimming.* Rimming is when a person performs oral sex on a person's anus. Although there is very little risk for getting HIV infection from rimming it can frequently result in the transmission of parasites. As such, although most escorts will allow themselves to be rimmed, they will not rim a client.

*Verbal Humiliation.* There are many clients who like to be verbally humiliated or have someone talk nasty to them while they are having sex. This is a light fantasy, and some escorts are very good at it.

There are several sexual activities requested less frequently. Although these types of activities can sound revolting these activities can be very erotic for some people. Some of these activities are unsafe, and require training (yes, there are training schools for sadomasochism). These activities are typically requested infrequently:

*Spanking.* This is when one person spanks another person on the buttocks with either a hand or belt. Typically, an escort does the spanking, but occasionally an escort will get spanked.

*Water sports.* This involves either urinating on a person or in their mouth. Some escorts will urinate on a client at their request, and very few will allow themselves to be urinated on. In rare cases a client will ask an escort to urinate while the client is being anally penetrated.

*Bondage.* This is when one individual gets tied up and then forced to perform sex. Generally, it is the escort who ties up the client.

*Sadomasochism (S & M).* Sadomasochism is a somewhat popular form of sexual fantasy. Most escorts who advertise sadomasochism tend to be the master or dominant role player. Some escorts will submit to the lesser forms of sadomasochism, but there are very few of these escorts. Forms of sadomasochism include strangling, gagging, blindfolding, cock and ball torture, whipping, bondage, verbal abuse, torture, electrodes, dildos, and other means that inflict physical or emotional abuse. When seeking out an escort who performs sadomasochism look for an escort who has a fully equipped dungeon and training in their field. Yes, there are training schools for this.

*Leather.* Many people have fantasies about sexual partners in leather. There are specific training programs for people into leather. There are also many unique clothing items that are made of leather including jock straps, chaps, harnesses, collars, armbands, hats, and vests.

*Fist fucking.* This is when someone is anally penetrated by the entire hand and sometimes continues to penetrate until the arm is inserted up to the elbow.

*Shaving.* Some people have the fantasy of shaving off all of their body hair or shaving off the body hair of another person.

Sexual exploration outside a person's normal behavior is healthy as long as the limits and boundaries of the individuals involved are respected. If the sexual activity has above normal danger it is best to hire someone who is trained in the specific form of sexual activity.

## Penis Size and Type

Many clients are interested in the penis size and type of an escort. On the whole, escorts have above average sized penis' otherwise they would not do very well in the market. There are many successful escorts with penis sizes that are of average size. However, many escorts lie about penis size.

First, many clients have a preference for either penis' which are circumcised or uncircumcised. Fortunately, most clients do not have an exclusionary preference. Uncircumcised penises are becoming more popular, but are still greatly less preferred than circumcised penises.

Second, clients have an interest in size. Generally, clients are more concerned about the length rather than the width. It is very rare for someone to have a penis size larger than nine inches in length, however, there are some clients who use nine inches as a benchmark for choosing an escort.

Penis size is typically a subjective matter. Many escorts will give an approximation rather than an exact size since many escorts have never actually measured their penises. There is average, above average, big and very big. Average is five to seven inches, above average is seven to eight, big is over eight inches, and very big is over nine inches.

There are several physical attributes that can affect the perceived appearance of a penis. A penis can appear larger or smaller based on width, whether it is circumcised, and the form of the head of the penis. Likewise, someone with a large penis may have more difficulty getting an erection than an individual with a smaller penis.

Typically a client who pressures an escort over the phone for their penis size is looking for phone sex. I would suggest that if penis size were part of a marketing strategy then the actual size should appear in the ad. If penis size is not a marketing strategy then size should only be expressed in approximate terms if at all. Client's who seek an escort based on a single attribute tend to make poor clients.

### Communications

Communications are how clients and escorts communicate with each other to make an appointment. Many escorts fail miserably because they do not realize it is not sufficient to just place an advertisement and have the world beat a path to their door. An advertised escort must make contact with a client through telephone communications.

Most escorts use pagers, however even this simple system has many flaws. Ideally, the potential client calls a pager number, enters a return number, the escort's pager displays the return number, and the escort returns the page within five or ten minutes. In reality, very few escorts can successfully master this system.

Typically, an escort will either operate through a pager system or a phone system or a combination of both.

### Pager Systems

Use of a pager to conduct business is a relatively inefficient way to conduct business for the following reasons:

- Potential clients generally want to make contact quickly, and do not want to wait for the escort to return a call.
- The client may be at a pay phone that does not accept the return of calls.

- For clients in a hotel, it may be insufficient to leave a return number since many hotels require callers to know the first and last name of the registered guest as well as the room number.
- Many clients do not know what information is required in order for the escort to return the call.
- Pager systems are subject to service problems. These problems include down time for the service, and a delay in forwarding pages.
- Many escorts forget to carry their pagers or even forget to change the batteries.
- Many escorts who have legitimate jobs do not leave messages on their pagers as to their availability.
- Many escorts do not return their pages in five to ten minutes.
- Many clients do not want to provide their name or phone numbers.

I estimate an escort who uses a pager system loses over 50% of their client business for these reasons. In fact, it is not unusual for only one out of ten escorts to return a page within five to ten minutes. For this reason, most clients will call multiple advertisements in the hopes of having maybe two or three return their pages.

If a pager system is used there are several ways to enhance service to potential clients:

- The escort should choose a reliable pager service.
- The escort should have voice and digital service on their pagers.
- Escorts should consider carrying a cellular phone so they can return pages promptly.
- The escort should record a friendly greeting message that clearly states what information must be left in order to return the call (however, this does not guarantee the client will follow directions).
- The escort should return pages within five to ten minutes.

One client writes about the difficulty of finding an escort in Los Angeles where there are hundreds of ads in the local papers:

*It's amazing how difficult it is to get an escort in Los Angeles. I've checked Frontiers, and "available 24 hours a day" doesn't seem to mean much. More often than not, I don't even get a return call on a page. Of course, I'm in a hotel, so pagers that only allow me to leave a digital phone number don't help. If I have the option, I leave the name of my hotel, my full name, and room number in a voice message. Of course, this has saved me a lot of money, but it has been surprising.*

### Direct Calling

Pager systems are very unreliable and are only used as a back up system by the most successful escorts. Typically, the most successful escorts have a fairly sophisticated telephone system that combines many of the features offered by the local telephone service combined with a reliable cellular phone service.

Typically, the most successful escorts invest a considerable amount of thought in their telephone systems. The objectives of their telephone systems are to allow clients to call them directly, to differentiate legitimate callers from troublemakers, and screen out problem callers. To achieve these results the escort will employ a number of telephone features. Among the features available from local telephone services are:

- *Caller Identification*. This feature allows the escort to see the name and number of the caller.
- *Anonymous Call Blocking.* This feature allows the escort to block people from calling them from unlisted phones numbers and some pay phones. Typically, 90% of calls to an escort from phones that list the caller as anonymous are crank callers. The caller receives a message saying the party called does not accept callers from blocked phones. The

caller needs to dial *82 to unblock their phone in order to call the escort.

- *Specific Call Blocking.* This allows the escort to block specific phone numbers from calling them. This can be used to discourage stalkers and repeat nuisance callers.
- *Signal Ring.* This allows the escort to have multiple phone numbers that ring on one telephone line. Typically, the telephone will have a distinctive ring for each phone number. This feature allows the escort to accomplish many things:

1. **One number is typically reserved for repeat clients.** Business cards are among the cheapest forms of advertising. The phone number on the business card is typically different than the one used for advertising. If a repeat client calls on the advertised number instead of the business card number it either means the client lost the business card or is calling around. If the repeat client is calling based on an advertisement rather than a business card number the client may or may not be interested in using the escort again.

2. **Different numbers are used in different advertisements**. This allows the escort to determine which advertisement generated the call. Oftentimes escorts charge differing amounts depending on which advertisement attracted the call.

3. **The escort can determine response rates from various advertisements.** Many escorts will keep track of the response rates from various advertisements to determine an optimal advertising strategy.

4. **The signal ring helps determine the honesty of the prospective client.** Typically, an escort's first question to a prospective client is "How did you hear about me?" The escort already knows the answer because of the signal ring. The client does not know the escort knows the answer. As such, if the prospective client is dishonest with their answer the escort knows the prospective client is dishonest. It is always best to

decline a client who is dishonest with their first answer because the situation rarely improves.

5. **Multiple phone numbers allow the escort to determine crank callers and prospective clients who are shopping around.** Typically, a client who is up to no good will responds to multiple advertisements. An escort with multiple numbers will easily expose anyone who is making bogus appointments or calling for phone sex.

- **Call Waiting.** The advantage to call waiting is the prospective client does not get a busy tone.
- **Call Forwarding.** Call forwarding allows the home phone to be forwarded to a voice mail pager or to a cellular phone.
- **Call Backs.** Many escorts will get the name and number from the client. Typically, this is to match the information displayed on the caller identification box. In the event the numbers do not match, the escort will call the number given to ensure the appointment is legitimate.

Typically, these are many of the same features an escort agency would use on their telephones. A successful escort knows over 50% of their potential business is lost by using a pager system. However, escorts experience the problem of having a high percentage of nuisance callers if they cannot screen for callers from anonymous numbers, block out repeat nuisance callers, identify calls from pay phones, and identify calls from cellular phones. The use of the methods outlined above screen out about 90% of all nuisance callers.

In addition to a well thought out home phone system many escorts also carry cellular phones. Typically, the home number is forwarded to the cellular number to take advantage of the security features established on the home phone. Many cellular phone services now offer many of the same features available on a home phone.

Some escorts and escort agencies have been known to use as many as four cellular phones in their business. This prevents calls from being traced to the final number. Although this is a standard practice for drug dealers, it is an unnecessary precaution for prostitution.  First, wiretaps are rarely used for prostitution. Second, the U.S. Supreme Court has ruled law enforcement cannot legally wiretap telephones to monitor prostitution activities unless there are other public safety issues involved such as drug dealing or the threat of violence.  There is, however, the risk of an illegal wiretap.

Many of the top escorts also have a significant presence on the Internet.  Business from the Internet is sometimes the only marketing outlet or the primary marketing outlet for an escort. An escort who is on the Internet typically has an additional line for Internet connectivity.

Communications is the main reason why many people who advertise as escorts are unsuccessful.   Many escorts have communications systems that make them unavailable to the majority of their potential clients.   Many clients cannot be reached directly for one reason or another or do not have the patience to wait for callbacks that may never occur.  As such, many clients will call several advertisements in a magazine in the hopes one escort will either answer the phone directly or will promptly return their page.

Many new escorts do not understand communications and advertising are interconnected.  Here is a letter I received from a new escort:

*I just placed my first professional advertising (Intense Fisting Top) in a local paper a month ago.  Based on the advice in your book, I'm changing my strategy.  A few more words and an extra line in the advertisement makes the advertisement read a whole lot better and I anticipate an increase in my call volume. I expect to get more calls in the future after I invest in a cellular phone over a pager.  However, I still recommend a pager for those who are starting as an escort as it is cheaper than a cellular phone and easier to disconnect than a regular telephone connection.*

**Location**

Where a client will meet an escort is a significant issue for both the client and the escort. The most successful escorts tend to offer in-call and out-call service. In-call is when the client goes to the escort's home and out-call is when the escort goes to the client's home or hotel room.

Some escorts will only do in-calls, others will only do out-calls, and many will do both. In many cases the cost to the client for an in-call is cheaper than the cost to the client of an out call.

There are pros and cons to in-call or out-call service for both the escort and the client. The escort benefits the most by being able to offer both services, however there may be overriding issues for only offering only in-call or out-call service.

The advantages to an escort for offering in-call service are:

- Clients who are married or have roommates have a place to go without getting a hotel room.
- Escorts can offer a lower price compared to other escorts because they do not have to charge for travel time.
- In markets where there is very little business or vacation travel in-calls appeal to the local market.
- Police are less likely to target escorts who have in-call service unless there are complaints from the neighbors.
- Several types of escorts including many transsexuals, many massage therapists, and escorts without transportation only offer in-call service.

The disadvantages to an escort for offering in-call services are:

- A high percentage of first time clients make appointments and do not show up for their appointments.
- Many in-call clients do not feel a need to show up on time or get lost and are late. This interferes with the scheduling of other appointments.

- Many clients do not want witnesses to their activities and will not keep the appointment if someone else is at the residence (such as a roommate of the escort).
- For some escorts, there is a risk of clients showing up without appointments or becoming stalkers.

The advantage of an in-call to a client is the client does not need to make arrangements for a place to meet an escort. Typically, a client who lives with other individuals would need to ensure their house is free or would need to rent a room.

The advantages to an escort doing an out-call are:

- Some clients do not have transportation.
- Clients are less likely to no show the escort.
- Out-calls are typically more profitable than in-calls.
- The escort maintains privacy at home.

The disadvantages to the client for out-call appointments: out-call appointments are typically more expensive, some escorts no show clients or are not on time, and there is greater risk for theft and violence. Typically, there is less risk using an escort who offers in-call as well as out-call service.

## Budget

Clients tend to have a budget in mind for escort services before calling the advertisements. Going rates and the variety of rates vary by market.

The rates on the top independent escorts will range between $100 and $150 depending on the market. There are also escorts in the $50 to $100 range and escorts in the $150 to $300 range. In general, the independent escort with the highest level of repeat clientele will be in the $100 to $150 price range.

It is generally best to avoid escorts and escort agencies that quote their prices as "starting from." These escorts and escort agencies generate a high level of complaints, and are typically high-risk situations for the clients.

There are many clients who will only hire independent escorts just as there are many clients who will only hire escorts through agencies.   Independent escorts are oftentimes less expensive than escorts from agencies, however this is not always the case. Escorts from agencies offer a higher degree of safety and dependability.   Most of the top independent escorts will price themselves at the same price quoted by the top agencies.

### Escort Myths

There are a lot of myths about escorts.   An experienced escort can tell whether another escort is experienced or not based on the escort's perception of the business.   Escorts get a lot of calls from other escorts, and work with other escorts.   There are many things an experienced escort would know that a client or inexperienced escort would not know.

- **Busy Times**.  It is commonly believed escorts are busiest after midnight.   In fact, the busiest times for escorts are between 4 p.m. and midnight.   Typically, clients who call after midnight are of low quality.   Clients who call after midnight are oftentimes drunk or on drugs and can be very difficult.   Many of the top escorts do not take calls after midnight and will only see clients after midnight by prior appointment.   Also, very few escorts are available in the mornings since they tend to sleep until 11 a.m. or noon.
- **Busy Days.**  It is commonly believed the busiest days are Friday and Saturday.   Actually, the busiest days are Sunday through Thursday.   Sunday, Monday and Wednesday are the busiest days.   Most clients are with family on the weekends and escorts are not generally regarded as family entertainment.   Most travel calls, however, occur on the weekends.
- **Number of Clients.**  Top escorts may have several hundred semi-regular clients, and will typically see two or three clients a day.   Top escorts may have three to five days a month when they do not see anyone.   The most successful escorts see clients every day seven days a week.

- **Age.** Most people believe the most successful escorts are relatively young. In fact, the most successful escorts are between the mid-twenties to forties in age. The reason for this is, older escorts tend to be more stable. Younger escorts do not generally have the business experience to operate their own business, and frequently change their residence or phone numbers. Younger escorts generally work for escort agencies, and even then may have difficulty with being successful due to unreliability.
- **Body types.** Most people idealize escorts as being young and muscular. The ideal escort for many clients is twenty years old, six foot in height, and weighs 200 pounds. This is an extremely rare occurrence. In fact, although many escorts take very good care of their bodies they tend to either be on the slender side or have muscular swimmers builds. In fact, clients who prefer escorts who are over six feet tall and weigh over 200 pounds report the most dissatisfaction with escorts. Many of these escorts are heterosexual and are in the business to exploit gay individuals.
- **Slow periods.** Many people think the summer is the busiest period for escorts. Most clients are on vacation during the summer, and so it tends to be the slowest period. The busiest months tend to be January, February, and March possibly due to cabin fever. The slowest periods tend to be around April 15th (when the politicians insist on their share), July (typically an escort sees a drop in business of about 50% from busier months), and around major holidays including most holiday weekends (escorts are not family entertainment).
- **High dollar clients.** Many escorts tell numerous stories on how much money they make. There are some clients who pay outrageous amounts to get what they want. However, these clients generally do not become repeat clients, and escorts who do not have a steady clientele typically live in feast or famine. The top escorts stick to a market price, do not hustle clients, and do not expect tips. In fact, many of the top escorts will decline some high dollar clients because

many of them are difficult clients or are involved heavily
into drugs.

- **Payment up front**. The media portrays payment to the
escort as money left out on a dresser. This is actually a good
way for a first time client to signal trust to an escort.
Typically, the top male escorts will rarely ask for money up
front after their first encounter with a client. Likewise, the
top male escorts will never pick the money up off the table
until after the session has ended. This is true even with first
time clients.

### Travel Calls

Many of the top escorts spend a significant amount of
traveling with clients. Typically, escorts who specialize in travel
spend 50% or more of their time traveling, and see very few
clients in their home market.

One escort recently jotted down his travels at my request:

*An example of my recent, current, and upcoming trips goes
something like this: In the last four weeks I have been to
Honolulu, Breckenridge, Phoenix, Las Vegas, San Francisco,
and Chicago. In the upcoming two weeks I will have been to
Guatemala, back to Honolulu and on several overnighters to
Idaho and places back east.*

*I don't like to do local calls betweeen trips. I really need
my rest and recovery between these travel calls.*

There are several types of travel clients. First, there are
many people who do not have travel companions. Many escorts
accompany clients on trips to Europe, Asia, and cruises. These
trips may involve a week to two weeks. Second, there are clients
who want a weekend companion. Then there are clients who
book an escort for a day of non-stop sex.

Having an escort for a day or a week can be a frightening
experience for both the escort and the client. There are horror
stories from both clients and escorts of drug and alcohol binges,

being abandoned in the middle of no where, and fear of violence. The risk of incompatibility is always present.

In many cases, the travel client has seen the escort in their home market before booking a travel call. The client is more assured of safety and compatibility if the client has already spent time with the escort. Alternatively, many of the top escort agencies will also arrange travel calls. Typically, an agency will steer a client to an escort who is suitable for travel calls. Another method used by clients to find travel escorts is word of mouth. This is also a good method prescreening a potential escort.

Escorts also have considerable risk in booking travel calls. Typically, the escort will employ the following subtle methods to ensure a prospective travel client is legitimate:

- The escort gets the client to set dates for travel.
- The escort gives the travel information to their travel agent to get airfare and itinerary.
- The escort gives the travel information to the client and the client calls the travel agent to arrange payment.
- The escort asks for a deposit of between 20-30% of the amount quoted.

This procedure is very subtle. The client who makes commitments and keeps their commitments is typically honest and not overly controlling. If the client is not honest in the process, there is a good chance the escort will not get paid. If the client attempts to control the process then there is the possibility of stalking. If the client balks at any of these procedures then it is a good sign that there will be trouble and the escort should not take the client.

The cost of a travel call varies significantly. The primary factors that determine the cost of a travel call are:

- Many escorts will cut the price if they are interested in the destination or if the itinerary presents a once in a lifetime opportunity such as a tour of Asia.
- The longer the trip the lower the cost per day.

- Whether or not the escort likes to go on travel calls.
- The top escorts are more expensive than local escorts though this is not always the case.

Prices vary considerably, but here are some general rules of thumb:

- Full day rates range from $300 to $1500 depending on the escort. The most quoted rate is $500 for independent escorts however there are also many in the $1000 range. Some of the top models and porn stars command over $1500 a day.
- Weekend rates tend to range between $1000 and $2500.
- Rates for a week range between $3000 and $5000.

There are many clients who cannot afford the travel rates of an escort. However, many of the most desirable escorts will rarely see a client except for travel.

I received this letter from a client who used an escort on a travel call:

*I took a break last spring and took an escort to an exclusive resort for a week. He was a stunner visually. He was a better golfer than I, handled a small boat well, was not as good at tennis, and was comically cute and inept on a horse. I had a great time and he seemed to enjoy himself too. It obviously was not seven days, twenty-four hours a day of sex. His fee what $3,000 plus direct costs. The rate was very reasonable, given his usual busy schedule.*

### Escorts Who Travel Around the Country or World

There are some escorts who travel from city to city or even country to country. In the United States the typical circuit is New York, Miami, and Los Angeles. Some escorts may split their time between cities. Other escorts have a regular travel schedule between a number of cities.

Escorts from other countries tend to see their market as being most of the world. Here is the letter I received from an escort planning to move to New York:

*I am a Croatian guy. I am 36 but look like 27, blond with blue eyes, very good looking, tall, with a very nice body. I am a passive type escort with a small dick but very nice buns. Due to the war I had to get out of my country ten years ago. Since then I have been wandering through Europe and America. I have lived most of the time in Spain, Brazil, and Peru.*

*I have also managed to get a good bulk of the faithful clients who call me oftenly. The Spanish market is the best of the three by far. This is because of the country's good economic situation. Brazil, even though there is a huge gay community, is far behind Spain in terms of fares. That is why most escorts try to work with tourists which are used to pay American fares. The worst market by far is Peru. With some luck a good escort can charge 30 dollars for two hours service.*

*In the three countries prostitution is legal, but hustling (looking for clients on the streets) is not. You have to work on your own place, in an agency or in a so called brothel. During all this years I have never had any problems with the police. I have never been arrested nor interrogated.*

*Most of my clients look for a second date not only because of my looks or skills, but because of my personality. I usually place my ads at the local newspapers and get phone calls almost immediately. The average client for an escort is in his 30's or 40's, who is lonely and needs not only sex but also company (someone to go out with for dinner, to a show, to dance, etc.).*

Escorts from other countries also tend to quote prices both on an American plan (an hour or less of quick sex) as well as a European plan that includes an evening of dinner and entertainment. Escorts in rural areas in the United States where travel times may be long also tend to quote a one hour and multi-hour rate.

### Risk of HIV Infection

Anytime someone has an infection that can be transmitted to others it is a cause for vigilant concern. However, although the risk of HIV transmission is a concern for both the client and the escort, the risk of transmission is probably less than the risk for contracting many of the other conditions listed in Chapter 11.

There are, in fact, many escorts who have HIV infections. There are also many clients who have HIV infections. There are many escorts and clients who do not disclose their HIV status or lie about their HIV status.

This means, escorts and clients should follow safe sex guidelines in their activities. This virtually eliminates the risk for HIV transmission. In fact, the primary groups at risk today for HIV transmission are intravenous drug users who contract HIV from shared needles and promiscuous young adults (gay and straight) who do not have protected sex.

Recently, there has been an increase in the number of escorts who advertise as "bareback bottoms". These escorts are typically HIV positive and do not practice safe sex. Unfortunately, there are many clients who prefer unprotected sex. Most escorts, however, insist on safe sex. This means, bodily fluids are not exchanged during sex and the use of condoms for anal sex.

Many law enforcement agencies perform blood tests on arrested prostitutes to determine if the prostitute is HIV infected. In most jurisdictions, it is a felony to operate as a prostitute while infected with HIV.

Although, I do not want to minimize the risk of possible HIV infection I believe most clients overemphasize its importance relative to the many other sexually transmitted diseases. These diseases, discussed in Chapter 11 can be transmitted more easily the HIV, are not as preventable through the use of safe sex techniques, and can have equally serious ramifications if contracted.

### *Stage Names*

Most escorts do not use their real names when working as an escort. Many escorts just use an assumed first name and do not give a last name. Escorts who have appeared in adult magazines or adult films will have a first and last name. Some escorts use three to five names for advertising purposes. There are many reasons for this:

- **Use of a real name encourages stalkers.** Unfortunately, stalkers are a real danger in the escort business, and stalkers will stop at no length to find out personal information on the objects of their desire.
- **Multiple names hide multiple advertisements.** In very competitive markets where there are several pages of advertising it is important to have multiple advertisements.
- **Multiple names identify which advertisement generated the prospective client.** Some escorts use multiple stage names to screen clients just as they use the signal telephone ring feature described under communications.
- **Stage names create a brand.** Many escorts have established national reputations. A good stage name becomes a standard for quality as it does for any product.
- **Stage names have unofficial trademark status.** There is an unwritten rule in the escort business not to use the stage name of another escort working in the same geographic area. There is also an unwritten rule of not using the stage name of a porn star regardless of location since porn stars have national reputations. In very competitive markets unscrupulous escort agencies (and even independent escorts) will oftentimes copy the advertisements for a popular escort word for word including the name and list the agency's phone number. Most reputable gay magazines will discourage this practice since individuals who engage in this form of deception are likely to be unscrupulous in other ways.

Most escorts will give clients their real names if they are regular clients. In general, however, an escort will be careful about giving out their real name until it has been determined the client is not a stalking risk.

## *The Sexual Issues of Escorts*

It may be surprising that many escorts have sexual identity issues. Many escorts do not fall into the convenient categories of gay, straight, and bisexual. In fact, there are many escorts who are somewhat asexual and rarely engage in sexual activities outside of work. Perhaps, these escorts could be called buy-sexual. If a client buys them the escort is sexual.

Many of the asexual types of escorts grew up in very religious families that were devoted Mormons or Catholics. Although many of these escorts from religious families enjoy their work, they are also consumed with tremendous guilt over having sex with anyone. In some cases, getting paid to have sex with someone is their rationalization for having sex with anyone. Getting paid to have sex gives the escort a high, followed by a down resulting from the onset of guilt.

Many escorts are very attractive and are highly sought after by both men and women in social settings. These escorts may be bisexual, but they have tremendous guilt over having sex with men. Just as in the example of the normally asexual escort these escorts rationalize they can enjoy having sex with men because they are being paid.

There are also many male escorts who will not have sex with women. Although female clients are rare, there are occasional clients who want to see an escort have sex with a woman. Many escorts see themselves as gay, and are capable of having sex with a woman. There are also many gay escorts who are extremely fearful of having sex with women.

The most dangerous type of escort is the escort that claims to be exclusively heterosexual. Many of these escorts see clients as prey, and oftentimes engage in theft and violence against clients.

There are many escorts who consider themselves heterosexual and feel their sexual identity is threatened by having sex with men. It is not unusual for male escorts to see a client and then turn around and spend the money on a female prostitute. Male escorts are oftentimes clients of other male and female prostitutes.

As mentioned before, many escorts are highly sought after by men and women. Some escorts will choose to have relationships with women because it is safer to them than having a relationship with a man. In some cases their girlfriends are also escorts or exotic dancers. In these cases, both the male and the female may be bisexual and these couples use business as the rationalization to have sex outside of their relationship.

Relationships are very difficult for an escort. Typically, an escort who enters into a long-term relationship with someone will retire from the business because it puts too much stress on the relationship.

Although there are some escorts who enter relationships with a client these are not usually the healthiest of relationships. First, there is usually a significant age difference and significant difference in emotional needs. Second, the client who enters the relationship typically has completely different reasons for entering the relationship than the escort. Third, living with someone is a lot different than renting an hour or even a week with someone.

Many escorts sincerely want relationships with someone around their same age and with similar interests. Many escorts enter into relationships with other escorts. These relationships may be healthy or unhealthy as in any relationships. Many escorts do not have healthy relationships to model their relationships after. As such, many escorts use the trial and error method in finding happiness in their relationships and may go through many short-term relationships before entering into a long-term relationship.

There are also many escorts who are sexual addicts and prefer to have multiple anonymous sexual encounters. When these escorts are not seeing clients they oftentimes seek sexual encounters in sex clubs and bathhouses. One escort said they chose to become an escort because it was an addiction that was marketable.

Many escorts have good relationships with their families. Many escorts are estranged from their families. There are many escorts with very few friends, maintain very private lives, and engage in self-destructive behavior.

These observations could describe anyone. However, the difference between most escorts and the general population is escorts tend not to live traditional lives. Their relationships and their behavior tend to be at the extremes of normal human behavior and relationships. There is no middle ground.

Despite the fact escorts live on the fringes of mainstream society, most of the top escorts enjoy their work and are relatively happy with life. Escorts choose to live outside the norms of society and see themselves as professionals.

I received this letter that seems to reflect many of the same feelings many escorts have about their involvement in prostitution:

*I suppose I fall somewhere between the elite and mainstream escort. I have had several sponsors over the years, one of whom is eighty years old, and with who I have been involved with since I was sixteen years old (nearly twenty years ago). This person enabled me to purchase my first car, and buy a small business. He has co-signed credit cards enabling me to have access to money any time I need it. He has been a kind and gracious benefactor. For this, I intend to care for him for the rest of his life.*

*Although my mother was highly educated, she did not earn very much money and I grew up very poor. She was a single parent and a wonderful person. I suppose I quickly learned in the gay world I could make money because of my looks. This does not mean I am not a hard worker. I worked my way through college, and later graduate school. I do not live in luxury, but I am comfortable. Shortly, I will be supporting my lover through college.*

*I learned about the world of massage from a very successful escort. I acquired a little schooling in massage, which I found to be consistent with my work as a fitness trainer. Within a year I had a full regular client base, both as a fitness trainer and massage therapist. Most of my referrals came by word of mouth although I did advertise in local publications. I did this for adventure, for the excitement of new clients, and many clients were quite attractive. I was shocked to discover so many attractive men used escorts. For those clients who have lovers or wives, the indiscretion of being seen was not worth the risk. Discretion and confidentiality is of the utmost of importance in our field.*

*I worked for a couple of agencies and found the work distasteful. Massage seemed to set the stage for a better experience. I was in control, and could determine the direction of the session much more effectively. It was not the appearance of the client that would determine attraction to the client. It was the client's energy. I have never had a violent experience. I trust my intuition, and one learns to screen effectively.*

# Chapter Four

# Escort Agencies

E scort agencies operate in many localities. The vast majority of escort agencies only offer women although some escort agencies specialize in men. Some escort agencies represent men, women, and transsexuals.

Although prostitution is illegal in all states with the exception of some rural counties of Nevada where brothels legally operate, local officials use escort agencies as an unofficial way to regulate prostitution. Escort agencies are seen as a lesser of evils. First, it keeps prostitution off the streets. Second, escort agencies typically police themselves and provide some assurance as to the safety of the escort and the client.

Escort agencies are subject to police sting operations, however many agencies either take appropriate action when a crime has been committed or cooperates with law enforcement agencies when crimes are being investigated. There are also fewer complaints against male escorts. Male escort agencies tend to be very concerned about the safety of their clients and their escorts.

In some markets, there is a strong adversarial relationship between escort agencies and law enforcement. Typically, these markets have laws that are very strict and actually are counterproductive to the safety of the escorts and the clients. In these markets the escort agencies charge an agency fee, and the escort is required to work for tips. As such, the client is hustled by the escort, and the most successful escorts in the market are hustlers. Fortunately, this practice is the exception and not the rule.

There are a few markets that have been very successful in preventing the operation of escort agencies including Houston and Indianapolis. These localities are very vigilant in policing the existence of escort agencies. However, the result has been an increase in the amount of hustling activity in public areas.

Markets where the law encourages the most successful escorts to be hustlers typically have the most client complaints in terms of theft, excessive charges, and problems with escort agencies. Seattle, Las Vegas and Denver are three markets with the most complaints when it comes to using escort agencies.

Hustlers tend to be the group of prostitutes with the highest level of dishonesty. Hustlers do not rely on repeat clients, and oftentimes see their clients as one-time victims. In markets where escort agencies do not charge flat rates the predominate type of escort who works for an agency is a hustler. In these areas it is much safer and less expensive to work with established independent escorts.

### Legal Issues With Escort Agencies

Many escort agencies specializing in male escorts operate with very little interference from law enforcement. The primary reason is that male prostitution represents 10% or less of the prostitution market in most areas. Also, law enforcement is primarily heterosexually inclined and has very little interest in pursuing male prostitution. There are several activities that will bring an escort agency to the attention of law enforcement authorities.

Currently federal law enforcement is on a crusade against the influence of organized crime. Organized crime is alleged to be very heavily involved in prostitution. Male escort agencies are generally very small operations and do not appear to be affected by the influence of organized crime. However, there are many agencies involved in providing male and female escorts. These agencies are much larger in size and may be subject to the influence of organized crime, and consequently scrutiny by Federal Bureau of Investigation.

A second activity that prompts scrutiny by law enforcement agencies is involvement in drugs. Several operators of escort agencies have been put out of business due to involvement in the sales or distribution of drugs. Escort agency involvement in drugs occurs for several reasons:

- The escort agency operator uses drugs.
- The escort agency operator is a provider of drugs to the escorts employed by the agency and their friends.
- The escort agency provides drugs to the clients of the escort agency.

The most serious activity that prompts scrutiny by law enforcement agencies is involvement with underage escorts. There are several reasons why operators of escort agencies may become involved in underage escorts:

- Several escorts report they worked with escort agencies when they were underage because they lied about their age.
- Several escorts have stated, some escort agency operators have a personal preference for young escorts and actively recruit escorts who are underage. In many cases this is to satisfy the sexual desires of the operator of the escort agency.
- Escort agencies are pressured by clients to provide underage escorts. There are many high profile and wealthy clients who are entertainers, entertainment executives, and fashion designers who have a nearly

insatiable appetite for young male escorts. Individuals who see underage prostitutes rarely see them more than one time. As such, escort agencies working with underage prostitutes must be continually recruiting additional males to work as prostitutes. Several agency operators have been apprehended by law enforcement because they catered to the wants of these high profile clients.

Most escort agencies are not involved in organized crime, drugs or underage escorts. In cases where escort agencies are involved with underage escorts the demand is client driven. Typically, only the customers of prostitutes who are caught soliciting prostitutes on the street are publicly humiliated in the papers and the Internet. Recently, however, a Detroit newspaper gained access to over 6,000 names of clients from one escort agency. There is a growing trend by the media and law enforcement to encourage the public humiliation of those who use any prostitute without regard to the consequences to the individuals involved. Some people would argue the customers of prostitutes did not think through the consequences of their actions. However, my position is sexual privacy should be a protected right, and sexual privacy should not be encroached unless there is a compelling public safety issue. Compelling public safety issues include murder, drug enforcement, organized crime, and other serious threats to public safety. The generalized fear that the activity might spread sexually transmitted diseases, or reflects badly on the character of the individuals involved are not compelling public safety issues.

A final issue for escort agencies is their increasing use of the Internet. Until recently, there was very little monitoring of prostitution on the Internet. This situation has changed significantly. There have been law enforcement sting operations conducted against escorts, escort agencies, and even web site operators who only provided advertising space on the Internet. It is expected this trend will continue at an exponential pace over the next several years.

### How Escort Agencies Get Started

Escort agencies tend to be small operations and may be run by one individual. Owners of escort agencies typically have multiple business interests and may even have full time jobs. As such the degree of service is variable.

Individuals start escort agencies because; they have an interest in the sex industry, have themselves worked in the sex industry, the skills to run a business, and enjoy the business. There are many escorts who have gone on to run escort businesses. There are also a lot of clients who have developed a fascination with the business and have started escort agencies.

Typically, the escort agencies started by escorts have the most respect for the escorts who work for them. These owners are less likely to expect sexual favors in return for work, and are more likely to carefully screen clients. Many escorts who start agencies are successful because they have many years of clients who trust them and contacts with several escorts who trust them. Many of these agencies receive the bulk of their business and escort staff through word of mouth.

Other agencies are established by middle aged individuals who want to be surrounded by young attractive individuals who will trade sexual favors for client referrals. Many escorts report that their first sexual encounter with a man was with the owner of an escort agency. Generally, with these types of agencies the prospective escort must exchange sex with the owner in order to be hired. However, it is certainly true escort agencies are not the only places of employment in the United States where people exchange sex for hiring and advancement. At least with an escort agency sexual harassment is part of the job description and the escort is compensated accordingly.

With the exception of individuals who expect sexual favors in return for client referrals, escorts are generally very respectful of each other. Many escorts work with other escorts and have sex with them on the job, but their behavior does not normally continue after work unless they are in a relationship with each other. In fact, the top escorts probably treat all individuals with more respect than most people give or receive on the job.

There are a many reports of agency owners who are involved in drugs. In these cases the agency owner provides drugs to an escort in order to control the escort. This activity is the exception rather than the rule since many escort agencies frown on drug use and will terminate an escort if their drug use interferes with job performance. Escorts on drugs typically are unreliable, have unsatisfied clients, and are a high risk for theft and violence.

Indeed there are some disreputable operators of escort agencies. Here is a report from one client who has had considerable experience with one agency in Denver:

*I have probably spent the past five years on high-class escorts. I have a number of degrees and am in the field of education and have been interested in the sex industry and its affects on men for years.*

*In the past five years I have met some very intriguing guys. I have seen them gain financial success, lose fortunes, become arrested (on various sexual and non-sexual charges), weave their way through the trappings of drugs, destroy the relationships in their real lives, and have severe health problems due to the stress related to their jobs.*

*These guys still give me a call to touch base, and are really quite reflective about their career paths. Though I have met these guys independently, they all have a common thread in their career. They are all from Denver and have worked with one manipulative man. You must know the man and you know all the guys too.*

### Working for an Agency

Escorts who work for an agency are independent contractors. Most agencies receive a percentage of what the escort makes as a fee. This percentage varies from 30-40% of the fee charged the client.

Many escort agencies have twenty to thirty available escorts, however there are generally two or three escorts who see most of the clients. There are several reasons for this:

- The owner of the escort agency will typically have their favorites.
- There will be one or two escorts who have broad appeal to clients based on appearances and personality.
- Many escorts only work part-time as escorts and have full-time jobs or go to school.
- Many of the more popular escorts are oftentimes booked by travel clients and are unavailable.
- Many new escorts do not return their pages promptly or are difficult to reach.
- Many escorts go on drug binges and are unable to work.

Escorts working for an agency are expected:

- To be honest with clients and the agency.
- To promptly remit agency fees after seeing a client.
- To return pages promptly.
- To notify the agency of availability.
- To be pleasant and professional with clients and the agency.
- To show up on appointments they accept.
- To maintain transportation and communications.

These expectations are no greater than the expectations of any employer. However, many of the escorts that work for agencies are young, lack business experience, and do not always recognize the consequences of their behavior. A good escort who works for an agency makes about $1,000 a week. There are many escorts who will jeopardize this income by being dishonest with a client or by not exercising basic business skills. Some escorts have been known to lose over $3,000 in business in one week because they do not return their pages.

About 50% of the escorts who are hired by an agency do not last more than a month with the agency. The most common reasons why an escort does not last with an agency are:

- **Failure to return pages**. Typically, after the third time an escort fails to return a page the escort will be terminated.
- **Disappearances.** If the escort disappears for a few days then the escort will be considered unreliable and dropped.
- **Client complaints**. Escort agencies take client complaints seriously and are well attuned to whether a client complaint is legitimate or not.
- **Availability.** If the escort is consistently unavailable to take appointments the escort will be dropped.
- **Dishonesty.** If an escort sees a client behind the back of the agency the escort will generally be terminated. Agencies are generally pretty good at catching this practice.
- **No showing a client**. An escort is terminated for not showing up for an appointment.
- **Percentage of calls cancelled**. If the escort has a higher than expected percentage of appointments that do not go through it generally means the escort is seeing the client without the agency's knowledge.
- **Personal issues**. There are many people who work as escorts simply to fulfill a fantasy. After an escort has experienced the fantasy the escort may no longer want to work as an escort.

Given the amount of money an independent escort can make, most people wonder why someone would work for an agency. There are actually a number of reasons why someone would work for an agency rather than work independently:

- Most escorts do not have the business skills to operate independently. Many escorts learn the business by working for escort agencies.
- Working for an escort agency provides access to more profitable clients.

- Many escorts prefer the anonymity of working for an escort agency.
- Many escorts prefer the flexibility of not having to work seven days a week.
- Many escorts prefer to have a third party screen potential new clients.
- Escort agencies generally provide many of the tools needed to run a business including beepers, advertising, and someone to answer the phone.
- Many escorts live at home or with other individuals and do not have the privacy to run a business.

Many escorts who start with agencies go on to work independently. In some markets, escorts will work independently and for escort agencies. There are some markets where agencies have the bulk of the business and independent escorts cannot compete against the agencies due to the loyalty of their client base and size of their advertising budgets.

### Client's and Escort Agencies

Many clients choose to use agencies exclusively to secure male escorts.

- Agencies have many escorts who do not advertise. Many of the escorts who work for agencies only do escort work part-time.
- Agencies tend to have a variety of escorts with body types desired by the majority of clients. Among the most popular escort types in agencies are younger escorts and muscular escorts.
- Agencies typically have a faster response time than independent escorts. Instead of having to call several numbers and wait for pages to be returned the client only needs to make one call to an agency.
- Reputable agencies give accurate descriptions.

- Many agencies have a wide selection of escorts. However, a broad selection is typically only available with advance appointment.
- Agencies generally guarantee security and discretion.
- Escort agencies are easier to reach late at night and early in the morning. Although escort agencies may not have a broad selection at these times. There are, however, some agencies with very limited hours.

Agencies loose in their hiring practices tend not to get repeat business. Just as with successful escorts, successful agencies have an 80% repeat clientele. Likewise, the top agencies have criteria for selecting clients.

The top agencies also tend to have criteria for selecting clients. As with the top escorts agencies the top agencies derive 80% of their income from about 20% of their clients. These are the things reputable agencies look for in deciding on whether to accept a client:

- Clients who have a history of turning escorts away at the door. If an agency is accurate with a description there should be very few instances when an escort is rejected. Any quality agency will value their time and the time of the individuals who work for them.
- Clients who have a history of trying to get pager numbers or phone numbers from an escort. Agencies have a lot invested in their business. Typically an escort caught working behind the back of an agency will be fired.
- Clients who do not pay or no show an escort. These clients generally will not be sent other escorts.
- Clients who make appointments are preferred to clients who call at the last minute. Oftentimes, the number of available escorts available at the last minute is very small.
- Agencies prefer clients with broad tastes. Clients with broad tastes tend to be repeat clients.

A client should keep in mind most escort communities are relatively small and the client will lose their client confidentiality if the client is dishonest with an agency. Information on dishonest clients is oftentimes shared between agencies throughout the United States.

There are several services an escort agency will provide to their regular clients. These services include:

- Reputable referrals when a client is traveling.
- Special rates on travel calls.
- Notification of new escorts. Many repeat clients get the advantage of being the first to see a new escort.
- Preferences in terms of scheduling. A repeat client is much more likely to get an escort at the last minute.
- Search services to find specific types of escorts.
- Screening services of escorts in other cities. This is especially useful to high profile clients.

If the agency is disreputable and is not looking for repeat clients the agency will not screen potential clients. These agencies engage in disreputable practices such as:

- The agency lies about the appearance of the escort.
- The agency will send over numerous escorts in the hopes the client will select one.
- The agency repeatedly calls a client for repeat business.
- The agency will lie about the agency fee and the client will only be told when the escort arrives about the tipping policy.
- The escort may show up to the door, take the money, and leave.

These practices primarily occur with agencies with high agency fees and then expect the escort to work for tips. With agencies such as this, the escort may only receive $25 of a $150 agency fee. These agencies exist because the laws in some jurisdictions and the enforcement of those laws create a situation where prostitution is more dangerous and victimizing. Laws against prostitution should not be written in a way to encourage the hustling of clients. Hustlers are the most dangerous types of prostitutes. These localities would be far better off enacting laws require escorts not to solicit tips, and look the other way on what actually occurs. As far as Seattle, Las Vegas, and Denver are concerned their anti-prostitution laws are not designed to create a public safety issue, but rather to preserve a public safety issue.

### Escort Agency Advertising

Escort agencies have several advantages over independent escorts in terms of advertising. These advantages generally allow escort agencies to dominate a market. The typical methods escort agencies use to advertises are:

- Escort agencies oftentimes have a place of business and have local business licenses. This allows them to advertise in the yellow pages as an escort agency or provider of adult entertainers.
- Escort agencies have larger advertising budgets than independent escorts. Escort agencies will run numerous classified advertisements. These advertisements actually appear to be advertisements for independent escorts. In some markets 80-90% of these advertisements are actually for escorts offered by escort agencies.
- Although many independent escorts advertise on the Internet, escort agencies are more likely to appear at or near the top of most search engines when using the keywords "escort" and "male".
- Some escort agencies publish their own magazines or have tie-ins with gay magazines. This allows them to dominate the local market.

There are ways for independent escorts to effectively compete against agencies. A new escort would need to have an advertising budget allowing for 5-10% coverage in a magazine in order to effectively compete against a dominant local agency. In many markets, this approach would be very expensive. Typically, the top escorts can expect to spend $500 to $1000 a month on advertising, although some escorts spend as little as $20 a month.

### Escort Agency Policies

Escort agencies tend to have very stringent policies when dealing with clients. These policies are designed to avoid problems with the appointment and to ensure the appointment is legitimate. Among the policies a prospective client may confront are:

- If staying in a hotel the client may be expected to provide the registered name and the room number.
- Some escort agencies will not provide service to certain motels. It is best for a client to ask if the agency provides service to a certain hotel
- An agency will ask for a call back number. A reputable agency will always be discrete when calling back to confirm an appointment.
- Many escorts who work for agencies are only available by appointment. Selection may be limited for last minute callers.
- Agencies will almost never negotiate rates. Clients who attempt to negotiate rates are almost never repeat clients.
- Escort agencies will never agree to have an escort meet a client at a neutral place such as a bar. These arrangements almost always never work out.
- Escort agencies will oftentimes not service certain neighborhoods or apartment complexes.

Clients who do not agree to these terms are invariably troublesome clients for an escort agency.

### Escort Agency Pricing

The cost of an escort through an agency is generally competitive with the rates a client would pay a high quality escort in the same market. The predominant fee in the United States is $150. The agency typically gets one third of the fee.

There are great variations depending on the market. In New York and Los Angeles the rate is typically $250. The Phoenix market rate is at $100. The rates for porn stars range between $200 and $500 for an hour, and some porn stars command $1500 for an hour. The most common rate for a porn star is between $200 to $300 for an hour.

There are many clients who do not like to pay agency fees. Customers dislike paying service fees to anyone whether it is their bank, real estate agents or travel agents. In general, the public has very little respect for anyone who makes money by processing transactions. In reality, anybody who works on commission has marketing expense and spends a lot of time at their business. Someone who works for wages or a salary rarely has any idea of what it takes to operate a business.

As such, it is the general nature of individuals to do everything possible to undercut someone working for commission. Certainly, there are alternative ways for someone to arrange a transaction without paying a commission.

- People try to sell their houses without using real estate agents.
- People will have their travel agent do the research for a vacation and then go to an alternative source.
- Clients will go around the backs of an agency to procure an escort.

Regardless of the field, there are customers who feel things can be done better, faster, and cheaper without having to pay for professional advice. Clients who do not follow professional advice and are dishonest with escort agencies typically report the highest level of dissatisfaction with the escorts they have used.

Typically, these individuals would have been much better off using the services of an escort agency.

The clients who use reputable escort agencies regularly are the clients who have the highest satisfaction from using escorts. The reason is a reputable agency works to maintain a quality product. With a good client, an escort agency will even share objective information on independent escorts. In many cases the independent escort worked for the agency at one time or another.

The reasons why escort agencies will provide objective information on independent escorts in the area are:

- Reputable escort agencies never oversell their available escorts. If the escort agency does not have an escort who meets the needs of the client the next best thing is to refer the client somewhere else.
- Reputable escort agencies have a genuine concern for the safety of their clients.
- Escort agencies realize clients use many sources for escorts. Many clients are well known by all of the escorts in an area. An escort agency would rather see the client satisfied and provide business at a later date rather than strain the relationship with the client.
- Escort agencies just like the top escorts rely on word of mouth referrals for much of their business. By referring business to other escorts the escort agency in turn receives referrals from escorts who cannot accommodate a client for some reason.

A client may be thinking about the degree of client confidentiality when using an escort or an escort agency. Clients who are dishonest with escorts or escort agencies should be concerned because information on dishonest clients spreads very quickly in the escort community. Clients who are honest in their dealings with escort agencies and escorts can be fairly assured their transactions are kept confidential. In the cases when information is disclosed it is in an attempt to satisfy a client request.

There are very rare cases when an escort agency discloses client information outside the escort business. Dishonest clients may find themselves open to retaliation including exposure and blackmail. Information on honest clients may be disclosed if the client was a victim of a criminal act.

## Specialty Agencies

Some agencies specialize in certain types of services. Several agencies handle porn stars. These agencies are typically very expensive and typically book travel appointments. These agencies oftentimes represent a number of models, bodybuilders, and porn stars. Many of these individuals do not ordinarily see clients.

These agencies tend to be very selective on who will be accepted as clients. There are perhaps only a few hundred individuals in the world these agencies have as clients. However, these clients expect and pay for the best in terms of escorts.

The average cost of an escort from one of these agencies is $800 to $1500 a day plus expenses and sometimes much more. It is sometimes very frustrating to a prospective client when the object of their desires is not within their budget. However, there are many individuals, including college students who will save their money in order to have the sexual fantasy of their lives.

Although many of these top models are truly very wonderful people, many of them are not worth the time or money. A reputable agency will try to steer a client away from someone who may be less than pristine in personality, however there are many clients who are totally infatuated with a particular person's appearances. These clients are oftentimes disappointed when their meeting with an escort does not meet expectations.

In most markets, however, the safest and most productive way to procure an escort is through an escort agency. There are exceptions to this rule and the prospective client is always best to get a word of mouth referral before dealing with an escort agency. In some areas, the best escorts work for escort agencies, and they do not have the hassles of screening clients or of running a business.

# Chapter Five

# Top Models and Bodybuilders

There is a very small group of individuals who turn heads wherever they go. These individuals cannot go into a bar without being approached by dozens of people. These individuals are celebrities to others through their work and reputation. Not only do these individuals have gorgeous looks; they also have a personal energy that attracts people to them.

Top models, dancers, and bodybuilders have always been highly sought after by potential clients. Many of these individuals are not available for escort work. The top models, dancers, and bodybuilders available for escort work tend to work very secretively. These individuals pick up clients through chance meetings, through their work, and through their connections with friends.

It is frowned upon in the areas of modeling, bodybuilding, and dancing to engage in escort work even though it is very common. People with these professions who engage in escort work are very discrete. A hustler has customers, an escort has clients, and these elite escorts have sponsors.

These types of escorts are very frustrating to clients because they are relatively unobtainable. Although these types of escorts are motivated by money, these individuals are also driven by a number of other factors. These escorts tend to have difficult to pierce complex defense systems. These escorts are highly sought after, and more often than not they will reject a client than accept a client.

### How Elite Escorts Choose Sponsors

There are several criteria these types of escorts use to select clients:

- **Money.** Money is not generally the deciding factor with these escorts although it may get their attention. It is not unusual for these escorts to be offered a thousand dollars or more to spend an evening with a client. Even at this price there is no guarantee these escorts will have sex with the client.
- **Trust.** These types of escorts have a lot at risk if they are exposed. Many of them are well known in their field, and most of these fields frown on employing individuals who are known escorts. The types of escorts at the highest risk are nationally known models, professional bodybuilders, and people who work in film and television
- **Opportunity.** Very few potential clients have the opportunity to meet these types of escorts. These escorts generally have a very small group of friends, and most of them work in a similar field. Consequently, the clients these individuals accept are in some way involved in the same field. Models tend to have clients who are affiliated with the fashion industry. Bodybuilders tend to have clients who go to body building exhibitions. Performing artists tend to have clients who are in the entertainment field.

Elite escorts do not seek out clients. Clients seek the escort out. This must be done very carefully, since most of these escorts are well aware of the potential stalker, and is generally wary of anyone who approaches them. These relationships develop over time. The client needs to feel comfortable with the escort since in many cases the client is very high profile. Likewise, these escorts must ensure they will be able to have a certain degree of independence in the relationship. These relationships are very carefully built on mutual respect.

I received this letter from a sponsor:

*Having been in a long-term relationship/arrangement, I understand and appreciate your description about the give and take involved in a sponsorship arrangement.*

*I'm looking for that special someone in my life. My last arrangement really came out of the blue. There been no matches as I have lurked on the net, but it doesn't stop me from looking.*

There are many clients who seek out these escorts with the expectation of total devotion. In reality, most of the escorts in these relationships maintain considerable financial and career independence. The escort may also be involved in another relationship, and even married. These escorts are in fields they enjoy, and will not retire from their profession in order to be controlled by another individual. The prospective client who expects to have a loving, nurturing, romantic relationship with these types of escorts is generally disappointed. Although there are elements of care and respect in the relationship, the core of the relationship is strictly financial.

An elite escort may have only one sponsor who provides housing, transportation, expenses, and a monthly stipend. At most, these types of escorts may have two or three sponsors who are sending monthly checks of $2-3,000 each.

These escorts will rarely see a client for an hour. There are some professional bodybuilders who will give private posing sessions for a considerable amount of money, but in general these escorts are looking for long term sponsors.

Although sex may be a part of these relationships, in general the client is seeking companionship. Typically, the client will see the escort once or twice a week or only use him as a travel companion. In many cases the clients are married and have a family. In some cases the wife knows about the special relationship, but it is typically agreed the matter is not discussed.

### The Life of an Elite Escort

These types of escorts have problems of success most people can only dream of having in their own personal life. These issues influence whether someone will take sponsors.

**Career Issues**. Top models, dancers, and bodybuilders are very successful in their careers. These individuals are in very high demand and work very hard to maintain their career.

Most people would love to have a job where their job duties include working out two hours a day, tanning three times a week, making regular trips to the beauty salon, and traveling to exotic locales to work for a thousand dollars a day.

In reality, these people are self-employed. These individuals must maintain a strict regimen to stay in shape for work. If something goes wrong on a set these individuals may never get work again. If these individuals gain an unsightly pound, it may take months before they get a call for more work.

These people spend a lot of time marketing themselves and staying in shape. Yes, these individuals may only have a day a week where they get paid, but they put in more than a forty hours week to get one day of work.

**Privacy Issues**. These types of escorts get continuous requests for their phone numbers. Privacy becomes a real issue. Stalkers are a very real problem.

To maintain privacy these people have unlisted phone numbers. Many of these individuals may not even have a phone in their name, and they may have someone screen their calls. These individuals use a post office box rather than give anyone their home address. These individuals rarely go out except in the company of other people, and they maintain a very close group of friends who protect them from unwanted advances.

**Time and Emotional Issues**. These types of escorts do not have a lot of time. These individuals typically only see people who they enjoy spending time and people who respect their need for private time.

These people spend their free time with one to three sponsors exclusively. The elite escorts are in high enough demand they have no trouble attracting a new sponsor. Typically, a sponsor is very generous and does not make high demands on the person's time. The sponsor may be married, travel a lot, or want occasional companionship during the week. Extravagant vacations abroad are not unusual.

### *Developing a Relationship with an Elite Escort*

Potential sponsors actively seek out elite escorts. Ineffective ways to get an elite escort's attention are personal advertisements, calling escorts, or even approaching individuals directly. There are some escorts who attempt to market themselves as elite escorts, but in general this is also ineffective. Subtlety, persistence, and good manners are how sponsors attract the attention of an elite escort.

There are some good rules of thumb when approaching this type of transaction:

- If the prospective sponsor needs to ask the price, the prospective sponsor cannot afford the arrangement.
- If the escort advertises for this type of arrangement, the individual is not suitable for this type of arrangement.
- Courtship is very important. A sponsor can expect to spend several weeks courting a prospective elite escort.
- Identify needs. It is very important for the sponsor to identify the financial, emotional, and other needs of the prospective elite escort. Any offer made to an elite escort should carefully consider all of these needs.

- Introduction is important. The first step that a sponsor makes must be as non-threatening as possible. Going too fast will generally cause the elite escort to back off.

Clearly, the manner in which these relationships occur is very different from the way a hustler or escort establishes business relationships. For an elite escort, it is not a business, it is an arrangement of opportunity. In many cases the escort is financially secure and does not need the relationship. For some dancers, models and bodybuilders who do not make much money, escort work is seen as a way to stay in their field of interest.

Most elite escorts have their relationships with sponsors over many years. Although, at some point or another the sponsorship stops, there are very few elite escorts who regret the arrangement. There are some cases of drug overdoses and domestic violence in these relationships, but these incidences are relatively rare.

### Finding an Elite Escort

Unless a prospective sponsor has ties to the particular field of the elite escort, it is unlikely the prospective client will get past square one. However, sponsors of elite escorts are very wealthy, and typically have contacts in a number of fields. In many cases, top entertainers and business executives will have close friends who will help search for an appropriate elite escort.

In the case of professional bodybuilders prospective sponsors will search certain athletic facilities known for their 24-carat facilities and members.

The search for the appropriate elite escort can be very time consuming and may require the courtship of numerous potential candidates before there is a match. Typically, very few of these sought after individuals will consent to an arrangement such as this. However, there are many top models and bodybuilders who would consider a sponsor arrangement even if they were heterosexual.

## *The Cost of an Elite Escort*

If the potential sponsor needs to ask the cost, the potential sponsor cannot afford this type of arrangement.

The typical compensation package offered to elite escorts includes independent housing, independent transportation, educational expenses, expenses for a trainer and a monthly stipend. Generally, the total compensation package comes to between $10,000 and $20,000 a month.

There are other elite escorts who may have two or three sponsors who pay between $2-3,000 a month each to have the elite escort on retainer. In the rare instances where the elite escort will see a client for an evening the cost is oftentimes a $1000 or more for just dinner and drinks.

There is more than one sponsor who has had to declare bankruptcy due to the expense of pursuing one of these elite escorts. These sponsors tend to cater to every whim of the elite escort showering them with cars, extravagant gifts, and expensive vacations. However, as in anything, there is a market for those who choose to market themselves to people with unlimited budgets.

# Chapter Six

# Porn Stars

W hen many clients think of escorts they think of porn stars. Porn stars are popular escorts with clients because many people have seen their visual images in adult magazines and adult videos. Many of the most popular porn stars do not work as escorts.

### *Getting Discovered*

Porn stars are discovered through a variety of methods. These are the most common means to getting into porn:

- **Sending pictures and a description to a producer of adult videos**. The addresses of many of the adult video companies appear at the end of many adult magazines. Specifically, the Adam Gay Video Guide is published annually and lists the top male adult porn stars, gay adult videos produced in the last year, and much more information including the addresses of all of the gay adult film production companies.

- **Referral to or discovery by an agent.** An agent for porn stars will market the individual to the studios, provide advice on appearance, prepare a model for a shoot, ensure all arrangements are made, and ensure the model gets paid. In return the agent will be paid 20% of any performance fees.
- **Discovery by a studio or director.** There are numerous people who work in the industry who are constantly on the look out for new talent. Typically, these people use several methods to find models; they run ads in gay papers, they go out to bars, and they get referrals from people who they know.

There are numerous stories told by models of being offered the world to do gay adult films only to find out they are getting paid less than expected or not paid at all. There are hundreds of adult film companies and very few of these companies are entirely reputable. There are a lot of con artists in the adult film business who continually prey on young and unsuspecting models.

A model with a bad experience in the adult film industry may have psychological effects from their experience for many years. A person entering the business is best to have their eyes wide open and seek the advice of reputable individuals in the business.

Here are some of the ways to prepare for the gay adult video business:

- **Ask the advice of well-known porn stars.** There are many well-known porn stars visible on the Internet who may be willing to refer models to specific video companies or agents.
- **Get advice on appearance**. Gay adult video stars are first chosen based on appearance. This includes hair and physical attributes. The top models are very conscientious about hair and appearance.
- **Availability.** Many gay adult film stars have jobs. A model must be able to get away from work in order to film. Since,

many models do six or fewer films during their career; it is best to keep the day job.

- **Read interviews.** Many gay adult magazines have interviews with porn stars. Many of these interviews give good insight into the porn industry though most writers tend to only write positive things about the industry. An excellent writer on the gay adult film industry is Mickey Skee. He has written a number of books on the gay adult film industry. Many of his books are based on interviews with scores of gay porn stars. His books are essential reading for anyone who is interested in becoming a gay porn star.
- **Comfort level.** A good model is comfortable having sex on demand and in front of other people. The demands of the director vary greatly, however many of the top film directors expect models to be able to get a penile erection on demand and be able to perform sexual scenes over many hours. Filming is difficult work, and directors are on a schedule.

A number of models receive satisfaction from filming adult gay videos. Typically, these individuals enjoy sex, enjoy the attention they receive, enjoy meeting new people, and view their career in gay adult films as a way to live out their fantasies.

### Class Structure

Individuals who seek to work in the gay adult video industry should try to work with the top companies and individuals. This is no different than pursuing any other career interest.

The gay adult film industry has its classes just like any other field. For descriptive purposes there are four classes: industry leaders, reputable, niche players, and scum.

### Industry Leaders

These companies or individuals have the highest reputation for professionalism, honesty, integrity, and for paying their bills.

They are very consistent in the market and in their dealings with other people.

The film companies with the best reputation for honesty and integrity are Falcon and Catalina. These companies are very well organized with their filming, put out a consistent product, market their models, and consistently pay their bills. Models report the fewest problems with these companies.

Among the most respected individuals in the business are Chuck Holmes (Falcon), Josh Eliot (Catalina), Chi Chi LaRue (director for several companies), Mickey Skee (writer and producer of the gay porn awards) and Peter Scott (agent).

Granted, many of these individuals have their detractors, however, in this business this sometimes translates into professional jealousy. It is a very competitive business, and there are very few individuals who are able to rise above the fray and consistently maintain their honesty and integrity.

Here are some descriptions in order to give a flavor of how the industry leaders operate.

## *Falcon*

Falcon is generally considered the highest quality producer of gay adult films. Every detail of their organization is well thought out from their secret high tech temple headquarters, to every aspect of the production of their films. The distribution and marketing of their films is without a peer in the industry.

Films produced by Falcon command the highest prices on the market. Falcon's films are of exceptional quality. The models used are among the highest paid in the industry and must have a certain appearance and be able to perform under demanding production requirements.

Falcon films have a certain look and feel. There is extreme care taken to ensure the best lighting, camera angles, editing, and presentation to the viewer.

As a company, Falcon uses the services of the best models, directors, production people, agents, and distributors in the business. These individuals and companies know that by using only the highest quality in their production of films they will attract the highest quality purchasers of their films.

## Chi Chi LaRue

There is perhaps no individual who evokes as many ambivalent feelings as Chi Chi LaRue. As a professional, however, there is no other individual in gay adult porn who can match his work schedule, his creativity, and ability to attract new models into the industry.

Chi Chi La Rue is constantly directing films for several film companies including All Worlds Video and subsidiaries of Falcon. When he is not filming he is staging productions around the world. He meets thousands of people each year and is responsible for discovering and attracting scores of new models into the world of gay adult videos.

Most people are amazed at his ability to remember every model, his ability to keep in touch with hundreds of people and his endless ability to produce more films. Chi Chi La Rue is the director every aspiring porn star wants to have the opportunity to work with even if they only do one film.

## Peter Scott

Peter Scott is the one agent who has the universal respect of all film producers. He is widely known for his honesty and integrity in an industry and profession not generally known for those attributes.

Peter Scott only represents the best models in the industry. He is known as the one agent in the business never to have attempted to have sex with a model. He is also the only agent who is not involved in the escort side of the business.

Peter Scott provides his models with good advice on appearance, professionalism, what to expect when filming, and is excellent at resolving public relations problems. Even when he does not take on representation of a model he treats individuals with dignity and respect. He provides very effective marketing for his models, and only works with the most reputable adult film producers.

Producers of films rely heavily on Peter Scott for advice. Models contracted through Peter Scott are known for their reliability and ability to perform on set. Nightclubs are assured performers contracted through Peter Scott will show up for their performance, and certainly be crowd pleasers.

Peter Scott has a reputation for providing good counseling to models, and providing opportunities to his models even when he does not make a commission. For this reason, a lot of film producers refer models to him after the model has finished exclusive contracts.

There are no guarantees any potential model will succeed at getting film roles. However, anyone who wishes to be in the business and only wants to work with the top companies should at least contact Peter Scott for his opinion.

Attracting the attention of the industry leaders is not always easy. These individuals and entities have established their reputations on their professionalism and tend to not only look for pretty faces, but individuals that exhibit professionalism.

## *Reputable*

Many of the remaining individuals and entities in the gay adult film industry fall in the category of reputable. These individuals and entities do not have the consistency, stature, or reliability of the industry leaders. These individuals and entities tend to pay less than the top video companies (although many of them will use the top performers from time to time). These individuals and entities may not pay their bills on time, and have been known to bounce a check or two (although they generally make good on them).

When dealing with these companies it is usually best to use a reputable agent who will ensure the terms of any contract are met. It is not unusual for a reputable film company to attempt to change contract terms at the last minute. In these cases, a model is at a distinct disadvantage without a reputable agent.

## *Niche Players*

This category includes a wide variety of persons involved in the gay adult film market.  These include photographers, new film companies, film companies that target a specific market, amateur video companies, and other entities that may or may not be involved in the business full time.

There are literally hundreds of these individuals and entities.  Many of them are legitimate, and many of them do not have the interests of the model at heart.  An agent is the best way to determine if an entity is legitimate or not.

## *Scum*

As in any business, the gay adult film business has its share of individuals and entities that use their involvement in the business to exploit others.  There is no central credit-reporting agency for the gay adult film business, but everyone who is involved in the business full-time, knows the scammers.

Many individuals involved in scamming others are tolerated on the fringes of the business for many years.  Typically, these individuals hop from one company or another or one scheme to another.  Here are some of the more common activities of these scammers:

- **Bounced checks.**  Many a model has signed a model release only to find the check received was written on an account with insufficient funds.  In some cases, the individuals who wrote the checks decide to stop payment on the checks.
- **Breach of contract.**  There are some companies that negotiate with a model for a certain amount or specific types of activities in a scene and change the terms during the course of filming.  There are numerous reports of producers trying to get an extra scene for the money, getting additional sexual activity or cutting the agreed upon pay on the set.
- **Cancelled shoots.**  Every company experiences the unexpected.  The difference with the scammers is cancelled shoots occur with some frequency and some times after the

model has shown up on the set. In some cases the model has paid for a cross-country flight and arrives on the set only to find out the shoot has been cancelled and will not get paid for their travel or expenses.

- **Disreputable agents.** There are many people who promote themselves as agents. Many agents in the business engage in disreputable activities. These are activities a potential model should watch out for when interviewing an agent:

1. **Trying to engage in sex with a model.** Some agents will attempt to engage a prospective model in sex. Granted, there is a need to know if a model can perform. However, this is usually determined by setting the model up with a reputable photographer for a photo shoot.

2. **Misrepresentation of the cast list.** Many agents misrepresent their cast list and may list names on their cast list they do not represent. This is sometimes difficult to catch because many porn stars work with several agents.

3. **Asking for money up front.** There are many agents who will ask a model to pay a fee for photo shoots or marketing expense. Reputable agents do not charge for marketing a new model.

4. **Misrepresentation of what is expected of a model.** Some agents recruit models by saying they are looking for models for Playgirl magazine since this appeals to heterosexual males who do not wish to engage in sex with men. In some cases, models are sent to film sets without being told they are expected to engage in sexual activity on film.

5. **Signing exclusive contracts.** Reputable agents may not even use contracts let alone exclusive contracts. The gay adult film market is somewhat fragmented, and there is considerable benefit to working with different agents.

6. **Find out which film companies an agent works with.** If an agent does not work with Falcon or Catalina there is generally a problem with the agent. Be sure to get the name of the models represented by the agent and the

titles of their films and check the box covers. In some cases, you might be able to find the model through advertisements or on the Internet. A prospective model should always check with other models on their experiences with the agent.

The only way to avoid problems with scum is to not do business with them. In the rare instances where a top model will deal with a studio with a bad reputation, the model will require payment up front or work through a reputable agent. The gay adult film market is a very small world, and everyone knows the reputations of nearly everyone else in the industry.

### *Trends in the Gay Adult Film Industry*

Over the last two years there have been several distinctive trends in the gay adult film industry.

- **Fewer reputable gay adult film producers**. In 1997, there were four first class gay adult film producers. By the middle of 1998 there were only two first class gay adult film producers. One of these producers went out of business, and the other has dramatically reduced the number of films produced in a year.
- **Increased reports of bounced checks and cancelled shoots.** At least four companies who had reputable reputations now have reputations for bad checks, and cancelled shoots.
- **Models are being used for fewer films.** At one time, a model could be expected to perform in twelve films (three with each of the major companies). At present, many models are being ignored or are only cast for two or three films before they no longer get offers for films.
- **Lower budgets.** A higher percentage of films are being filmed at much lower budgets than in the past. Models who were making $1,000 for a scene in the past are now being offered $400 to $500 to shoot a scene.

- **Greater market segmentation.** There are a number of new gay adult film companies filming fetish videos. The themes for these videos include bare backing (sex scenes without condoms are banned with the major companies), water sports, fist fucking, and sadomasochism. Many of these new video companies use models with a "real man" or natural look. Many of these models perform in the films to fulfill a fantasy and are either not paid to perform in the films or are paid very little.
- **Fewer films are being produced.** Overall, there are more films being produced because there are more producers of gay adult films. However, the top film producers are producing fewer films, or the same number of films with lower budgets.
- **Fewer porn stars command premium salaries.** There are fewer porn stars receiving higher than normal salaries. Whereas, a few years ago there were many porn stars receiving scene rates of $2,500 up to $10,000, there are very few individuals currently receiving these rates.
- **Fewer personal appearances.** There are fewer nightclubs willing to pay the price for personal appearances. In the past, porn stars routinely traveled around the country appearing at many nightclubs and strip clubs. Fewer of these clubs use porn stars as an attraction. Whereas the typical fee paid to performers was $1,000 or more for a personal appearance, the average fee has dropped to $500.

There are several reasons for these changes in the gay adult video industry:

- The Internet has in many cases replaced adult films and magazines as the medium of choice for viewers of gay pornographic material. One group of gay adult magazines has reported a 40% drop in their

subscriptions over the last year and has stopped
publishing..
- The wholesale and retail prices of gay adult videos have
  dropped dramatically over the last several years.
- Buyers of gay adult videos have been buying more
  videos from amateur and non-mainstream producers of
  gay adult videos.

It is unclear if these changes are temporary or permanent.
Nevertheless, the Internet and the ability of many new gay adult
film producers to enter the market have had a definite impact on
the industry.    For the viewers of gay pornography, this means
there are more viewing choices at a lower price.  For prospective
models, this means they can expect to perform in fewer films,
and get paid less for their performances.

Recently, I received this letter from a successful porn star:

*You are absolutely correct about your observations on the
porn industry.  I think part of the problem is there are many
hungry models who are willing to work for next to nothing.  I
spoke with someone today with whom I did a scene a couple
weeks ago and he turned down a scene that would have paid
only $400.  I wish the industry was filled with more individuals
like him and then the rest of us would get paid what we are
worth (even if what we are worth is still small potatoes).*

One truism in the gay adult film industry is it still pays to
produce quality.  During the gay porn awards season for 1998
nearly every film that won awards had the involvement of Peter
Scott.   Peter Scott consistently provided quality models and
many new faces.   Those individuals who decry the lack of
quality in gay adult films should look for a "casting by Peter
Scott" label on the films they purchase.

### The Escort and the Adult Industry

Having described the good, the not so good, and the ugly it
would be helpful to analyze how an escort uses the adult film

industry to their advantage. With the advent of the video camera and the computer it is possible for anyone to effectively create an adult video for sale. Likewise, there are many people associated with the adult film industry such as photographers, magazines, Internet webmasters, and agents who that can even be helpful to people who do not necessarily want to be in gay adult videos.

Becoming a successful model in gay adult films is essentially a crapshoot. The difference between being a one-film model and having a long and prosperous career in the business involves a lot of variables:

- **Appearance.** Many escorts take considerable care with their appearance, but being camera ready requires special attention to hair, body hair, muscle tone, and extra concern for the appearance of the abdominal and buttock muscles.
- **Desirability of look.** Although there may be hundreds of producers of gay adult films there may only be twenty or so individuals who cast the bulk of the films for the top producers of gay adult video films. These individuals make or break people in the business.
- **Personality.** The ability to make friends and develop business relationships is very important. Many of the top film stars do not develop a large following of fans even after they have performed in twenty or more films a year. However, they are reliable performers on video and have developed a good network of directors and producers who offer them constant work.
- **Performance.** Being able to have sex on demand is essential for a new model. Most people are not given a second chance, and word of mouth travels very fast in the industry.
- **Representation.** There are many companies with an insatiable appetite for new talent. Some companies are notorious for promising new models the world and then never using a model again after their first film. A good agent will market a model to twenty or more of the most reputable companies, directors, and producers.

Representation is especially important if a model does not live in the Los Angeles area.

- **Location.** The top companies will fly the top models to California from all over the country. However, models living closer to Los Angeles tend to get the bulk of the work since film companies typically produce their films with low budgets. A model not frequently in Los Angeles or San Francisco is oftentimes out of sight, out of mind, and out of budget.
- **Personal Issues.** Many models perform in one adult film and decide they do not like to perform in adult films. Filming is very difficult work, and requires a great commitment of time. In some cases, it is not profitable for an escort to film frequently. Some of the most successful escorts will only film once or twice a year.

Many escorts profit handsomely from being one-film models, and there are many one-film models assured of a long career as an escort through their involvement in the gay adult film industry. There are many ways for a male escort to exploit the gay adult film industry more than the gay adult film industry exploits the male escort:

- **Photo shoots.** The top agents in the gay adult film industry work with some of the top male nude photographers in the country. Most photographers will agree to shoot a roll of film for the model's personal use. This roll of film can be used for marketing and promotion.
- **Photo spreads in magazines.** Photo spreads in magazines provide good references for clients. Clients are generally excited and more loyal to escorts who have appeared in the gay adult magazines.
- **A homemade jack-off video.** Producing a home made jack-off video is always good marketing. These videos are easy to produce, and sell very quickly to clients. Homemade videos can be easily marketed on the Internet.
- **Agents.** By having an agent, an escort may get a number of possible opportunities. These opportunities include

modeling jobs, client referrals, dance engagements, and personal appearances.

- **Film companies.** Many film companies promote their films through dance tours throughout the country and advertising in various magazines. The film companies can provide valuable exposure to male escorts.

### The Los Angeles Market

There are certain distinctions that need to be made about the Los Angeles market. The majority of porn stars and the majority of gay adult film companies are based in Los Angeles.

This means there are many more opportunities for filming if a person lives in Los Angeles. The variety of opportunities is also greater. Many porn stars film one, two, or even three films a week. Some porn stars develop a wide and varied network of contacts and work almost continually.

Many successful porn stars do not live in Los Angeles, but tend not to film as often, and see their involvement in the gay adult film industry as a part time avocation.

### Working in the Industry

Working as a model in the gay adult film industry is a job and requires commitment and good work habits in order to be successful. Granted, there are very few jobs that require a person to maintain a tan, work out for two hours every day, and have regular sex.

Nevertheless, as with all jobs there are some drawbacks. A model is considered self-employed. As such, a prospective model needs to consider the following issues:

- A model needs to provide for health insurance.
- Film companies will report income on 1099 forms to the IRS and will not withhold taxes. Porn stars need tax advice.
- Income can be erratic so it is important for a model to save their money to cover expenses during slow periods.

- If a model breaches a contract it will typically result in very unfavorable word of mouth, loss of representation, and possibly result in being blackballed in the industry.
- The failure to be able to perform on set, showing up on the set on drugs, or showing up on the set with a communicable disease may result in being sent home and not getting paid.

Many of these issues are the same issues an escort normally encounters. However, the major differences with working for a film company as opposed to being an independent escort, an escort is working for other people and with a number of other people. Escorts who do not work well with others may find it difficult to work within the gay adult film industry. The gay adult film industry is a close knit group that has worked together and as competitors for decades. Word travels fast.

A prospective model usually has a lot of questions about working in the gay adult film industry. The questions are pretty standard, and so are the answers.

*What do gay adult film stars get paid?*    The standard answer is about $1000 a day, but there are a lot of variations to this. Some companies pay models $400 to $500 for a scene, whereas the top companies pay about $1000 a scene. The difference is typically based on the grade of the model, the grade of the company, and whether the model has an agent or not.

*What other payments might be made?* Some models might receive extra payments for photo stills, a box cover, dialogue, and personal appearances. An agent is usually needed to negotiate these extra payments since many scene rates do not assume extra payments. An agent will also ensure the studio provides travel expenses and accommodations.

*How do gay adult film stars get paid?* Rates are quoted per scene. Scene rates vary by the type of sexual activity. Jack-off scenes pay the lowest. Oral scenes pay more. Scenes involving anal sex pay the most.

*Who gets paid the most?* Very few models ever make more than the standard pay. The reason for this is, there are very few models that develop enough popularity to translate into more video sales. The porn stars with the highest earning power are Jeff Stryker, Ryan Idol, Hal Rockland, Kevin Williams, and Ken Ryker. These porn stars can command $25-50,000 to perform in one film.

*What will a model need to do on set?*   This is generally agreed to when the director books the model. Typically, models will not be asked to do anything they feel uncomfortable doing. Typically, what will be done is agreed upon at the time a contract is made.

*Will the model be told their co-star before the shoot?* Studios tend to be very protective of their models and will generally discourage contact with a co-star before a shoot.   For new models, there is a good possibility they will be working with a relatively new, but experienced model.   It takes three to six months before there is any material available in the market on a new model.  However, most studios will give a description of the co-star to a model.

*What will happen on set?*  Typically, a first time model will be driven to the set by someone from the studio.   When the model arrives at the studio he will meet the other models, meet the crew, and meet with a makeup artist to prepare for the scene. If the model is expected to bottom in the scene he will need an enema.

*What does a model need to bring to the set?*  A model is expected to come to the set:

- with costumes unless costumes are provided for by the studio
- ready to perform
- clean and sober
- with picture identification and a social security card

It is generally best not to bring valuables to the set.

*What will be provided on the set?*  The studio will provide for makeup, food, beverages, condoms, lubricant, enemas, and props.  The studio may also provide drugs to enhance or allow for performance on set.

*What happens during filming?* The director controls the filming. The director will give the models direction on what is trying to be accomplished. A scene may take a couple of hours to complete, or the scene may take a few days to complete. During this time a model will be expected to work under hot lights, work in uncomfortable positions, and act as if he is enjoying the situation.

*What happens after filming?* After filming the model will get paid after filling out a model release, W-9 tax forms and miscellaneous other forms. It is best to cash any checks at the bank it is drawn on after filming. Some studios will cash the check on set.

*Why don't models get paid sometimes?* There are numerous stories of models not getting paid or getting paid less than the agreed amount.

- If a model is unable to perform on set the model may not get paid.
- If a model shows up on the set drunk or on drugs the model may be rejected on set.
- If a model refuses direction or fails to carry out their contract (whether oral or written) they may be paid a lesser amount.
- If a model shows up on the set with a sexually transmittable disease the model may be rejected on set.
- If a model has drastically changed their look or appearance without the knowledge of the studio the model may be rejected on set.
- If a model is late the model may be rejected.
- If a model walks off set for any reason the model will not be paid.
- If an agent substitutes a model without the studio's express permission, the model will probably be rejected.
- Some studios write bad checks.
- Some studios may attempt to bargain down the model fee either during the shooting of the video or after shooting the video citing budget reasons. This is generally a con. Some

gay adult film companies have a reputation for using this con on a regular basis.

- Some studios may attempt to renegotiate what a model will do on screen during shooting.
- Some studios have a reputation for committing to a shoot and then canceling the shoot when the model appears on set. Some models have even traveled cross-country only to be told they will not be paid. This rarely if ever happens when an agent is involved.

*How long will it take before a film is released?* A film will be released within three to six months after filming. Typically, a studio will send a model a free copy after release of the film.

*What is the best way for a model to get marketed for additional films?* The top male porn stars market themselves in a variety of ways. First, the top porn stars have an agent. Second, the top porn stars attend the industry functions such as the Probe awards in July, the Gay Video Awards in December, and the Consumer Electronics Show held in Las Vegas in January. The key is to meet as many people as possible, and follow up when these individuals express interest. There are numerous other gay porn events. Most are by invitation, and most agents get invitations for the models on their cast list.

*What about performing in straight adult videos?* There is a very limited market for males in straight adult videos. Typically, males get paid more to do gay adult videos than females get paid to perform in straight adult videos. Males who perform in straight adult videos get paid on average one hundred dollars to be in a scene. Some of the male models in straight adult videos do not get paid at all.

## Difficulties on Set

A porn star may encounter some difficulties on set. Even if the porn star is ready, able, and willing to perform, there are a number of things that can go wrong when working on a film set. Generally, the problems are minor since many of the directors and studios have considerable experience in filming. However, there are also times when things can go seriously wrong. These are a partial listing of what problems a porn star can expect:

- **Heterosexual Models**. The number one complaint from models is working with heterosexual models. Many heterosexual models are difficult to work with, or are unwilling to perform on set. Many studios will only use gay or bisexual models for this reason. Unfortunately, many studios and the viewing public have a fascination with heterosexuals. In some cases, the studios, directors, and agents have lied to the model about the expectations on set.
- **Delays**. Many directors do not start on time. This can be very difficult for a new model if the model is not aware of the punctuality habits of a particular studio or director.
- **The Director**. There are a few directors who are known for having temper tantrums on set.
- **Cancellations**. Occasionally shoots are cancelled at the last minute or rescheduled. This can be expensive to a successful escort.
- **Police Raids**. Although police raids are rare, police raids do occur from time to time. It is not a serious matter unless the model is caught with drugs. Many adult films are filmed in residential areas. Prying neighbors are oftentimes the source of a complaint that leads to a police raid. Typically, film companies keep their filming locations secret to avoid any problems.
- **Injuries on set**. Many studios are filming riskier forms of sexual behavior including fisting, sadomasochism, and other forms of non-vanilla sex. Many of these activities involve some form of physical risk. Unfortunately, as studios venture into these new areas, the studios do not always hire models trained in the sexual activity to be performed on set. In one instance a model had their colon ruptured by a model with had no prior experience fisting.

A successful escort would typically find it more profitable to stay home and see clients rather than film. However, filming does bring increased exposure to potential clients and allows the porn star to raise their rates. This is true whether the escort does one film or dozens of films. In some cases, it is most profitable to only do one or two films.

### Porn Stars as Escorts

Being a porn star requires far more discipline than most escorts are accustomed. For some people, knowing what day it is, to show up on time, and to follow direction from others are terribly onerous inconveniences. Just the thought of having to wake up before noon for a shoot is enough to discourage some of the most successful escorts from pursuing a career in porn.

An escort who has performed in gay adult video has greater income potential as an escort than an escort who has not performed in an adult film. The reasons for this are:

- An escort who has performed in gay adult video develops free national exposure.
- An escort who has performed in gay adult video will be able to market themselves as a porn star. There are many clients who will pay more to see a porn star than a non-porn star.
- An escort who has performed in gay adult video has more opportunities to make personal appearances in strip clubs around the country.
- Escorts who have performed in gay adult videos attract higher income clients and these clients are more likely to hire escorts who have performed in gay adult videos for travel engagements.
- An escort who has performed in gay adult videos develops a national following of fans.
- Many clients will hire escorts who are porn stars because they have an interest in the industry.
- Contacts in the gay adult film industry are good referral sources for clients.

There are many clients who are intimidated by the prospect of hiring a gay adult film star as an escort. For this reason, a porn star will use a variety of marketing methods.

- A gay male adult film star may not disclose their adult film star status in their advertisement. This gives the escort the option of disclosing this information to a client during the telephone conversation.
- Telling a client over the telephone about an appearance in a certain issue of a gay magazine is oftentimes a good selling point for an escort.
- Telling a client over the telephone about an appearance on the box cover of a certain film is a good selling point for an escort.
- There are many clients who have no interest in gay adult films. As such, it is a turn off for an escort to market themselves as a porn star.

An escort who is a porn star will increase their overall marketability to clients and will get less price resistance from clients. In some markets an escort who is a porn star will be able to get a price premium. There are, however, some things for the escort to keep in mind in terms of advertising:

- Porn stars intimidate some clients.
- Clients perceive porn stars as more expensive.
- Clients perceive porn stars as having a bad attitude.

There are clients who seek out porn stars for several reasons:

- Some clients have a fantasy of having sex with a porn star.
- Porn stars are perceived as having better bodies than non-porn stars.
- Some clients have seen the porn star in magazines and films.

There are many non-porn star escorts who have developed the same wide following as porn stars. These escorts have developed their reputation through body building careers, web sites on the Internet, personal appearances in strip clubs, and reputations for being Colt or Playgirl models. Typically, however, it is easier to develop the same reputation through involvement in gay adult video.

It is important to remember most careers in gay adult porn are short lived. However, by doing even one film a successful escort can increase their earning power and gain valuable experience.

# Chapter Seven

# Specialty Escorts

There are a number of specialty markets in the world of escorts. One of the reasons clients hire escorts is to experience their sexual fantasies. The market for some of these specialties tends to be small, so many of these same escorts also advertise in the mainstream as well as their specialties.

When dealing in a specialty market it is always best to get a referral by word of mouth. Clients in these niche markets tend not to be repeating clients, so there is a greater tendency for the escorts in these markets to be less honest. Likewise, the types of activities in these markets are inherently more dangerous to the client.

### The Bisexual Market

There is an increasing group of clients who hire a male and a female. Essentially, these clients have sexual fantasies to fulfill. Just as many heterosexual males have the fantasy of being with two women, many bisexual individuals have the fantasy of being with a male and a female.

These clients tend not to be repeating clients, but see this experience as a one-time fantasy fulfillment. The types of clients for this service are:

- Individuals with no previous sexual experience. These clients may be a-sexual or have physical handicaps that have made it difficult or impossible to have sexual encounters.
- Couples who have the fantasy of bisexual experiences.
- Heterosexual males who want to experience a homosexual experience, but would feel more comfortable if a woman was present.
- Homosexual males who want to have a heterosexual experience, but would feel more comfortable if a male was present.

The clients who are looking for a bisexual couple may be looking for several things:

- Some men want to experience being anally penetrated in the presence of a woman.
- Some men and couples enjoy seeing a sex show.
- Some men have the fantasy of being anally penetrated while penetrating a woman.
- Some men have the fantasy of double penetration of a woman. Double penetration is when the woman is penetrated both anally and vaginally at the same time.

Unfortunately, however, advertisements for a male and a female attract a lot of crank callers and a very small percentage of the callers are legitimate prospects. The types of independent escorts who normally advertise this service are oftentimes husband and wife or boyfriend and girlfriend. In some markets these couples may use their advertisements as a way to lure victims. In these cases, they set up the client in order to steal from them.

Finding a male and female couple can sometimes be difficult. In some markets there are couples who advertise. In other markets escort agencies handle males and females. When hiring from an agency it is best to request a male who is bisexual. There are many male escorts who will not work with women. In markets where males advertise themselves as bisexual the client can ask the escort if there are any females who work with them. Likewise, the client may ask a female escort if they work with any males.

## Male Escorts for Women

The dream of every heterosexual male is to make a living providing sex and companionship to appreciative women. In reality, the market for male escorts who cater exclusively to women is very small.

There are several reasons why this market is very small. First, women generally do not have problems finding sexual partners. Second, women tend to prefer having sex with someone familiar, and do not tend to like anonymous sex. Third, women generally do not have as much disposable income as men.

The market for male escorts for women tends to fall into the following categories:

- Male strippers who perform at bachelorette parties. These engagements sometimes involve more than stripping, just as bachelor parties oftentimes include sex with female prostitutes.
- Strip clubs with women clientele. Women and men are both likely to make sexual overtures to male strippers. There are many male strippers who will make arrangements for private performances involving sex after their performance.
- Male/female couples. There are many married couples who enjoy engaging male prostitutes. Typically, the male likes to watch while another male engages in sexual relations with their female partner. There are also cases where the male will engage a female prostitute and a female will engage a male prostitute.

- Single females. It is extremely rare for a single female to engage a male prostitute through an advertisement or an agency, however reports of this activity are increasing.

Typically, when females or couples hire a male prostitute their budget is less than when a male is paying for a male prostitute. A very high percentage of these clients are involved in drugs or the male has sexual impotency problems.

The most successful male escorts for women are strippers since they have more personal contact with potential clients. Many of these relationships are not monetary, but involve gifts. It is not unusual for some of these strippers to make several women think they are in a relationship with them while asking for loans, gifts, and other forms of support. As with any type of hustler, many of these escorts are con artists who see women as prey.

The market, however, for male escorts for female clients is very small, and these escorts do not make as much as male escorts for men. Typically, these escorts will charge no more than $100 or $150 for a private performance and oftentimes will see someone privately for much less.

The demand for male escorts for female clients or couple clients depends greatly on geography. The greatest demand for these types of escorts seems to be in the Midwest where some male escorts report that up to 20% of their business is comprised of females and male/female couples.

Despite the lack of work for male escorts for women, it does not keep men from having the fantasy. This letter is fairly typical of the heterosexual male fantasy:

*I am a 30 year old male. I am 5'8", 170 pounds, blond hair, blue eyes, have dimples, and a great personality. For a long time I have been interested in becoming a male escort for women. I am strictly heterosexual and find myself attracted to beautiful older women (40 and up). I consider myself very open-minded and have great respect for all people regardless of their sexual preference.*

*I am writing to you because I am looking for some guidance on how to get started. I live outside of Boston. I believe the market for male escorts for women is slim but growing. I would like to be part of that growth. I own my own business and am looking to supplement my income and depending on how it goes I would consider being an escort on a more permanent basis.*

## Wrestlers

There are some clients who like to wrestle. There are very few escorts who do this type of work for a number of reasons. These reasons include safety, prevention of injuries, lack of training, and inadequate body type.

In major markets there will generally be a few escorts who advertise wrestling as their specialty. These types of escorts can be found on the Internet and in local publications.

Again, this is a sexual fantasy. In some cases the prospective client sees wrestling as a way to explore their homosexual desires while denying any homosexual desires. Wrestling is seen as a legitimate way to have physical contact with another man without having sex with them.

## Bodybuilders

Competition level bodybuilders are probably the most popular group of escorts. These escorts are generally around 250 pounds of pure muscle.

Although there are many escorts in this category who would be considered among the elite escorts discussed Chapter 5, there are also many escorts who are bodybuilders and work full time as escorts. Many of these individuals are well past their prime for competitive bodybuilding. Many of these escorts are in their late thirties and early forties. A few of these escorts are in their mid to late twenties.

Bodybuilders attract the most fanatical of clients. Clients of bodybuilders generally subscribe to fitness and bodybuilding magazines, attend competitions, and belong to athletic clubs attracting bodybuilders. Clients who want bodybuilders tend not to seek out other types of escorts. For the client it can be very frustrating since there are very few escorts who fall into the bodybuilding category, and the ones who do oftentimes generate numerous complaints.

This type of escort is also very high risk to the client. Many of these bodybuilders are straight and work as escorts in order to victimize clients. Most bodybuilders will allow body worship only and keep hustling clients for more money. There are numerous reports of clients being warned not to use certain body building escorts. The warning typically goes unheeded, and the client reports back later about being victimized by the escort. There is no other type of escort who has a following based on blind fanaticism as competition level body builders.

The cost of hiring a bodybuilder is among the more expensive types of escorts. A client can expect to pay a minimum of $300 for an hour with a competitive bodybuilder. This will entitle the client to spend an hour watching the bodybuilder pose. There are some exceptions to this observation, but these exceptions are few and far between.

In general, clients who are interested exclusively in bodybuilder type escorts are considered among the most difficult to satisfy, and many agencies will not take a client with an exclusive interest in competitive bodybuilders. The reasons for this are:

- Many clients have had bad experiences with escorts who were bodybuilders. These experiences including theft and physical harm.
- Bodybuilder escorts are very expensive and there are very few clients who will pay $300 to $500 for an hour.
- Bodybuilder escorts very rarely meet the client's expectations.
- Agencies have a very hard time recruiting high quality bodybuilders who do not get client complaints.

When it comes to hiring bodybuilders as escorts word of mouth referrals are very important to the client. As stated above, very few clients who are fixated by bodybuilding escorts will accept outside advice on the escort's professionalism. Unfortunately, these types of escorts, in general, are the source of most of the public safety issues in terms of advertised escorts.

### Transgender Escorts

This part of the market is becoming increasingly popular. It is also a very unique market. It includes transvestites and transsexuals.

Transvestites are males who dress as females. Transsexuals are men who are in varying stages of becoming women. Some are under hormone treatment, others have had their breasts enlarged, and others have had their male sexual organs changed to female sexual organs. There are many post-operative transsexuals who advertise themselves as both women and transsexuals. Generally, the client will not be able to tell the difference.

If a transsexual is pre-operative (meaning the transsexual still has male sexual organs), the transsexual may not be able to get an erection because of hormonal therapy. A client who is expecting performance should ask the transsexual if they are capable of getting an erection or consider hiring a male escort at the same time.

Transgender escorts are very popular and tend to have a large repeating clientele. Transgender escorts have a very loyal following due to their rarity and mystique. The occasional news report of a famous celebrity being caught in a compromising position with a transgender prostitute has done much to popularize these types of escorts. Some escort agencies specialize in transgender escorts, and in some localities transgender escorts are the escorts who make the most money.

Transgender escorts are very popular with men who see themselves as generally heterosexual. Transgender escorts can generally be found at the popular nightclubs whether or not the nightclub has a straight or gay orientation. Transgender escorts oftentimes work in nightclubs as hustlers.

There are many stories of men picking up transgender prostitutes who never found out the transsexual's true sexual identity. One famous porn star I know dated a transsexual for two weeks before finding out he/she was a transsexual. If in doubt, it might be best to ask, however there is no guarantee a transsexual will tell the truth about their status. There are many military men who report being seduced by transsexuals in Tijuana tequila bars only to have second thoughts about their encounter while nursing a hangover.

Although there are many reputable transsexual escorts (generally, these are escorts who advertise on their own and have a good clientele), this is also a group of escorts who can be high risk. Obviously, these are individuals who are very good at deception. It is best for a client to take precautions with their wallet and valuables when picking up a transgender hustler in a bar or off of the street. Using advertised transgender escorts and transgender escorts who work for agencies are usually the safest way to procure a transgender escort. Many transgender escorts will only do in-calls, however some will also do out-calls.

## *Tandems*

Just as every heterosexual male has the fantasy of being with two women, many gay or bi-curious males have the fantasy of being with two males.

The typical client who will hire two male escorts is someone who frequently uses escorts. Typically, the client will use one escort with whom he has familiarity, and ask for the escort to bring along a friend. Clients will rarely call an advertisement and ask two strangers to come to their hotel room or home.

Escorts will run advertisements for tandems in the major markets. Oftentimes, an escort will work together with their boyfriend. In some cases, a couple will only work together and not separately. If a client is interested in two escorts it would be best to use an escort seen in the past, use an agency, or use a word of mouth referral.

As with the male and female couple the primary reason for hiring two guys is to fulfill a sexual fantasy. These fantasies include watching a sex show, being double penetrated, or just being with two men at the same time.

Since many clients see multiple escorts in a given market, offering tandems can be a strategic advantage to an escort. Many clients will stick with a small group of escorts rather than risk contacting new escorts. There are many clients who like variety, but also like to stick to a known quantity. For established clients, a tandem with an escort they have used previously offers safety as well as variety.

## S & M

In some markets there are escorts who are into sadism and masochism. Most of these escorts will only play the dominant role. There are a few escorts who prefer being submissive, but these are few and far between.

The most respectable of these escorts have their own fully equipped dungeon. If the client likes humiliation, bondage, various types of torture, and other types of out of the ordinary sexual experiences it would be best to call someone who advertises these special services. Many of these individuals have undergone special training in these specialties and respect the limits of their clients.

This type of activity is not for everyone, but it is becoming more popular. Among the most popular female escorts are dominatrixes who provide torture and no sex. These activities involve a certain amount of risk, and it would be best for a client to go over their expectations and determine the escort's training before engaging in these activities.

Recently there was an article listing the top search terms used on a particular search engine. For the period of time analyzed the word spanking was used 187,940 times and ranked number 58 of all terms used. The word bondage was used 185,434 times and ranked number 61 of all terms used. The term IRS was used 183,475 times and ranked number 62 of all terms used. These examples should leave no doubt as to the prurient interests of people who use the Internet. Sadomasochism is clearly part of our collective culture.

The Scarlet Letter in San Francisco holds seminars on sadomasochism as well as a number of other sexuality programs. They have held seminars on a number of topics throughout the country. The Internet web site for the Scarlet Letter is http://www.hooked.net/~wcow/scarltr.html. The e-mail address for the Scarlet Letter is Scarltr@aol.com or the organization can be contacted by calling (415) 621-4145

## *Concluding Observations*

The purpose of this section has been to describe in as much detail the various market segments of the male prostitution market in the United States and how various types of escorts operate. With the advent of the Internet, there have certainly been changes to the way male prostitutes operate. However, even on the Internet there are distinctions between hustlers, escorts, porn stars and other types of escorts. There are now electronic street corners, electronic advertising, and access to many people (both escorts and clients) who would not have been accessible just a few years ago.

Certainly, male prostitutes who have learned to exploit the Internet are among the most profitable male prostitutes. If anything, the Internet has broadened client access to male prostitutes. Clients have near instant access to pictures, descriptions, references, and phone numbers. Male prostitutes are more accessible than ever. There are some male prostitutes who use the Internet exclusively to develop clientele.

However, as long as there are clients there will be entrepreneurs to meet the needs and desires of clients. As long as there are sexual needs and fantasies to be fulfilled there will be prostitutes. In the vast majority of cases the relationship will be mutually beneficial. Perhaps 95% of prostitutes who enter the market only see clients occasionally or see clients to fulfill a fantasy and then retire from the business.

In essence, there are many ways to become a male prostitute, and many opportunities to become a male prostitute. However, as in any business, the people who succeed are the ones who are the most professional. Likewise, the clients who are most satisfied are the ones who have done their research before purchasing a product.

# Business Issues In Male Escorting

This section is devoted to the business issues of escorting. The first chapter in this section describes how the top escorts run their businesses and what differentiates them from other escorts. The second chapter deals with the various types of clients and what makes someone a desirable client. Most successful businesses model themselves after quality, both through a series of reactions to risks encountered as well as by profiling the characteristics of a profitable customer. The same is true of escorts.

The last four chapters in this section deal with various risks. There is an attempt to outline these risks in an objective manner. The risk is outlined, the risk is described, and there is information provided on what, if anything, people can do to avoid the specific risk.

# Chapter Eight

# Qualities of the Top Male Escorts

T he first section of this book dealt with the various market segments for male prostitutes. The descriptive material on escorts differentiated the top male escorts from the bulk of the escorts who advertise. As in any business, there are professionals who are in the top of their league and those who have less than desirable reputations.

There is a similar pattern that sets top escorts apart from the competition. A common comeback line from an escort to a client who thinks their price is too high is "you get what you pay for." In fact, the escort who would use this line is rarely worth the price. In actuality, a top quality escort would rarely say this to a client, and would instead refer the client to someone in the market who meets the client's budget.

The top escorts get their reputation through the respect and courtesy shown to all individuals. Certainly, all escorts have bad days. Escorts have bad days when they have been hammered by numerous prospective clients, but in general the top escorts are more interested in projecting a sense of professionalism and higher standards than the norm for the industry. This is but one example of how to identify a top quality male escort.

## How to Identify a Top Quality Escort

Top quality escorts can be found in any of the market niches described in Section One. Although hustlers tend to be transient, there are a number of high quality hustlers. Many of these hustlers have the same attributes as the high quality escorts. The major factors that differentiate the top escorts from the other 95% of the market include personal appearance, marketing and advertising, professionalism, how they screen their clients, business practices and how they run their personal life.

Although personal appearance is very important to the success of an escort, it is by no means the only factor. Some of the most attractive escorts are among the most disreputable. Unfortunately, many clients think with only one head when hiring an escort, and many of these disreputable escorts can do quite well over a period of time. These disreputable escorts succeed by moving to new markets with great frequency.

## Personal Appearance

Maintaining personal appearance is very important to the top quality escort. Staying pretty not only costs a lot of money, but it takes a lot of time. Here is the general regimen for the top escorts:

**Exercise.** The typical high quality escort spends two hours in a gymnasium six days a week. The work out regimen consists of 30-60 minutes of cardiovascular exercise, about fifteen to twenty minutes of abdominal exercises and another hour of lifting weights. The most common weight lifting program is a split routine where different muscle groups are worked different days. Typically, the muscle groups worked are chest/triceps, back/biceps, and shoulders/legs on successive days followed by one day off. Many of the top escorts have personal trainers at

$30-50 per hour. There are also many escorts who work as personal trainers.

**Hair/Nails.** The escort business is one of looking good, and not just any hairdresser is acceptable. The typical high quality escort will go to a hairdresser who has considerable experience with entertainers and other individuals who need to look good for their jobs.

**Diet and Nutrition**. The food budget for a typical high quality escort is probably two to three times the amount normal individuals spend for food. First, most of the top quality escorts are on a low fat diet. Second, in order to maintain muscle mass the escort must eat two to three times what a normal individual eats. Meals are supplemented by various dietary supplements including vitamins, creatine, protein shakes, and possibly three or four other dietary supplements. The average cost per month for dietary supplements may run between $150 to $200 per month.

**Plastic Surgery.** Many of the top escorts are in their late twenties and thirties biologically even though their real ages are oftentimes closely held secrets. Unfortunately, age and genetics are not always kind to people, especially if they abused their bodies with drugs and alcohol during a reckless youth. Fortunately, with the help of high quality plastic surgeons escorts can prolong their youth until after forty years of age. The most common forms of plastic surgery are liposuction, chest implants, hair transplants, and facial surgery.

**Tanning.** The typical escort will make use of a tanning bed about three times a week or will spend a lot of time out in the sun.

**Clothing.** The clothing of choice for the top male escorts varies, and generally they will look good in everything. However, there are some definite preferences for Versace, Armani, and DKNY. For the client who likes to take their escort shopping it is best to have a high credit limit.

Escorts are always good sources for health and beauty tips. There are many cases where clients start a self-improvement regimen because of their experiences with an escort. Many escorts felt they were ugly ducklings in their youth and only developed their looks when they matured.  In fact, some clients have taken advice on fitness from escorts, developed a program of fitness, and become escorts themselves.

## *Marketing and Advertising*

A high quality escort spends a lot of time thinking about their marketing.  Most clients think all an escort does is run and advertisement and wait for the phone to ring.  A lot of novice escorts think the same thing.  Successful marketing is a fine art in any field.  The escort business is no exception.  Here are the marketing attributes of the high quality escorts:

**Consistency.**   Top escorts are very consistent in their advertising. Top escorts advertise in the same places month in and month out and change their advertising once or twice a year

**Pictures and description.**  A top quality escort will usually use a picture with their face.  A picture will typically be updated every year.  If the escort uses a classified advertisement it tends to be accurate in terms of description.

**Stage Name**.  A top quality escort uses the same name for advertising month in and month out.    Escorts who are disreputable tend to change their names frequently.

**Look at the Quality of the Advertising.**   Top escorts understand the value of their advertising. Top escorts know what words attract high quality clients.  If anything, the advertising of a high quality escort is understated.

**Top quality escorts do not generally advertise price**. There are exceptions to this in markets such as Los Angeles where rates vary considerably between escorts.  However, where prices are quoted the price is all-inclusive and tipping is not expected.

**Top quality escorts advertise with quality**.  Quality markets with quality.  The top escorts give a lot of thought to differentiating themselves from escorts with bad reputations. Many of the top escorts simply refer to their Internet web page in their advertising.  Some escorts only advertise through national mediums such as the Internet or Unzipped magazine (formerly the Advocate Classifieds).  Top quality escorts will generally refrain from advertising in magazines or Internet sites known to have advertisers with bad reputations.  Magazines with a stated policy of investigating complaints and refusing to take advertising from escorts known for stealing or physical violence will tend to have a higher quality of escort.

Top quality escorts give a lot of thought to their marketing. Top escorts market themselves in a manner that attracts a certain type of client.  Unfortunately, escorts who are prone to be physically violent or steal from clients advertise in an almost identical manner to those escorts who advertise for repeat clients. The most common difference is, the disreputable escort will almost always advertise their rate as "starting at" or describe their rate over the phone as "starting at".

Many of the top quality escorts now get most of their clients by advertising on the Internet.  These escorts maintain a presence on the Internet by participating in various forums and advertising on multiple sites. Typically, the escort will maintain their own site on a reliable server.

In most cases web pages contain a telephone number and an e-mail address.  However, due to the number of crank callers, many escorts avoid using a phone number on the Internet. Publicity on the Internet can generate 50-100 crank callers a day.

### Professionalism

Top quality escorts are very experienced in dealing with people.   Typically, many escorts and hustlers view nearly everyone as a potential threat.  The top escorts view potential clients as opportunities.  Essentially, this means the top escorts have a way of making people feel special.  To some this would seem like common courtesy, however, in a world where common courtesy is expected it is oftentimes a scarce commodity.  These are some of the ways the top escorts treat their clients:

**Top escorts return phone calls**.  Many escorts are very slow to return telephone calls or pages.  Although the top escorts generally have the telephone turned off when they are with clients, they return telephone messages as soon as possible. The top escorts also travel a lot, and typically will leave a message on their answering service they will be unavailable for a time. Top escorts do, however, return phone calls promptly or as soon as possible. The exceptions to this rule are:

- When the caller leaves a beeper number.
- When the call is from a pay phone number (many pay phones cannot accept incoming calls).
- When the call is from a cellular phone number (many clients make calls from cellular phones and then turn off their phones).
- When the caller leaves a message for the escort who implies the interest is for phone sex.
- When the call is late at night.
- When the escort is on travel or has taken the day off.

**Top escorts are prompt**. The top escorts are prompt for their appointments or never more than 15 minutes late. The top escorts realize time is money for both themselves and their clients.

**Confidentiality**. Top escorts treat their clients with the utmost confidentiality. Top escorts do not keep records on their clients, and do not typically call their clients except to return a client's message.

**Courtesy**. Good escorts are good listeners. Top escorts have typically made up their mind on the suitability of a client after the first three sentences of a conversation. If the potential client makes it past the first three sentences without being rejected the client can expect to be treated with good manners.

**Honesty**. The top escorts have built their reputations on honesty, and they also expect a certain degree of honesty with their clients. Top escorts are very adept at detecting lies, and make judgement calls on whether the lie is material or not to the relationship with a client.

The top escorts build their relationships with clients on respect, trust, and integrity. These are the basics of any good personal or business relationship. These characteristics follow through with how the top escorts choose their clients.

### How the Top Escorts Screen Their Clients

There are many clients who believe they are the ones who are making the purchasing decision. This would certainly appear to be the case in markets where there are hundreds of advertised escorts. In reality, in every market there may only be a handful of escorts who work full-time as escorts. The other escorts in the market only work part-time as escorts to supplement their income.

The top escorts do not typically earn the bulk of their income by talking to prospective new clients who are responding to an advertisement. The top escorts typically earn the bulk of their income from a core group of regular clients. These escorts may travel about 50% of the time, and the remaining time is typically spent with repeat clients.

These escorts do not spend their time waiting for the phone to ring. Top escorts stay pretty busy seeing two or three repeat clients every day. Top escorts tend to be very selective about who they accept as a new client, and advertise only to fill in holes in their schedule and replace regular clients who move away, stop calling, die, or get fired.

The clues a top escort looks for in selecting new client are referral source and specific client attributes:

**Referral Source**. The top escorts will always ask a client how the client found out about the escort. In many cases, the escort will know by what the client says in the first few sentences or by which phone number the prospective client called. It is amazing how many clients will lie to an escort about how they heard of the escort. Many prospective clients will give a very vague answer. A top escort who detects the lie will then politely decline the client since if the client lies about the referral source, which is a relatively innocuous question, the relationship will rarely get better. Escorts who advertise in a number of venues, will accept clients based on this hierarchy:

- **Word of mouth referrals**. Top escorts will typically always take a client if the client is a word of mouth referral. These are the best types of clients because the prospective client's expectations are based on the judgement of a third party.
- **Unzipped Magazine**. This has always been regarded as the place where the top escorts in the United States have advertised. This magazine was formerly called the Advocate Classifieds. Unfortunately, when the name was changed, the advertising rates were raised by 40% and many of the top escorts have elected to stop advertising in Unzipped magazine. Many of the top escorts have moved their advertising dollars to the Internet.
- **The Internet**. Although the appeal of the Internet has broadened, the demographics are still very good for the average user of the Internet. There are several ways to advertise effectively on the Internet. Most of the top escorts now have web pages, they also advertise on any number of web sites that feature escort advertising, and many publications now publish their advertising on the Internet. When a publication has a web site, the quality of the clients who call based on the advertisement on the web site as opposed to clients who call based on the printed publication is of a higher quality.
- **Escort ads in local papers**. Although many escorts base their portfolio of clients on residents of a local market, these clients tend to get more scrutiny than business travelers do. Advertising in local publications is a major source of nuisance callers, price shoppers, and prank calls. In some markets there are multiple papers or the escort runs multiple advertisements. The escort has a mental ranking of the quality of client each publication attracts and which advertisements attract the best client.
- **Massage ads**. Many of the top escorts run advertisements for both massage and escort services.

The top escorts are more likely to refer out a potential massage client to another escort. Massage clients are less desirable than escort clients. Typically, top escorts will only accept a new massage client when they are in the middle of a slow period or if the client is particularly persistent and pleasant.

**Specific Client Attributes**. High quality escorts look for high quality clients. A high quality client does not necessarily mean high paying clients, although clients who pay higher than the stated rate definitely receive quality treatment.

The top escorts look for the following factors in determining whether to accept a client:

**Tone of voice.** Top escorts will only take clients with a professional and pleasant tone of voice. Clients who are difficult typically ask too many questions, try to control the conversation, or express fears of being ripped off. These individuals rarely make desirable clients. The top escorts would prefer to make these types of clients someone else's problem.

**Appointments.** Most of the top escorts work by appointment only. Although many of the top escorts will try to accommodate their repeat clients, they will generally not go to any great effort to accommodate a new client at the last minute. Many of these escorts do not work past midnight, although these escorts may make an exception for a client who gives advance notice.

There are some clients who will call and ask for an appointment at 11 p.m. and then ask if they can call at 10 p.m. to confirm the appointment. These clients rarely call to confirm and most escorts take clients on a first come, first served basis. Generally, the escort will agree to the terms knowing the client is unlikely to call back and will double book the time. About 50% of the time escorts will inform the prospective client they booked someone else for the appointment. The other 50% of the time the client will be lucky the escort is available.

**Keeping of Promises**. The top escorts keep mental notes on clients who keep their promises and which clients do not keep their promises.  If a client no shows the escort, if the client does not keep his promise to call back, or if an expected deposit does not arrive the escort will generally write off the client.  The same saying applies in the escort business as in any other business: "Many buyers are liars."

**References from other escorts**.  Many escorts will ask clients if they have seen other escorts.  Most clients lie about this, but there are many reasons not to lie about this with a top escort.  The reason for this is, it instantly qualifies a client for the escort, especially if the other escort has a less than desirable reputation.  Top quality escorts make it their business to know the reputations of as many escorts in their market as possible.  The first reason for this is, escorts oftentimes work with other escorts on tandem appointments.  The second reason is, the top escorts receive 20-30% of their business from referrals made by other escorts.  If an escort works alone, it is not generally a good sign.

**Where the call is originating from.**  An escort will oftentimes ask prospective clients where they are calling.  The purpose of this question is to compare the information given by the client with the information on the caller identification.  It is amazing how many prospective clients will lie about where they are calling.  If a prospective client lies about where the origin of the call, the escort will typically come up with an excuse and decline the client.  Top escorts typically block all calls from unlisted numbers which requires the prospective client to dial *82 in order to allow the call to go through.  Escorts will typically scrutinize calls from cellular phones, pay phones, and certain hotels before accepting a client.

The basic question of the client's location uncovers a number of scammers.  It is not unusual for prospective clients to say they are calling from out of state and say they will be visiting the area in the near future.  However, a high percentage of these individuals will be unclear on the date or be staying at a hotel that has been recently closed for renovations or has even been demolished.  In these cases, the prospective client should be told to call back when their travel arrangements have been completed, and to be sure to make reservations at a hotel that is still open.

These methods are all subtle but effective means to screen prospective clients without having to meet a client or even spend much time in conversation. Many prospective clients use means of deception because of a perceived need to hide their identity. In reality, prospective clients who lie on the matters outlined above or attempt to block their identity are generally up to no good.

Clients who truly need to shield their identity because of the prominence of their name have other means to ensure they are not discovered. In fact, many of the most famous clients of male escorts are well known in the escort business, but their privacy is typically well protected in the male escort community. The only times when confidentiality is breached are in cases where the individual has died or the client has been dishonest.

### Business Practices of the Top Escorts

The top escorts all follow pretty much the same business practices. Many of these practices are very subtle, and have been devised to both protect the escort and build trust with the client.

**Honesty**. This is a characteristic stressed for both escorts and clients throughout this book. There are certainly a number of dishonest male prostitutes, and they may well outnumber the honest male prostitutes. However, the top male escorts are generally extremely honest with clients. These escorts meet their commitments to clients, they are honest in their advertising, and they have good relationships with everyone in their life.

**Business Cards**. The top escorts all have business cards. Although some of the business cards may be risqué, the most successful business cards simply list a name and number or list the escort's occupation as massage therapist. Many of the top escorts will give their clients their real name, and a phone number different from the phone number advertised.

**Phone Systems**. Top escorts tend to have sophisticated telephone systems as described in Chapter 3. The purpose of these phone systems is to ensure clients can reach the escort and to screen out undesirable callers.

**Taking the Money Up-Front**. Although the stereotype of an escort is someone who asks for payment before performing services, the majority of the top escorts never ask for payment up front. In the case of a first time client the escort may ask for payment up front, but most first time clients typically place the money in an open place where the escort can see the money. In those cases the escort will typically not take the money until after the session is completed.

These are all subtle business practices that consider the needs of clients. These practices are designed to build trust with new clients so they will feel comfortable becoming a repeat client. The top escorts all realize repeat clients are far more valuable than one-time clients are, and do their best to cultivate ongoing relationships.

## Why Some of the Top Escorts Use Agents

Many of the top escorts use agents to some degree. Clients believe this arrangement results in unnecessary fees. However, in reality the agent fee is typically 20 to 30%. In return, these agents provide the following services:

- The agent handles all advertising.
- The agent handles all phone inquiries. For the top escorts about 90% of the inquiries are crank callers, from individuals who have no intention to use the escort, or cannot afford the services of the escort.
- Agents handle the development of web sites, answer e-mail (and although agents may answer in the name of the escort they keep the escort informed of the contents of all e-mail). Again, 90% of all e-mail is fan mail and not serious inquiries for services.

- The agent handles all scheduling, travel arrangements, photo shoots, model engagements, and filming arrangements.
- The agent handles public relations, rumor control, and provides advice on how the escort should act and behave.

The advantage to the escort from this arrangement is:

- It frees up a lot of time.
- This arrangement virtually eliminates bogus appointments and phone sex callers.
- Many of the top escorts travel about 50% of the time so it eliminates communications difficulties.
- There is no need for telephone tag since most agents answer the phone during most of the day.
- An agent can very quickly identify stalking risks.

Typically, potential clients who will not work through an agent are up to no good. Clients who work through an escort's agent are typically of very high quality, and are oftentimes repeating clients. The goal of any top quality escort is to establish a group of repeating clients for travel. Discerning high quality travel clients from the bulk of the inquiries takes a lot of time and effort. Through the use of an agent many top quality escorts are able to concentrate on the revenue producing side of the business, and leave the business issues to someone else.

### *How the Top Escorts Run Their Personal Lives*

The top escorts very much guard their privacy. Typically, these escorts may or may not be in a relationship and stick to a very close knit group of friends. It is not unusual for people who are outside of the escort community (or even other escorts) to make attempts to disrupt the life of an escort. As such, many escorts prefer to keep a low profile.

Successful escorts tend to be very responsible in their personal lives. Perhaps the two sweetest words in the English language are "paid for". Many escorts pay their bills in cash and oftentimes have excellent credit. Many of the top escorts own their own homes, and have their cars paid off. Most of the top escorts also carry individual health insurance.

In keeping with this profile, very few of the top escort's drink or do drugs of any kind. There are many escorts with drug and alcohol dependencies. A telling sign of these problems is, the escort is always short of money. The top male escorts would never complain of a shortage of money.

The top male escorts generally enjoy travel and many of them are very well traveled. Many escorts have traveled around the world with clients and many are fluent in more than one language. The top escorts are also very well educated. Many escorts have a college degree or some college.

The top male escorts take their business very seriously. Although most people can hardly sympathize with someone whose job is to work out two hours a day in a gym, eat a lot, tan three times a week, and shop for clothes, being an escort is certainly a full-time job. Likewise, the top escorts must have excellent business sense, good marketing skills, be able to read people very quickly, and think well on their feet. Having sex with people is certainly the least important part of the business for the full time escort.

The top male escorts enjoy their chosen profession, and spend a great deal of time on self-improvement, and on ways to improve their business. Escorts are subject to emotional burn out as in any other field. In general, however, most escorts who choose to retire as an escort do so because they have entered into a relationship or they have found other interests. In many cases, escorts go on to become successful business owners in other fields.

# Chapter Nine

# Clients

---

T his book touched on client issues in the previous chapters, but the concentration has been on the various types of escorts and how they run their business. Most escorts will tell a client they have never directly solicited a client. In almost all cases clients have solicited the escort. As in any business, customers drive the market.

The market for sex is very broad and diverse. The market for sex ranges from quick sex with a hustler in an adult bookstore for ten or twenty dollars to several thousand dollars for a weekend with an elite escort.

The vast majority of clients are nice people. To an escort this attribute is far more important than the personal appearance of a client. In fact, many of the top escorts prefer their clients to be older, heavyset and not particularly attractive. The reason for this is, these types of clients are not generally very demanding and are easy to please.

*Types of Clients*

Clients come in all sizes, shapes, and ages. What differentiates one client from another is their motivation for calling an escort or looking for a hustler. What motivates the client to seek out an escort oftentimes determines if a client is desirable to an escort. Other prostitutes base the desirability of a client on timing and opportunity. This means the client has called at a convenient time and the escort is available to make the appointment.

Here is a listing of the various types of clients and their desirability:

**Business Travelers**. These clients travel regularly to a location and use escorts when they travel. These clients may be married or come from an area with very few male prostitutes. These clients are very desirable because they are frequent and tend to be very loyal to one or a group of escorts.

**Married Clients**. These clients are either local or regular visitors. Many of these clients are fifty to seventy years of age with a wife and grown children. As such, these clients have a legitimate need for discretion. These clients tend to be bisexual and are perhaps the happiest of all clients because they tend to be successful and have happy relationships. These clients are desirable because they tend to be loyal and regular clients.

This is a letter I received from one married client:

*In my case, my wife is handicapped and we cannot have sex. My alternatives are to be celibate, play around with the local ladies, hire a lady escort, or a male escort. The problem with playing around in the local social circle is, word travels faster than e-mail and some of these ladies are interested in commitment. I have no intention of leaving my wife, or of embarrassing her by starting some really juicy local gossip. Although high quality lady escorts are easy to find, they tend to be more expensive than high quality male escorts, although high quality male escorts are harder to find. Many male escorts are reasonably well educated, good conversationalists, good companions, as well as hot sex.*

**Single Clients**. There are a lot of people who are forty years and older who are not in relationships for one reason or another. Many of these clients are dedicated to their jobs or own businesses. These clients use escorts exclusively for sexual relations. Some of these people make good clients, but the vast majority of them have insatiable tastes for new faces and bodies. Also, since these types of clients use escorts frequently they tend to spend a lot of time researching the market for what is available. These clients also tend to be price shoppers. Price shoppers do not make desirable customers in any business.

**Couples.** Couples who use escorts are primarily male couples, however there are a number of husband and wife couples. In the case of male couples, these clients tend to have monogamous relationships and are looking for a one time sexual fantasy. Husband and wife couples may also be looking to fulfill a sexual fantasy, but typically there are other factors. In some cases the male is impotent due to prostate problems or substance abuse. In other cases, the husband allows his wife to procure an escort because the husband is seeing female escorts. It is very rare for a single female to call an escort advertisement, although it does happen. These clients are rarely repeat clients.

**Experimenters.** There are two categories of experimenters. First, there are very young clients who may be in their late teens and early twenties who wish to have their first experience with a man. These clients use an escort because it allows them to experiment sexually without the prying eyes of their parents or their friends. Many escorts take these clients because they realize the emotional issues of developing a sexual identity. The escorts who take these clients typically spend a lot of time being supportive to the client, and will encourage them to continue to explore their sexuality with others.

The other type of experimenter is older and has thought through their decision to have sex with a man. These clients may be in their late twenties to seventies. The thoughts of this reader reflect the opinions of this group:

*I am a 31 year-old bi-curious guy and avid reader of many of the forums on the Internet. So far, my only sexual experiences have been with women (although believe me, in my mind I've had sex with many men). I now have the confidence and information I need to start exploring the pleasures of male on male sex. I've decided that the best way for me to experiment with gay sex is to start out with the services of an escort. I think that's the best way for me to really enjoy the experience to the fullest.*

**Life Changing Situations**. There are many mental health professionals who suggest to patients the use of an escort. The reason for this is, when people go through stressful and life changing events such as the death of a loved one or a period of depression they withdraw from friends and family. During this period these individuals oftentimes lose the desire to have sex or develop relationships. Seeing an escort is oftentimes the first step in regaining a connection with other people. Likewise, many escorts are very knowledgeable about health and nutrition, and many of these clients have gone on to take the advice so they can move on with their life. It is not unusual for these clients to call back many months later or even years later to thank the escort for helping them make positive changes in their life.

One client wrote me this letter:

*After my lover of nine years died of AIDS, I used a New York City agency to hire a male prostitute. He stayed the night and really enabled me to get back in touch with my sexuality. I felt he was extremely good and helpful. The very next week on a blind date we ended up in the sack. This never would have happened if the compassionate guy hadn't prepared me.*

*I was typical in that I never thought I would hire anyone for sex. I am very glad that I did. I have not done so since. It is almost too easy and I fear that it could be a substitute for a real relationship, however if I ever feel the need, I might do it again.*

**Other Escorts.** Many escorts also use escorts. In fact, many escorts get into the business because they have used an escort. Escorts use escorts for many reasons. First, a prospective escort will use an escort to learn about the business.

Second, a prospective escort will use escorts to check out the competition.    Finally, many escorts use other escorts for pleasure.

**Relationship Seekers**.  This is the most dangerous type of client.    Typically, these clients do not have very many social relationships and have great difficulty in entering a relationship. Their motivation for hiring an escort is to convince the escort into entering a relationship.    There are many escorts who enter into long term relationships with clients, and some of them are long-term and healthy relationships.    In many cases, the client who is seeking a relationship with an escort is looking for a trophy wife to control.    Escorts do not generally make the best loyal, monogamous partners because most of them are very independent entrepreneurs, and are often sexual addicts.    These clients have a high risk of becoming stalkers, and can be very disruptive to an escort's life.

There are many variations on this theme.    I received one letter from an individual explaining his reasons for using escorts:

*I noticed you categorized clients who are relationship seekers as dangerous.  I tend to agree with you but would like to add my own experience to your discussion.*

*Let me mention that I was born with a genetic disorder, and even though I consider myself quite attractive my uneven gait did not exactly do wonders for my social life.    When I started graduate school I got to know a couple of body workers.    My interest grew because sexually I had not been very successful.    I had a couple of appointments with body workers, a pursuit I quickly abandoned because as a graduate student I was in no position to continue paying for their services.*

*I ended up calling some of the escorts and body workers inquiring about their services and asking them if they wanted to meet just for a drink or something.    Nine times out of ten that approach failed.    After all why would they spend time with me while they could be making money?    But occasionally, the approach worked and I got to meet some very nice and colorful people.  I actually maintain a couple of friendships with some of these escorts.*

*I have found that with the sex workers that I did end up befriending I never need to worry whether they will become uncomfortable with my situation. Sex workers have experienced so much both socially and sexually they do not give a second thought to the fact I do not walk as others walk.*

More typical is the letter from this well-meaning gentleman:

*Can you give me some advice? I am a 55 year-old man who has been in the closet all of my life and am only recently coming out. I fell that I wasted most of my life trying to live the heterosexual life (wife, three children, house in the suburb, the good job) and now I am trying to make up for lost time. I have told my wife and children that I am gay but can't come out on my job, as I would probably be fired.*

*My dilemma is that I have become obsessed with sex and spend most of my time responding to escort ads and spending money on escorts and then feeling guilty about it and even abused. I turn to escorts because I think I am too old to have sex with a nice guy without paying for it and I guess I like the thrill of pursuing escorts. The problem is that I have been with a few escorts that I like and then I fall in love with them and want them to fall in love with me. But I can't afford to keep an escort full time, so they are not really interested in me unless I am able to pay.*

*Do you know any instances where an escort has really fallen in love with a client? How do I learn to separate real emotions on the part of an escort from them just hustling me? How do I know they are only saying the things they know I want to hear? If I can't have a love relationship with an escort, how can I learn to enjoy the experience of being with an escort for an hour or two without expecting it to last longer or to become something more profound?*

*I hope this does not sound stupid to you. The entire escort scene is driving me crazy and is taking over all of my life. I am in counseling and the therapist tells me about looking for love in all the wrong places and intellectually I understand this. I just can't tell my heart to behave otherwise.*

*What can I do?*

My response to the client was as follows:

*I understand your feelings.  And yes, you are looking for love in all the wrong places.  If you want a young lover, you will typically find one that is very needy and expensive to support.*

*One of the things I suggest is that you run a personal ad and see what happens.  Get a beeper so they can call you.  Just be honest about yourself and what you want in the ad.  There are some younger guys that are truly attracted to older men.  Believe me.  I know from a lot of observation.  The key is to not push a string uphill, and try to avoid an exceptionally needy relationship.*

*I think you would be a lot better off spending the time and the money on courtship and developing an emotional relationship first, and then a sexual relationship.  That is not going to happen with escorts, or at least it happens very rarely, and even then the relationships are not generally all that successful.*

**After Midnight Clients**.  Clients who call after midnight tend to be among the worst clients for an escort.  Generally a client who calls after midnight is drunk or on drugs.  It is not unusual for a client who calls after midnight to pass out before the escort arrives at the door.  Clients who are sexually stimulated by drugs may want to have sex, but are unable to get aroused.  This type of client can be a lot of work for an escort.  Many of the top escorts do not work after midnight for this very reason.  Clients who call after midnight tend to call advertisements on a whim, and do not typically make good repeat clients.

**Drug Clients**.  These have oftentimes been considered among the highest paying clients in the industry.  However, most of the top escorts refuse to take clients who are heavily into drugs because many of them have had substance abuse problems in the past, and do not want to be tempted by someone who has a ready supply of drugs.  These clients will typically call escorts and ask them if they "party". Some of these clients will attempt to pay for services with drugs or ask the escort to procure drugs for them. The top escorts will not accept this arrangement because typically they are not involved in drugs.

Law enforcement officials would be very wise to use this line when trying to entrap escorts, since the vast majority of problem escorts are ones who are heavily into drugs. If the escort refuses to take clients who party, then the police should move on to another escort. The escort who does not take drugs and does not take drug-related clients is of little risk to the community.

**Trade**. Trade is a term for individuals who are primarily heterosexual, but engage in homosexual activities typically without reciprocation. Although massage therapists receive the bulk of this business, there are a number of clients who will engage a male escort to fulfill some sexual fantasy of being seduced by another male. These clients are generally very attractive, and most escorts can readily identify them on the phone.

There are also clients who tell escorts it will be their first time with a man, however, many of these clients have indeed have had many sexual experiences with men, and simply use the line to peak the escort's interest. Escorts can readily tell if someone's fantasy is the have their 500th virgin experience by tone of the prospective client's voice, and by what the client says, and what the client does not say. In fact, over 50% of the time, clients will not admit it is the first time they are having sex with a man, though it is readily apparent upon meeting them and in the way they engage in sex.

The sexual fantasies of clients who have never had sex with a man and hire an escort include kissing, cuddling, and oral sex. The way to tell if someone has never had sex with a man before is in the performance of oral sex. These clients have only had sexual experiences with a man by watching adult videos. As such these clients perform oral sex with gusto only seen in adult videos. Very few people want to fulfill the fantasy of having anal sex during their first sexual experience with a male. However, there are individuals who have previously experimented with sexual devices, and want to fulfill their fantasy of anal penetration, though this is rare.

I suspect the use of prostitutes (male or female) is a fairly common practice even if most individuals only use a prostitute once or twice during their lifetimes. By one estimate 16% of all adults have used a prostitute at some time in their lives. The core group of regular clients is relatively small compared to the entire market, but there are very few people who have not at least fantasized about being with a prostitute.

For some clients, procuring a prostitute is a rite of passage into an age of expressing sexual feelings, for other clients it is a normal part of their sexual practices. Regardless, of the motives of the client the result is a very large market for aspiring prostitutes.

### Client Expectations

Regardless of the client's motives for procuring an escort, it is always best for clients to have some idea of the type of escort they are interested. Some clients have very broad tastes, and some clients have very narrow tastes.

The two most popular types of escorts are bodybuilders and escorts who are in their late teens and early twenties. Bodybuilders are oftentimes disappointing to clients because many of them are very expensive and only available for body worship. Clients are also very frustrated with younger escorts because most of them lie about their age, and the escorts who are truly young tend to be unreliable.

Clients should be very clear about their expectations with escorts. The primary characteristics important to clients are age, height and weight, endowment, versatility, hair color, and personality. The biggest problem is, mathematically it is very easy to eliminate most escorts in a market if a client has specific requirements for each variable.

One client wrote me the following letter:

*As an occasional client I have to say that I agree with you when you say that clients who insist on their physical ideal report the least amount of satisfaction with the escorts. The escorts whose company (among other things) that I've enjoyed mostly have been pretty far from my physical type, yet they had the ability to put me at ease both in the initial phone conversation and first meeting. I like to think that I've done my part in these meetings by treating the escort with courtesy and respect from the start.*

For example, clients who want an escort 21, blond, over 6 foot, over 200 pounds, with a 9 inch penis, and versatile are likely to be disappointed.    Although escorts come in all ages, sizes and shapes, if there were to be an average escort it would be 26 years old, brunette, 5'8" to 5'10", 150 pounds, with a 6 to 7 inch penis and either a top or a bottom (but not good at both). This same escort would advertise as 21 years old, blonde, 5'11", 160 pounds, with an 8.5 inch penis, and versatile.

In reality, there are very few clients who know the difference in many of these attributes, which is why most escorts get away with this type of deception.    However, all reputable escorts give relatively accurate descriptions even if they take license with some of the attributes.

### Things A Prospective Client Should Not Say

There are many standard ploys used by prospective clients to get the escort's attention.  Many of these standard ploys are in fact an attempt to con an escort into giving more favorable terms or to make the client more attractive to an escort.  The top escorts have pretty much heard everything, and realize there are certain comments that will make a prospective client unattractive or unsuitable.  Here are the most common things clients should not say in their initial conversation with an escort:

- **Clients should not say they are from Los Angeles.**  Clients from Los Angeles are known as the worst possible clients and are rarely repeat clients.  Clients from Los Angeles are accustomed to a broad assortment of available escorts and typically see someone new every time.  Clients from Los

Angeles are also accustomed to lower pricing than exists in much of the country since rates typically start at fifty dollars. Clients from Los Angeles also have a reputation for being dishonest. Clients from Los Angeles who do not say they are from Los Angeles are generally exceptions to this rule. This analysis may seem unusual, however it is valid. The reason the analysis may be valid is, individuals who are dishonest give clues to their dishonesty. One of the clues to dishonest individuals is, they will say something like "trust me", which is generally a sure sign to not trust the individual. The phrase "Hello, I'm visiting from Los Angeles", seems to be synonymous with the phrase "trust me". Clients from Texas and the Midwest are known as the best clients.

- **Clients should not say they are attractive**. Top escorts are attracted to a wide variety of clients and typically do not play favorites. In fact, many of the top escorts enjoy and prefer clients who are over forty, balding, and overweight. The most attractive clients are generally more work, and not as likely to be repeats.

- **A client should not state their need for discretion**. Top escorts are very discrete. Clients who truly need discretion take precautions for discretion. Clients who feel a greater than normal need for discretion oftentimes do not show up for their appointments, or are crank callers who are deliberately setting up bogus appointments.

- **Clients should not hang up on an escort**. Top escorts trade notes on clients who are rude. All escorts have caller identification systems and trade notes with other escorts on people who are calling around and being rude. Clients who are impolite oftentimes find out every escort in the community has information on them before they call.

- **Clients should not ask an escort if they would take a check or credit card.** Top escorts only take cash. A very high percentage of clients will write bad checks or use fraudulent credit cards. Many clients are also known for requesting charge backs on their credit cards. There are a couple of exceptions to this rule. First, some escorts will take checks from long established clients. Second, for escorts who travel it is always a good sign when the client's credit card works in purchasing plane tickets. Escorts will also generally accept traveler's checks, money orders, and bank checks.

- **Clients should not ask an escort about their policy if they are rejected at the door**. Top escorts will not take clients who have histories of rejecting escorts. Many agencies provide accurate descriptions of their escorts, and will not accept a client who has previously rejected an escort. These types of clients have very limited tastes, and have typically rejected some of the top models in the country in the past. The chance for any escort to be deemed acceptable in their eyes is very small. This type of client is typically a waste of time.

- **A client should not ask to meet an escort in a neutral place.** Top escorts will only meet clients at their home or hotel room. Clients who want to meet an escort in a neutral site have a history of not showing up for their appointments and rejecting escorts. Many of these prospective clients have a history of setting up bogus appointments. There are many ways for a client to check an escort's references before calling an escort. These methods include researching an escort on the Internet and calling other escorts and agencies for opinions. There is no need for an escort to meet a client in a neutral place.

- **Clients should not ask for a discount in exchange for drugs.** Most of the top escorts do not do drugs, and many of the top escorts do not take clients who are doing drugs on an appointment.

- **Clients should not telephone from a pay phone.** Many callers from pay phones are not legitimate clients. There has also been an increase in spurious callers from cellular phones. It is always best for a client to call from a telephone that does not have its number blocked from caller identification systems.

- **A prospective client should not say money is no object.** The highest paying clients never say money is no object.

The top escorts quote a price and do not expect tips. Clients who do tip are generally remembered, and an escort will make extra efforts to accommodate the client in the future.

- **A client should not ask a general question on availability.** This is a sure sign of a client who is shopping around or the client is calling for phone sex. The top escorts will be hesitant to discuss anything with a client unless the client has a specific time and date in mind for an appointment. The top escorts will typically tell a client they have some availability and to call back when they are ready to make an appointment. The types of callers who ask general questions on availability are rarely serious callers, and if they are looking to procure an escort they are typically making multiple calls. In many cases, these prospective clients are calling every escort and massage advertisement in a publication.

- **Prospective clients should not generally say they are looking for their first time with a man.** There are many clients who use this line to peak the interest of an escort. However, most escorts will be able to readily determine by tone of voice and what the client asks as to whether the client is being honest or not. The top escorts have a scoring system for honesty, and when this phrase is combined with a number of other dishonest comments it raises a red flag in the mind of the escort.

- **Prospective clients should not say they are looking for a regular escort.** This is usually a con to get the escort to provide a lower price. Prospective clients who say they are looking for a regular escort are typically calling every advertisement in a publication, and are rarely repeat clients.

- **Prospective clients should not ask if there is a special rate for locals.** Any escort who offers special local rates should quote the local rate based on the information displayed on a caller identification system or based on the information provided over the phone. Typically, prospective clients who ask for local rates are travelling and generally are not repeat clients.

- **Prospective clients should not start the conversation by asking price.** Price shoppers are rarely serious clients, and tend not to be repeating clients. Very few prospective clients who start the conversation by asking price actually book an appointment.

There are a number of reasons why prospective clients use these tactics when calling an escort. The primary reason why clients use these tactics is, in many cases these tactics work. Although experienced escorts will see through these cons, there are thousands of new entrants into the escort field every year and many of these cons play to the ego of the unsuspecting escort.

New clients are high risk to an escort for a number of reasons. If an escort accepts in-calls, generally 50% of the new clients do not show up. This can be an expensive waste of time for an experienced escort. Also, a high percentage of new clients shop around and use multiple escorts. These clients will typically ask if the escort is available later in the day, and tell the escort they will call back and make an appointment. An experienced escort will rarely take these types of calls seriously.

An established escort prefers to accept new clients who will provide repeat business. There is a distinct pattern to a conversation with a client who is likely to become a repeat client. These prospective clients tend to keep their conversations short, ask a few direct questions, and book an appointment within three to five minutes. Clients who are deceptive, ask open-ended questions, and do not make commitments (or do not keep the ones they make) do not make desirable clients.

A top quality escort generates 80% of their income from repeat clients. Typically, the advertising budget for top quality escorts equals the amount they expect to earn in a month from new clients. At most, an established high quality escort expects to gain one or two new clients a week who they will see three or four times a year. The typical advertising budget for many of the top escorts is $400 to $500 a month. This figure ranges from $20 a month for Internet connectivity to $1,000 or more for escorts who advertise in multiple publications on a weekly basis.

There are many weeks when a top quality escort will not take new clients. If the escort is busy, a prospective client should always ask for a referral to another escort. If the escort provides a referral to another escort it is always a good sign the escort giving the referral is a high quality escort. A client should always contact an escort and tell the escort their advice was taken. Generally, this is a near guarantee the escort will accept the client in the future. Likewise, if the escort does not give a referral it is a good sign the escort is not acceptable. The top escorts always refer clients they cannot see to other escorts. In return, an escort can expect to receive 20-30% of their new business from the word of mouth referrals from other escorts.

If the prospective client does not take the escort's advice it is almost certain the escort will know about it. Escorts who receive word of mouth referrals from another escort will almost always call the escort to thank them for the referral. In cases where the client does not take the referral it is almost a sure sign the client is not desirable. Just as with any other professional the top escorts try to give good advice to their clients. When clients fail to take good advice it is a good sign they would become difficult clients.

Top quality escorts will always accept a word of mouth referral even if they are not accepting new clients who call off of their advertising. As in any business, clients who are derived from a word of mouth referral generally make the best clients.

### The Use of Search Services and Agencies

Clients with special needs are increasingly using search services to find high quality escorts. The client may be looking for a specific type of person, have special needs in terms of discretion, or may have a need for escorts in various cities.

Clients use various resources for their searches:

**Local Agencies**. Local agencies typically have twenty to thirty available guys. Most of these escorts do not advertise individually. A client will oftentimes maintain a relationship with a reputable agency in his own city or in the cities where he travels.

**National Agencies**. There are three or four agencies with escorts in most major cities. These agencies typically represent porn stars, but may maintain a list of non-porn stars available throughout the country. These agencies typically advertise in Unzipped magazine. These agencies oftentimes specialize in escorts who are available for travel. Although, these services are oftentimes at the higher end in terms of cost these services also offer some very high quality escorts at prices comparable to independent escorts.

**Retainer Searches**. Many clients are now putting agencies on monthly retainers for searches. This works well for clients with specific tastes, geographical requirements, or other special needs such as privacy. The cost for a retained search is typically $100 a month. Typically, 90% of escorts approached by an agency retained for a search do not pass the screening process. This would indicate that maybe only 10% of the escorts who advertise meet basic standards of professionalism described in the previous chapter.

### What A Client Can Expect to Pay

Clients should always have a budget when hiring an escort. The cost of a professional escort will vary from $50 to several hundred dollars depending on the market, the escort, and the services desired.

In general, the highest quality escorts are priced between $100 to $200. Escorts who are priced above this level are rarely worth the price. Although, the exception to this rule is the once in a lifetime opportunity of being with certain bodybuilders, top models and porn stars. These elite escorts are not generally looking for clients, and see very few clients, but like everyone they have their price.

Clients are certainly better off seeing a small group of escorts and not spending a lot of time looking for new escorts to see. It is generally the least expensive and safest approach to the escort market. Clients should always seek out word of mouth referrals.

The client who typically runs into problems with escorts does not heed advice, does not look for the warning signs of a disreputable escort, and is overly infatuated with a pretty face. There are some clients who have certainly learned from their mistakes. However, there are also a number of clients who feel they will be victimized every time they use an escort. Nearly every client who has been victimized has been victimized because he did not take reasonable and prudent precautions to avoid being victimized.

# Chapter Ten

# Legal Risks

There are many possible legal ramifications for both the client and escort engaged in activities related to prostitution. In some cases the risks are small, and in other cases the risks are quite significant.

The cost of any legal entanglement can be quite significant. The cost of a fine is miniscule compared to the cost of loss of income from possible job loss, cost of a resulting divorce, embarrassment, legal fees, impoundment of personal property, and time spent on community service. There are even many reported suicides of persons who have been arrested for sexual crimes.

The legal systems of many societies have an unhealthy voyeurism into the private sex lives of individuals. There are some countries that still inflict the death penalty on those who are guilty of sex crimes such as sodomy and adultery. For the most part, however, many countries have reduced the sentence for a sex crime from hanging, stoning, crucifixion, or breaking on the rack to a fine and community service. Nevertheless, the cost of being embroiled in a sexual indiscretion is very real.

There are many possible sex crimes in the United States although many of them are not prosecuted. The possible crimes include loitering, indecent exposure, adultery, sodomy (homosexual and heterosexual), solicitation of prostitution, sex with a minor, incest, public sex, bestiality, rape, and certainly a number of other sexual acts. Individuals can also bring civil lawsuits against others for sexual harassment, inappropriate touching, and sexual molestation. An increasing issue is the transmission and receipt of pornographic material over the Internet. Although most of the efforts of law enforcement have been directed at individuals who produce, distribute or collect images of prepubescent individuals, there have also been cases against individuals who have sent pornographic materials over the Internet to minors.

There is certainly no consistency to the laws or enforcement of the laws from state to state or from community to community. Some laws are not enforced at all, others are enforced sporadically, others are enforced in election years, and still others are enforced only when there is a complaint.

### Public Policy

Most of the laws for sexual acts are based on historical prejudices. The basis for some laws such as the exclusion of gays in the military and the sodomy laws were in large part based on the belief homosexuality was a disease. The American Psychiatric Association eliminated homosexuality as a disease three decades ago, but long held prejudices can hardly be changed overnight.

Law enforcement officials do not spend a lot of time prosecuting sexual crimes because it is very hard to find evidence of consensual sex crimes. There are no corroborating witnesses when two people have consensual sex, and very little physical evidence. Even Kenneth Star with his unlimited budget to pursue allegations of consensual sex in the White House has trouble making a case. Most law enforcement agencies do not have unlimited budgets.

However, there are still sodomy laws in thirteen states where oral and anal sex is against the law for homosexual and heterosexual couples. Between 1988 and 1994, two thousand individuals were cited in Louisiana for committing sodomy. The law has not been enforced since a civil action was brought to declare the law unconstitutional. However, convictions under sodomy laws have been upheld by the United States Supreme in the past.

The other problem with enforcing laws against consensual sex is, many politicians are well aware of their own indiscretions. Those who are vocally judgmental of others oftentimes do so with serious consequences. There are numerous examples of politicians who are ardent in their support of anti-gay initiatives yet are blind sighted when it comes to the disclosure of their own sexual indiscretions including adultery, sex with minors, and even gay affairs. The few politicians who have survived such sexual scandals have been individuals who never hid (or only thinly disguised) their sexual activities, and had always shown tolerance toward the sexual activities of others.

Many law enforcement officials are also elected and subject to public opinion (and revelations about the secrets in their own closets). This includes judges, sheriffs, and district attorneys. With get tough on crime measures designed to get hard core criminals off the streets there are very few resources to pursue sexual crimes. When sexual crimes are pursued it is either to pursue a legitimate public safety objective, due to a high profile citizen complaint, or harassment. It is not unusual for law enforcement agencies to clamp down on sexual activity during an election year. When neighbors complain of sexual activity in a public park it is a public safety issue. At other times, when police actively seek opportunities to prosecute sexual crimes it can be a case of attention grabbing and unhealthy voyeurism at work.

*Public Safety and Public Policy*

Sexual activities are generally pursued when there are legitimate public safety issues. These are the general rules of thumb employed by law enforcement officials when a decision is made to devote resources to the enforcement of laws related to sex:

**A high crime area.** Street prostitution oftentimes goes hand and hand with drug dealing, robberies, gang activity, and violent crime. Especially, when this activity occurs in residential areas there is a high risk to residents. In general, people do not want to live in areas where criminal activity is occurring in their front yards. In order to clean up the neighborhood police will install police substations, have bike patrols, use undercover street patrol, canvass the neighborhood for information on suspected illegal activity, and have officials enact specific laws aimed at cracking down on crime in the area.

**Establishments promoting illegal activity.** Typically reputable establishments due not promote illegal activity on their premises. Many establishments that cater to individuals looking for consensual sex between adults are very careful to discourage other types of illegal activity. Businesses that are involved in drugs, located in areas with high crime, allow underage patrons and lack regard for their neighbors will find themselves subject to periodic police raids and possible forced closure.

**Escorts and Escort Agencies.** The penalties for prostitution in most localities are very minimal. The purpose of sting operations by police on escorts and escort agencies is not necessarily to enforce the prostitution laws since most people arrested for prostitution are released within hours of arrest. Generally, the purpose of a sting operation is to find individuals who have knowledge of other illegal activity. Prostitutes tend to have considerable knowledge of drug dealers, gang activity, money laundering, persons who are wanted on warrants, persons who have committed robberies, and persons who have committed violent crimes.

Law enforcement will typically devote most of their resources to female prostitutes rather than male prostitutes for several reasons.

- Female prostitutes tend to work for pimps and have a larger network of knowledge than do most male prostitutes.
- There are more female prostitutes and fewer male prostitutes.
- Most law enforcement officials are heterosexual, and do not have a voyeuristic interest in male prostitutes.
- Female prostitutes are more frequently the targets of violent crime and exploitation.

Typically, law enforcement officials engage in sting operations against advertised male escorts in the following instances:

- When there is a suspected link to drugs.
- When there has been a high profile violent crime.
- A lot of sting operations occur during election years.
- When there are a number of males operating as escorts in the area.
- When male escorts bring attention to themselves.
- When there is evidence the escort agency is using individuals who are underage.

In general, the number one rule in the business of the male escort business is to be discrete and not bring any unwanted attention. While most male escorts who are in the business for any length of time encounter a brush with the law at some time or another, typically the encounter is not a deterrent to an established escort. The penalties are minimal, and most established escorts will simply revise their criteria for accepting new clients. Since established escorts make 80% of their money from repeat clients, most can afford to stop taking new clients for several months.

For these reasons sting operations are rarely a deterrent to established prostitutes. Police activity can combat street prostitution when the operation lasts several months if not longer. Most established escorts can make a decent living off of their established clients for periods of at least six months if not longer.

## High Risk Activities

Law enforcement authorities put very little emphasis on private consensual sexual activities. The reasons are simple: there are no witnesses and no physical evidence. The key is to keep sexual activities private to avoid unpleasant experiences with law enforcement authorities.

Here is a list of areas by area of relative risk:

- **Public Parks.** Most police regularly patrol and make sweeps of public parks where there is suspicion of suspected sexual activity.
- **Public restrooms.** Police typically use undercover and surveillance equipment to monitor sexual activity in public restrooms. This tactic was even used in the U.S. Capitol where a congressman was caught engaging in oral sex. Despite the congressman's obvious commitment to publicly servicing his constituents his political career came to an abrupt end.
- **Rest areas.** Highway patrol officers regularly monitor rest areas.
- **Public streets.** Driving around public streets for hustlers is an increasingly dangerous activity. Many cities have enacted anti cruising laws for some areas, and have enacted laws that allow the forfeiture of automobiles used when a client solicits for prostitution.
- **Adult bookstores**. Adult bookstores are subject to frequent sweeps by uniformed police and undercover operations by plainclothes police. Many adult bookstores are monitored for sound and by surveillance camera.
- **Adult movie theatres.** Adult movie theatres are commonly targets for police raids.

- **Sex Clubs.**  Sex clubs are frequently subjected to raids because sex clubs are generally unlicensed businesses. Typically, patrons are not cited if they leave peaceably. However, there are exceptions to this rule.

- **Bathhouses.**  Local authorities generally tolerate bathhouses operated in a way that is courteous of their neighbors, is well maintained, discourages the use and distribution of drugs on premises, promotes safe sex and does not allow underage patrons.  Most local authorities recognize a need in the community where adults can safely have consensual sex. Tolerance of a bathhouse is seen as a lesser evil to having other areas in a city used for sex in public.  Typically, when a bathhouse is raided it is for the purpose of sending a message to the owners to clean up the operation or the condition of the property.  Patrons are not generally cited, but are intimidated into leaving the premises.

- **Hustler Bars.**  Hustler bars are also tolerated in some cities although hustler bars may be subject to frequent undercover surveillance.  Hustler bars many be tolerated because the employees monitor the comings and goings of transients into the community, hustling is kept off the street, and it is not unheard of for a bar owner to pay off local officials.  In return for the operation of a hustler bar the owner generally agrees to; avoid being a nuisance to the neighbors, keep the hustlers off the street, not allow underage patrons, discourage the use and distribution of drugs on the premises, and be cooperative with any police investigation.  If the bar owner breaks this social contract with the local authorities the bar will generally be shut down as a public nuisance.

There is a familiar pattern to police sting operations involving public facilities.  First, there is usually a complaint from the neighborhood.  The police then assign several officers over a period of several months to check out the location.  The officers assigned are typically attractive and in their twenties and thirties.  When the suspect attempts to have sex with an officer, or is caught masturbating, or is caught having sex with another individual it typically results in an arrest. In some cases, anyone who is at the location at the same time is also arrested.

Over the period of a sting operation the police may arrest between fifteen and twenty individuals. Persons arrested generally vary in age from twenty to seventy years of age.

In many communities where there is a large gay population, the American Civil Liberties Union will typically provide advice to individuals caught engaging in public sex. It is strongly advised that anyone caught in a sting operation consult with an attorney.

There are very few ways to prevent arrest in a sting operation. However, there are several things someone should keep in mind if arrested:

- A police officer does not have to reveal their identity as a police officer until after the arrest. Yes, officers of the public are permitted to lie, and oftentimes do when asked if they are police officers.
- If a number of individuals have been entrapped at the same time the charges oftentimes will be dropped. It is best for the group to collectively hire an attorney or group of attorneys.
- District attorneys and judges do not like to have their workloads clogged up with minor misdemeanors (keep in mind public sex is considered a felony in some jurisdictions). Many district attorneys and judges refuse to allow prosecution of minor sex cases because it can waste valuable time when there are more serious matters pending. However, this does not mean someone who is arrested for this crime should not take his or her defense seriously.
- All in all, it is better not to be entangled in either the criminal justice system or the civil justice system.

Clients have the least risk of detection by using advertised escorts or escort agencies. Many escorts (and even escorts who work for escort agencies) do in-calls. Otherwise, it is advisable to rent a room at a local motel.

## *Public Embarrassment*

Law enforcement and local media are increasingly using public embarrassment to deter public sex crimes. These crimes include sex in adult bookstores and the solicitation of prostitution on public streets. Typically, the media will print the names, occupations and even the addresses of individuals who have been caught by law enforcement engaging in public sexual activities.

There is significant evidence this sort of treatment can lead to suicide. Although there is no accurate count of these cases, suicides are not infrequent in the areas where there are frequent sting operations by law enforcement officials.

If the number of cases of divorce, job loss, and other forms of financial loss are included with suicide in the figures for the economic cost of this unnecessary exposure then it becomes clear this form of media coverage serves very little if any public benefit. Granted, the solicitation of prostitution is detrimental to communities especially when it occurs near residential areas. However, the crime itself does not justify complete emotional and financial destruction of an individual.

Individuals who engage in public sexual acts certainly have emotional problems. These individuals typically engage in anonymous sex for a number of reasons including dealing with sexual identity issues, attempting to have intimate contact with others when the individual has very few social contacts, and in many cases due to sexual addiction. A high percentage of these individuals may be manic-depressive, chronically depressed, or be at risk for major depressive episodes. A high percentage of individuals suffering from depression are at risk for committing suicide.

Public humiliation through media coverage can trigger a major depressive episode. This can result in an individual committing suicide. Persons who are arrested for public sexual acts are not generally a risk to the community for theft, robberies, or murder. Public sex crimes have penalties that are generally less than driving while intoxicated and certainly present less risk to the general public than driving while intoxicated.   As such, programs of public humiliation and embarrassment at best represent unhealthy voyeurism on the part of the media and at worst a depraved indifference to human life.

## *Legal Penalties*

Typically the penalties for being ensnared by local law enforcement agencies are relatively light.  The exceptions are when the initial charge is complicated by any of the following factors:

- Resisting arrest.
- Sex with a minor.
- Being uncooperative in any way with the arresting officer or the detention officers.
- Being found with drugs.
- Having a car that is unregistered, not having identification, or not having the car properly insured.
- Being a repeat offender.
- Being found to have outstanding warrants.
- Unpaid parking or moving violation citations.

A person who is arrested is more likely to be released if they are cooperative with the officers than if the person is uncooperative.   How someone acts from the moment of entrapment has a big effect on the severity of the final penalty. These rules apply whether a person's car is pulled over for a suspected moving violation or entrapped for a sexual offense:

- An arresting officer will generally identify himself or herself in a calm manner.  The arresting officer will instruct a person to stand or sit in a certain manner and with their hands out of their pockets.  The suspect should remain calm and follow the instructions of the arresting officer.
- The suspect will be asked for identification.  This should be willingly provided.

- A suspect should not try to talk an arresting officer into not making an arrest. It is best to maintain a calm demeanor and have thoughts that everything will go well. A positive mental attitude, despite the obviously stressful situation, will go further than resistance.
- An arresting officer will ask several questions before reading someone their civil rights. It is generally a good policy for suspects to be cooperative without saying anything that could be self-incriminating.
- Typically an arresting officer is using this time to perform a background check on the suspect. Even if the record of a suspect is not clean, it is quite possible by being pleasant and cooperative the suspect will receive lighter treatment from the arresting officer.
- The arresting officer may ask questions about knowledge of other illegal activities in the area, knowledge of other crimes being investigated, and other individuals involved in criminal activities. In some cases cooperation in these areas will cause the charges to disappear. This may be an especially useful tool if a person has good hearsay knowledge of the illegal activity, but does not have first hand knowledge.
- Do not lie to an arresting officer. Police officers are well trained to detect lies. Evasive answers or false answers to questions will generally result in more aggressive treatment by a police officer. Suspects who do not want to answer a question or feels uncomfortable answering a question should be polite and say they feel uncomfortable answering the question.
- An arresting officer will ask suspects if they are carrying any weapons or drugs. If the suspect has these items in their possession it is best to provide the information. This will oftentimes result in the suspect not being charged for concealed weapon or drug charges. This also builds up trust between a suspect and an arresting officer.
- Do not make any threatening remarks to an arresting officer. The comments include "Do you know who I am" (unless the

suspect wants to appear on television or in the newspaper so everyone in the community will know who the individual is, and what the individual allegedly did), "What is your badge number", or any other comments to express indignity. Comments such as these only serve to antagonize a situation.

- The degree of trust a suspect can build with an arresting officer in the critical first moment of apprehension can make the difference between whether a suspect will be arrested, given a citation, or allowed free. Passivity and cooperation are oftentimes the key to a get out of jail card.

- If the arresting officer decides to make an arrest he will read the suspect their rights, although in some areas suspects of misdemeanors are not read their rights. The fact the suspect has not been read their rights should not be taken as a sign an arrest has not taken place. At this point the suspect should not say anything and should ask for an attorney if anyone attempts to question them.

The suspect should consider the following issues after an arrest has been made whether or not he has been read their rights. At this point the suspect will be handcuffed and transported to a local detention center for processing. Typically, a processing warden will have the suspect interviewed, fingerprinted, photographed, and given a brief medical examination. It is very important to be honest and cooperative during this process. Also, it is important to remember anything said in jail can be used as evidence in court.

Once a suspect has been processed there are several potential scenarios. If the suspect is lucky there will be an overcrowding condition at the jail. This situation might require the jail to release suspects immediately on their own recognizance to reduce overcrowding. The other alternative is bail or bond. The cash bail amount for most of these crimes is very low and can be easily raised. Some jails allow people to post bail with a credit card. The alternative is to wait for an arraignment and generally a judge will release a suspect on own recognizance (OR) if the suspect has a job and steady place to live. It is best to use the one free phone call to call someone who will post bail.

After the suspect is released from jail it is time to prepare for a defense. Provided the suspect has exhibited model behavior during apprehension, arrest, and the unfortunate period of incarceration there may be very little to worry about. Most district attorneys do not relish the idea of prosecuting a single charge of sexual indiscretion. However, suspects who displayed any annoying behavior during the arrest process could be faced with a virtual laundry list of charges filed against them and serve some jail time.

It is important to hire an attorney. The attorney should be a criminal attorney who has considerable experience and respect in the legal community. There are usually a number of attorneys who specialize in prostitution. If the suspect does not know of an attorney an escort agency should be able to provide a referral.

An attorney should cost about $500 to defend a simple case of sexual weakness. If the suspect decided to take a swing at the arresting officer it will cost more.

Many first offenders make a serious mistake of not consulting an attorney. Lawyers do not like competition from amateurs. Defendants should keep in mind judges and prosecutors are well trained in the law. Judges and prosecutors have very little patience for individuals who do not respect their years of education and training. To have equal standing in the eyes of the law a suspect needs an attorney.

The criminal legal system is not based on whether someone actually committed a crime; it is based on intricate rules of procedure, long held customs, and personal relationships. There are studies that suggest we have a legal system with biases based on the income, race, gender, ethnicity, religion, and manner of dress. The defendant who does not have a lawyer is at a definite disadvantage.

A lawyer will be able to perform many functions that would be difficult or impossible for someone ignorant of the legal system. The services provided by an attorney on a charge of sexual misconduct include:

- The ability to plea-bargain a case with ease.
- The ability to discover procedural problems with the arrest.
- The ability to make discovery of relevant information to defend the case.
- The ability to make deals with the prosecution.
- The ability through procedural tactics to wear down the prosecution into a plea bargain.
- The ability to get the court record sealed or expunged after a period of time.

A defendant who goes to court without an attorney generally expects to be given courtesy and the ability to defend their case. In reality, most successful cases are fought through written motions and procedural tactics. These activities require intimate knowledge of the law and the individuals involved in the proceedings. It is very unlikely an individual with an attorney will ever have a trial. The chances of a dismissal or favorable plea-bargain agreement are very high.

A defendant who defends his or her own case will most likely be rushed through the proceeding. The judge will typically listen to the arresting policeman, find the person guilty, and not be lenient on sentencing. Most judges have overburdened court dockets, and very little patience for people who do not have respect for the law. Showing up to court without an attorney is considered a lack of respect for the court and the legal system.

The penalties imposed for crimes involving sexual misconduct are generally light if the defendant behaves themselves during their arrest and seeks out the services of an attorney. The operative words and phrases for getting through the criminal justice system with the least amount of damage are politeness, cooperation without self-incrimination, seek out a professional, and follow professional advice.

There are many possible penalties that can be imposed during the criminal process:

- The suspect can be let go after apprehension and before arrest.
- The charges can be dismissed after arrest.
- A fine can be levied.
- Community service can be imposed.
- Counseling can be ordered.
- Jail time can be imposed.
- Assets such as a car or bail can be forfeited.
- Be required to register as a sex offender.
- There are now schools for sexual offenders, customers of prostitutes and prostitutes. These classes are usually held for a day and the successful completion of the classes will usually result in the conviction being expunged from the offender's record.

Although the days of arbitrary raids are mostly over, raids can still occur. Some overworked District Attorneys will sometimes stop prosecuting lewd behavior because the number of arrests are obvious harassment and merely clutter an overburdened court system with no great benefit. Some judges routinely dismiss certain sexual crimes including those for prostitution to clear their overburdened court dockets. In some cases the police departments are so strapped for man power the arresting officer does not even show up to court. This is called luck of the draw, but there is no guarantee these events will occur. It is still best to have an attorney.

### *Legalization of Prostitution*

There are many people who have little experience with the legal system. Most of us experience the legal system through television and newspapers. We are not participants in the process with the exception of the occasional speeding ticket. In that rare case we go to the judge, ask to be sentenced to traffic school, go to school for a few hours, and the ticket is removed from our record. Very few of us get to experience the entire process of being arrested, going to jail, and having to go through the criminal justice system.

Today, there is an increased ferocity in prosecuting all types of crime. Some of the laws being enforced today were either never enforced twenty years ago or were enforced very lightly twenty years ago.

It is very easy to cast judgement on others and insist people who commit crimes should pay for their crimes. It is very easy to say there should be harsher and longer sentences.

In comparison to other crimes the penalties for prostitution are light and border on nonexistent. The only reason for having laws against prostitution is because many prostitutes have knowledge of or is involved in other illegal acts. Prostitutes who receive stiff sentences for solicitation are the ones who are guilty of far more serious crimes and have made a plea agreement. As such, the laws for sex crimes are simply tools used by a prosecutor to achieve other purposes. These include the pursuit of public safety issues, other crimes, and the cleaning up of neighborhoods.

For most prostitutes the criminal justice system is simply a tax on their earnings. Every once in awhile prostitutes must skip work for awhile and occasionally pay a fine. If things get difficult for a period of time the prostitute will simply move to greener pastures. There are many escorts who make the circuit between New York, Miami, Los Angeles, and San Francisco.

There are many escorts who do not believe they are breaking the law. Here is one letter I received:

*I feel your definition of prostitution is overly broad. I will say you are correct when someone exchanges money for sex it is prostitution. However, escorts only charge for their time, and if I have sex with a client it is because I want to have sex with the client. However, they are paying for my time and not to have sex with me.*

This individual very strongly believes he is not engaging in prostitution in a legal sense. There are very few, if any instances where law enforcement officials will accept this distinction during a sting operation. However, even prostitutes who believe they are breaking the law do not see anything fundamentally wrong with their activities. Ironically, the laws in many jurisdictions support this idea since many jurisdictions have penalties for prostitution lower than the penalties for many moving violations.

In fact, the United States Supreme Court ruled against the State of Florida in a decision prohibiting the use of wiretaps unless there is evidence of serious criminal activity with a serious threat to the community. The Supreme Court found since prostitution was only a misdemeanor under state law, it did not qualify under federal law for the use of a wiretap. State laws are subject to the guidelines of federal law in the case of wiretaps. Federal law requires evidence of serious criminal activity such as murder, drugs, or organized crime involvement in order for a wiretap to be authorized by the courts.

### Concluding Observations

It is doubtful prostitution will be legalized as long as politicians are in competition with the world's oldest profession. Most politicians are lawyers, and as I have stated before, lawyers do not like competition. Granted, if someone cannot live off of their looks, the alternative is to sell their principles and integrity. Yet, it is clear those who make the law must make the selling of one's body a greater evil than the evils politicians and lawyers commit in the ordinary course of business.

Yes, governments could make money by licensing prostitutes and the earnings from prostitution would become taxable. However, many prostitutes have chosen their line of work because they like to be self-employed and prefer not to have government interference. Granted, there is certainly jealousy by those in the bourgeois communist right wing establishment who believe every individual should carry the yoke of government interference, taxes, and family values, but most escorts prefer the advice of Yogi Berra, "Include me out."

Granted these observations are made firmly tongue in cheek. The legal issues of being caught involved in prostitution or involved in other sex crimes can be devastating for many people. For some, it can be the hideous mark in the permanent record mentioned in grade school. For those who fear the consequences of a criminal record it is best to find another field such as investment banking, politics, or telemarketing. On second thought, you might want to take a six-dollar an hour job where there is no responsibility or contact with people.

Given the current climate of investigating the private sex lives of individuals, escorts generally have no intention to seek public office. In part, because it would bankrupt the country to launch an investigation of their sex lives. No self-respecting prostitute would want to unnecessarily burden the public.

However, society is creating greater incentive for all individuals to live on its anonymous fringes. There many startling statistics to indicate the underground economy will increase dramatically in the coming years because of the disincentives offered by government to participate in mainstream society. Among the reasons for increases in individuals working in the underground economy include:

- Ten million people per year are arrested. Many of these individuals are emotionally and financially ruined in the process. An increasing number of individuals arrested are white-collar with no prior arrest record.
- Four million individuals are held in prison or jail at any given time.
- The increased severity and consequences of drug laws and increased penalties for private behavior is creating a larger underclass.
- The United States has the highest rate of disenfranchised individuals of any civilized society since felons cannot vote for life in many states.
- The penalty for failure to pay child support provides additional incentive for millions of individuals to live underground.
- The increasing use of civil forfeiture of property to exact criminal penalties.

- The increased use of wage garnishment.

Essentially, we are living in a society that is increasingly unforgiving. In the past someone who had wanted to start a new life could move west, and people would ask very few questions. National databases and the growth of the traditional areas of resettlement have greatly diminished the available habitats for the reformed scoundrel.

Prostitution is but one part of the underground economy. However, all of the parts of the underground economy will experience growth in the coming years as individuals who are denied employment, denied loans, denied the right to live peaceably in their communities, and denied basic civil rights seek a refuge free from the prying eyes of government intervention.

# Chapter Eleven

# Sexually Transmitted Diseases

S exually transmitted diseases (STDs) are a very real danger for both escorts and clients. Fortunately, most STDs are readily treatable. However, many STDs can have serious long-term effects and may be resistant to treatment.

Clients and escorts should be well aware of the dangers of STDs and should only engage in safe sex.

In researching this book I was shocked by the limited available information in other books on STDs, and I felt it was important to add a chapter specifically addressing health issues for an escort and client. Additionally, what is known about STDs has greatly increased in the last ten years, and some of the diseases themselves have changed. Likewise, much has been learned about STDs since the advent of HIV. Unfortunately, much is still unknown and the diseases continue to change their nature. Many STDs such as Hepatitis C are very much a concern because very little is known about the disease.

Many clients and escorts are sexual addicts and have many sexual contacts. Hand in hand with sexual compulsive behavior are other compulsive problems such as drinking, drugs, and unsafe behavior. These compulsive behaviors add to the risk of contracting a STD.

Most of the top escorts take their health very seriously, as do most clients. However, there are many escorts and hustlers who either lack access to medical care or do not have sufficient knowledge of the consequences of unsafe sexual behavior. There is increased risk because many prostitutes (and clients too) are intravenous drug users. Intravenous drug use multiplies the potential risk for contracting many diseases due to the sharing of needles.

These are the most common forms of sexually transmitted diseases:

## *Chancroid*

**Description.** This bacterium causes sores in the genital area.

**Symptoms.** Symptoms appear within a week of infection and consist of a small boil or sore in the genital area. The boil can then become an open sore and pus can be discharged from the sores. The lymph glands in the genital area can also become swollen.

**How it is contracted**. It can be contracted through intercourse and oral sex.

**Diagnosis.** The sores are oftentimes confused with other STDs and lab tests may be necessary.

**Treatment.** You will need to go to a doctor for diagnosis and get a prescription for antibiotics.

**Preventable through safe sex?** Yes, this condition can be avoided through the use of condoms.

## *Chlamydia*

**Description.** This is considered the most frequently transmitted STD in the United States. A recent study found thirty percent of sexuality active female teenagers had evidence of a chlamydia infection. It is a microscopic parasite. It can result in Reiter's syndrome, and can include eye infections, urethritis, and arthritis. It can also lead to sterility.

**Symptoms.** Symptoms appear seven to 21 days after infection and will appear as a urinary tract infection. Typically a person will notice discharge from the penis and pain during urination. There may also be inflammation of the rectum and swelling of the testicles. About 25% of the men who contract this diseased are asymptomatic.

**How it is contracted.** Chlamydia is contracted through intercourse, and occasionally from hand to eye.

**Diagnosis.** The sores are oftentimes confused with other STDs and lab tests may be necessary.

**Treatment.** You will need to go to a doctor for diagnosis and get a prescription for antibiotics.

**Preventable through safe sex?** Yes, this condition can be avoided through the use of condoms.

### *Cytomegalovirus (CMV)*

**Description.** This virus can be sexually transmitted, but generally only becomes active in individuals with compromised immune systems. It is especially active in individuals with HIV infection or hepatitis B infections. The virus is normally dormant in healthy individuals.

**Symptoms.** Most people do not show symptoms if they have a healthy immune system. Persons with compromised immune systems may show swollen glands, fatigue, fever and general weakness. More severe cases may result in nausea, diarrhea, and loss of vision.

**How it is contracted.** CMV can be contracted in a number of ways including close personal contact such as kissing. It can be contracted through any exchange of any bodily fluids.

**Diagnosis.** CMV can be diagnosed through a blood test.

**Treatment.** There is no cure for CMV though there are treatments available to control the disease.

**Preventable through safe sex?** No, this disease can be spread through kissing although the use of condoms can offer some protection against transmission. Typically, however, this disease is only serious in individuals with a compromised immune system.

## Genital Warts

**Description.** Some forms of human papilloma virus (HPV) cause genital warts. Although many forms of HPV do not have any symptoms these viruses can result in a higher risk for certain cancers. The most noticeable form of HPV causes genital warts.

**Symptoms.** Genital warts will appear around the genitals, in the urethra, in the anus and occasionally in the throat from two to three weeks after infection.

**How it is contracted.** It can be contracted through intercourse and oral sex.

**Diagnosis.** A doctor can identify genital warts through visual inspection. This can be difficult and uncomfortable depending on where the warts are located. If any unusual growth or discomfort is noticed a person should go to a doctor.

**Treatment.** Genital warts can either be treated through a topical solution or through surgery of some type.

**Preventable through safe sex?** Generally yes, but the virus can enter beyond the area protected by a condom.

## Gonorrhea

**Description.** Gonorrhea is a very common STD in the United States. It is a bacterium, and there are currently many strains resistant to treatment.

**Symptoms.** Symptoms appear in men in one to fourteen days and include the discharge of pus from the urethra and pain during urination. About 10% of men will be asymptomatic.

**How it is contracted.** It can be contracted through intercourse and oral sex.

**Diagnosis.** The sores are oftentimes confused with other STDs and lab tests may be necessary.

**Treatment.** You will need to go to a doctor for diagnosis and get a prescription for antibiotics.

**Preventable through safe sex?** Yes, this condition can be avoided through the use of condoms.

### Hepatitis A Virus

**Description.** Hepatitis A was formerly called viral hepatitis. This virus affects the liver.

**Symptoms.** A person will notice fatigue, headache, fever, nausea, vomiting, and lack of appetite and tenderness in the lower abdomen. Later, symptoms include dark urine, changes in the stool, and jaundice. Many people do not notice symptoms.

**How it is Contracted.** It is normally assumed eating contaminated food results in the contraction of Hepatitis A. Food contaminated with infected fecal matter can cause Hepatitis A. Inasmuch as contaminated fecal matter is the cause of Hepatitis A, it can also result from any oral exposure to contaminated fecal matter. This can include not washing hands after anal sex and from rimming.

**Diagnosis.** You will need to go to a doctor. Hepatitis A virus can be detected through a blood test.

**Treatment.** There is no known treatment for Hepatitis A virus. It can be prevented through a vaccine. If a person is exposed to Hepatitis A virus a gamma globulin shot may provide some protection.

**Preventable through Safe Sex?** Although we would like to think everyone practices good hygiene, the truth of the matter is, people frequently do not wash their hands after defecating, and people do engage in anal sex. As such, safer sex probably does not lessen the chances of contracting Hepatitis A if a person engages in any form of anal sex.

### Hepatitis B Virus

**Description.** This virus affects the liver. About 10% of individuals who contract this disease will not be able to recover from the disease, will suffer chronically from the disease, and run a high risk of liver disease and death. The disease is preventable through vaccination. Any individual who is sexually active with multiple partners should be vaccinated for Hepatitis B virus.

**Symptoms.** Symptoms typically occur within four weeks of contracting the virus. First, a person will notice fatigue, headache, fever, nausea, vomiting, and lack of appetite and tenderness in the lower abdomen. Later, symptoms include dark urine, changes in the stool, and jaundice.

**How it is contracted.** Hepatitis B virus can be contracted through intercourse, and any exchange of fluids. Using the same glass can even result in the contraction of Hepatitis B virus.

**Diagnosis.** You will need to go to a doctor. Hepatitis B virus can be detected through a blood test.

**Treatment.** There is no known treatment for Hepatitis B virus. It can be prevented through a vaccine. If a person is exposed to Hepatitis B virus a gamma globulin shot may provide some protection. Up to ten percent of people who contract Hepatitis B virus will be contagious for the rest of their lives and be susceptible to liver disease and liver cancer.

**Preventable through safe sex?** No, the virus can be spread through kissing and intimate touching. The use of condoms may provide limited protection.

## Hepatitis C Virus

**Description.** . This virus affects the liver. There is still very little known about this virus.

**Symptoms.** Hepatitis C typically has very mild symptoms that are many times not noticed by the patient. This disease can, however, cause very serious liver damage.

**How it is Contracted.** There is very little known about this disease. It is believed this virus can be contracted through intercourse just as Hepatitis B and HIV can be contracted through intercourse.

**Diagnosis.** You will need to go to a doctor. Hepatitis C virus can be detected through a blood test.

**Treatment.** There is no cure for Hepatitis C, however alpha interferon is showing promise as a way to prevent deterioration of the liver.

**Preventable through Safe Sex?** Risk of Hepatitis C transmission is probably reduced by practicing safe sex, however, very little is still known about this disease.

## Herpes

**Description.** Genital herpes is carried by more than 30 million Americans. An outbreak of herpes results in cold sores and blisters.

**Symptoms.** Symptoms may occur within 20 days of infection, however many people are asymptomatic. The most common symptoms are clusters of blisters, painful, or itchy sores around the genital areas and mouth. Herpes may remain dormant for long periods of time and reemerge during periods of emotional stress.

**How it is contracted.** Herpes can be contracted through intercourse and the exchange of bodily fluids. It can also be contracted through touching. Herpes is most contagious when there are sores present on the body, however there is evidence some people are contagious even without the presence of sores.

**Diagnosis.** You will need to go to a doctor to have a culture done of the sores.

**Treatment.** There is no cure for herpes though the symptoms can be relieved through various medications prescribed by your doctor.

**Preventable through safe sex?** People should refrain from physical intimacy when sores are present since the virus is very contagious when there are open sores. Condoms may offer some protection.

## Human Immunodeficiency Virus (HIV)

**Description.** This is considered the most dangerous and most feared sexually transmitted disease since it attacks the immune system and in its final stages will result in death.

**Symptoms.** There are many possible symptoms associated with HIV. However, many people now get regular HIV tests to detect the presence of HIV and start treatment before there are any symptoms. Any sexually active individual with multiple partners should get an HIV test every six months. Escorts should get tested every three months if not more frequently.

**How it is contracted.** HIV is typically contracted through intercourse, the sharing of needles, and blood transfusions.

**Diagnosis.** HIV is diagnosed through a blood test. These blood tests are readily available at a doctor's office, local health clinics, and even through the mail.

**Treatment.** There is no cure for HIV, though there are many effective treatments that can slow down the damaging effects of the virus.

**Preventable through safe sex?** Yes.

## *Jock Itch*

**Description.** This is a fungal infection of the genitals.

**Symptoms.** The fungal infection results in an itchy reddish, scaly rash.

**How it is contracted.** It is contracted through a combination of failure to dry thoroughly after bathing and tight fitting underwear.

**Diagnosis.** This condition can be self-diagnosed, however it is possible for someone to confuse the symptoms with those of body lice or scabies.

**Treatment.** This condition can be easily treated with the same over the counter medication used for athlete's foot. The condition should clear up within a week. If it does not get better or gets worse it is possible you have misdiagnosed the condition and should go to a doctor.

**Preventable through safe sex?** Jock itch is not contracted as a result of unsafe sex.

## Molluscum Contagiosum

**Description.**    Molluscum Contagiosum is a virus that causes growths around the genital area and the thighs.

**Symptoms.**    Many people may be asymptomatic for years, but many people show symptoms within two to twelve weeks after infection.    The symptoms are the appearance of small, pinkish-white, and waxy, round growths around the genital area or thighs.

**How it is contracted.**    This virus is contracted through intercourse, oral sex, and intimate contact.

**Diagnosis.**    You will need to go to a doctor and microscopic examination of tissue must be performed.

**Treatment.**    The growths can be removed by a number of methods by a doctor.

**Preventable through safe sex?**    No.    Condoms may offer some protection, but it can be spread through intimate contact.

## Prostatitis

**Description.**    This is the enlargement of the prostate gland. It can be the result of fluid build up in the prostate gland or from a bacterial infection.

**Symptoms.**    The symptoms of prostatitis include a dull persistent pain in the lower back, testes, and scrotum.    There may be some discharge.    In advanced cases there may be a blockage of the urethra resulting in a reduced stream of urine and burning sensations when urinating.

**How it is contracted**.    Build up from fluid can occur from the failure to ejaculate on a regular basis.    If the condition occurs due to a bacterial infection it could be due to unsafe anal sex.

**Diagnosis.**    You will need to go to a doctor for a prostate exam.

**Treatment.**    In cases that are due to a build up of fluid it can be alleviated through more frequent ejaculation.    If it is caused by a sexually transmitted disease it will require antibiotics.

**Preventable through safe sex?**  This is one of the few conditions that can be prevented by having regular sex such as masturbation.  Anal sex may cause bleeding.  This can lead to the development of prostatitis.

## *Pubic Lice*

**Description.**  These parasites are commonly called crabs.

**Symptoms.**  A person will typically have intense itching in the genital area within five days after infestation.  A person who bathes twice a day may not notice the infestation for a longer period of time.

**How it is contracted.**  Pubic lice can be contracted through touch, infected bedding, furniture, clothing, steam rooms, saunas, and even toilet seats.

**Diagnosis.**  Typically lice attach themselves to pubic hair and can be seen through a magnifying glass.  In some cases, there may be very few parasites or the parasites may be very small.  In these cases, it may be hard to find a sample to see.  Self-diagnosis can also confuse lice with jock itch or scabies.

**Treatment.**  There are several over the counter remedies for lice.  A treatment to the body should be repeated within three days.  The treatment can be toxic to the skin and can result in an inflammation to the skin.  Moisturizing the skin after a treatment can prevent skin inflammation.   All clothing, bedding and furniture will need disinfecting.   Other members of the household may also need treatment.

**Preventable through safe sex?**   No, lice can be spread through casual contact.

## *Scabies*

**Description.**  This is a parasitic mite.   These parasites burrow underneath the skin and cannot be detected by the naked eye.

**Symptoms.**  Symptoms may take several weeks to develop.  A person will have intense itching and small bumps or rashes in the genital area, between the fingers, on the buttocks, and around the navel.

**How it is contracted.** Scabies are contracted through close personal contact, bedding and clothing.

**Diagnosis.** This condition is difficult to self diagnose. A dermatologist or personal physician who can perform a microscopic examination of a skin scraping best diagnoses this condition.

**Treatment.** There are several over the counter remedies for scabies. A treatment to the body should be repeated within three days. The treatment can be toxic to the skin and can result in an inflammation to the skin. Moisturizing the skin after a treatment can prevent inflammation of the skin. All clothing, bedding and furniture will need disinfecting. Other members of the household may also need treatment.

**Preventable through safe sex?** No, this condition is spread through casual contact.

### Syphilis

**Description.** Syphilis is an organism that can remain in the body for a lifetime and result in death.

**Symptoms.** Syphilis has many phases. During the first phase there may be painless sores or ulcers around the genital area, lips, mouth or anus. During the second phase the symptoms include body rashes. These early symptoms can be confused with many other diseases, but if syphilis is left untreated it can result in severe neurological damage and death in the latent phase.

**How it is contracted.** Syphilis can be contracted through intercourse, oral sex and kissing.

**Diagnosis.** Syphilis is typically diagnosed through a blood test.

**Treatment.** Syphilis is easily treatable through the use of antibiotics.

**Preventable through safe sex?** Safe sex offers good protection from syphilis.

## *Urinary Tract Infection*

**Description.**   Bacteria transmitted from the rectum to the urethra can cause urinary tract infections.

**Symptoms.**   The symptoms for a urinary tract infection include a burning pain during urination and blood or pus in the urine.

**How it is contracted.**   Essentially, a urinary tract infection is contracted when fecal matter finds its way to the urethra. Unprotected anal sex presents a high risk for a urinary tract infection.

**Diagnosis.**   A doctor should be consulted to confirm diagnosis and provide medication.

**Treatment.**   This condition is easily treatable with antibiotics.

**Preventable through safe sex?**   The use of condoms should prevent a urinary tract infection.

This section is primarily written for men who engage in sex with other men.  However, many men are bisexual and have regular female sexual partners.  As such, several things should be considered:

- Other sexual partners should be treated when these conditions are discovered.
- Many of these conditions are harder to diagnose in women than for men.
- Women may have different symptoms than men for many of these conditions.
- Pregnant women may have severe effects from these conditions.
- Many of these conditions can be contracted by the child of a pregnant woman, and have severe effects.
- It is also possible to contract these conditions from women.

**Anal Sex**

Many sexually transmitted diseases are contracted through anal sex. The reason for this is, many of these diseases can be found in fecal matter. Because it is relatively easy to dismiss these conditions as a result of eating raw food, the reported transmission of these diseases through sexual activity is probably greatly understated.

Far more people, both heterosexual and homosexual, engage in anal sex than will readily admit to engaging in anal sex. Things have changed greatly since thirty years ago when books generally discussed anal sex briefly and then only to dismiss it as an activity only the most depraved individuals engaged in for sexual satisfaction. However, in many states anal sex between heterosexual or homosexual couples is against the law even in their own homes.

Both heterosexual and homosexual erotic films have probably popularized anal sex. Many individuals have consequently practiced anal sex privately at home either by themselves with the help of a sexual aid or with their sexual partner.

It is clear there are many people who enjoy anal sex regardless of their gender or their sexual orientation. However, anal sex does have greater risk for the transmission of STDs than other forms of sexual activities. In women, the risk of pelvic inflammatory disease is very great if fecal matter finds its way into the vagina. This disease can result in infertility and even death.

As such, it is very important for individuals who are engaged in any form of anal sex to use safer sex practices and to be especially vigilant in maintaining good hygiene.

### Safer Sex

Safer sex guidelines have been established that will reduce the risk of contracting HIV. Many of the conditions listed above are not preventable through safe sex since these conditions can be contracted through casual contact. As such, any type of sex or intimate contact poses some type of risk. This means abstinence from sex or a monogamous relationship is the safest means to avoid a sexually transmitted disease.

Safer sex means using condoms for any form of sexual intercourse. There have been very few cases of HIV infection from oral sex. However, there is risk of HIV infection during oral sex if a person has bleeding gums or open sores on their genitals. As such, some people require the use of condoms even for oral sex.

Safer sex also means bodily fluids should not be exchanged. This means people should avoid ejaculating in the mouth or anus of others.

Persons who have multiple sexual partners should be regularly tested for HIV and get regular physical exams. Many sexually transmitted diseases are difficult to detect, and can only be diagnosed by a medical clinician.

### Unsafe Sexual Activity

There is an increase in unsafe sexual activity occurring in the United Sates. The highest risk groups for HIV in the United States are now young adults with multiple sexual partners and intravenous drug users.

In the gay community there is also an increase in unsafe sex among individuals who already have HIV. There is increasing popularity of having anal sex without condoms. This is commonly called bare-backing. There are both many clients and some escorts who will engage in bare-backing. Some disclose their HIV status, but most do not disclose their HIV status.

Bare-backing is an unsafe sexual activity, and the potential consequences should be considered before engaging in sex without a condom.

### How to Get Treatment for a STD

People with multiple sexual partners should consider how they are going to get treated in the event they contract a sexually transmitted disease.

Escorts should have a regular physician. The physician should be aware of their line of work, and have a practice geared towards the treatment of gay men. An escort should also be regularly tested for HIV either by their physician or through a clinic.

The essentials of a good doctor/patient relationship are mutual respect, good rapport, and the ability to follow medical advice. All good escorts carry good medical insurance even if they have high deductibles.

Clients who contract a sexually transmitted disease may feel uncomfortable going to their private physician or to a public health clinic. In reality, both are very good choices. However, many people retain a different physician for sensitive medical issues they want to hide from their insurance companies.

One good option is to go to one of the many quick care facilities maintained by hospitals and doctors groups. These facilities tend to be inexpensive, quick, and provide a degree of anonymity.

Many clients will also ask escorts for a recommendation on a doctor. Typically, doctors of escorts receive many word of mouth referrals from escorts. In some cases these doctors will always find time to squeeze in a word of mouth referral from an escort even when they have no appointments available. Typically a word of mouth referral from an escort to a doctor makes a very good patient and pays cash.

# Chapter Twelve

# Mental Health Issues

There are many escorts and clients who are mentally healthy. It is not unusual for a psychologist to refer clients to escorts after they have suffered an emotional loss in order for them to become reacquainted with sexual activity.

Sexual activity and the exploration of sexual fantasies are emotionally healthy activities. Human sexuality is very complex, and people develop their zone of comfort and safety through experimentation. Everyone makes mistakes, everyone may do things once to determine their individual tastes, and since we only have one life to live we might as well live our fantasies.

The sex industry does, however, attract more than its share of individuals with serious mental health issues. First, it is important to understand and recognize the types of behaviors threatening to an escort or clients. Second, it is important to understand how to deal with these behaviors.

## *Sexual Disorders*

There was a time when homosexuality was considered a mental illness. Currently, sexual identity is considered an adjustment disorder if a person has marked distress in excess of what would be expected and there is significant impairment in social or occupational functioning.

Sexual experimentation has been generally considered normal when people are in their teens or twenties. I have found many people miss the opportunity to experiment sexually at this age, and may enter a period of sexual experimentation at any age.

Sexual experimentation is also a function of fads seen in younger individuals. It is currently very popular in college and high school aged individuals to openly explore bisexuality. As such, many older individuals are also exploring their bisexual fantasies. In many cases, these individuals are experimenting through the use of escorts.

In fact, many sexual activities once considered disorders are now only considered disorders if the fantasies, sexual urges, or behaviors cause clinically significant distress or impairment in social, occupational, or other important areas of functioning.

The types of sexual activities no longer considered mental illnesses are:

- Exhibitionism, which involves the exposure of one's genital to a stranger. Generally, I would not recommend doing this in any place where it would not be considered in good taste. Bath houses and sex clubs are appropriate places for this activity.
- Sexual masochism involving the act of being humiliated, beaten, bound, or otherwise made to suffer.
- Sexual sadism involves deriving sexual excitement from the psychological or physical suffering of the victim.
- Transvestic fetishism involves cross-dressing.
- Voyeurism involving the act of observing strangers, who are naked, in the process of disrobing, or engaging in sexual activity. I would not suggest looking in people's windows,

but there are many acceptable places where this can occur such as nude beaches.

- Other sexual activities no longer considered as serious as in the past include phone sex, exclusive focus on one part of the body (such as foot fetishes), scat (feces), enemas, and water sports (urine).
- The Diagnostic and Statistical Manual of Mental Disorders (DSM-IV) also lists bestiality and necrophilia as less serious than in prior editions.  I do not, however, agree these are acceptable forms of sexual behavior even if engaging in these behaviors do not result in significant distress or impairment of social or occupational functioning.

### *Approach/Avoidance in Sexual Activities*

All sexual experimentation is a process of approach and avoidance.  First, the individual has the desire to engage in the sexual activity.  Despite the fantasy of engaging in a certain sexual activity, the individual will have feelings of resistance.  These feelings include guilt and fear.  Most people are brought up to believe that any sexual activity must follow narrow rules in order to be acceptable and fulfilling.  As such, they avoid in engaging in this sexual behavior.  In reality, very little of the sex that occurs falls within the narrow rules set by society.  However, because of these rules the individual may pursue their fantasy with some caution.

The manner in which individuals overcome their feelings of guilt and fear is through denial.  If an individual can deny that the activity is not actually sex through some internal rationalization then the activity can be justified.  Rationalization and denial are the key ingredients in shedding inhibitions and pursuing otherwise forbidden sexual experiences.  The final key ingredient is the expectation of privacy since other individuals may not see the activity as non-sexual.

There are many examples of activities that the participants have rationalized as being non-sexual:

- Teenage girls who are exploring sex with their boyfriends do not see petting, masturbation and oral sex as sexual acts.
- Young adults experimenting with same sex sexual relations do not necessarily see these relations as sexual.
- Heterosexual males who have anonymous sex with other males do not see this as a sexual encounter.
- Clients of massage therapists do not believe being masturbated is a sexual encounter.
- Many married individuals believe sex that does not include penetration or ejaculation does not constitute as sex.

Individuals who engage in this behavior look through a one way mirror. They do not believe their activity constitutes sexual behavior, yet they would describe the same behavior performed by others as sexual behavior. The reason the rationalization and denial is successful is because of the expectation of sexual privacy. Without the veil of sexual privacy, all sexual activities look dirty and disgusting to a world of critics. Unfortunately, the veil to sexual privacy is oftentimes lifted. The result is a reclassification of sexual activities from being the healthy exploration of sexuality to immoral and inappropriate.

The fear individual sexual privacy will be invaded by others has tremendous ramifications for the healthy development of relationships and sexual identity. Healthy relationships and normal emotional development occurs with the expectation of privacy. When this privacy is pierced and relationships and activities are viewed unnecessarily by the prying eyes of others, it can result in significant, unnecessary, and irrevocable damage to innocent individuals.

### Pedophilia

Typically, pedophilia involves acting out a sexual interest by someone who is over sixteen years of age on someone who is thirteen years or younger. The age of consent among the states varies from thirteen to eighteen.

There are escorts who admit they first started hustling when they were fourteen (and some were younger). There are many children who are thrown out of their homes at an early age and resort to prostitution to support themselves and some times others such as a sibling or friend.

It is also not uncommon for young gay adults under the age of eighteen to have their first sexual relationship with someone who is much older. In many cases it is consensual sex.

An escort under the age of eighteen will typically not be able to work for an escort agency or place an ad in a paper offering their services as an escort. As such, underage prostitutes typically must work on the street. Sometimes underage prostitutes exchange sex for meals and a place to live.

Typically the client of a young hustler is only interested in using them for sex. The young hustler typically has very severe emotional needs, and may possibly have an antisocial personality disorder. Although in some cases the hustler is told to leave home after telling their parents they are gay. However, there are generally other behavioral issues such as dishonesty, violence towards family members, and other troublesome behaviors.

I do not condone or advocate someone under the age of eighteen to engage in prostitution (and believe anyone who enters into prostitution as a career should enter it of their free choice). I would prefer to see children grow up in an environment where they can make choices about what they choose to do with their life. Unfortunately, reality is, many children without homes may not have other choices.

There is no doubt children who enter into prostitution at an early age have a higher rate of HIV infection, higher rate of intravenous drug use, higher rate for criminal activity and a higher suicide rate. These children tend to live fast and die young.

There are many children who are exploited for sex in the world and do not willingly enter the sex industry. There are many children who engage in sex out of coercion and not of their free will. Fortunately, there are now programs in many areas that do not treat juvenile prostitutes as criminals, but rather as victims.

Although many juvenile prostitutes can be rehabilitated to the point where they can make choices about what they want to do with their lives, the same is not true for pedophiles. The evidence seems to be increasing that pedophilia is not a curable condition.

Healthy sex is about choice. It is the ability to choose sexual partners, and on what terms. Typically, when someone seeks a very young sexual partner the motive and sexual pleasure comes from being able to control another individual.

I am not certain at what age a person has the emotional ability to make rational choices and effectively enforce their limits and boundaries when it comes to sex. The problem with this argument is, some people believe they were able to make those decisions at fourteen, and some people feel they have not developed the ability to make sexual choices decades later. The issue is even more muddled when the age of consent varies among the states from thirteen to eighteen.

In an ideal world people should have the skills to make healthy, rational, and responsible sexual choices when their bodies reach the age of sexual maturity. In reality, most people are not emotionally able to make healthy, rational and responsible choices when their hormones start to kick in. However, in a world where eleven-year-olds can be tried as adults for violent crimes, I will argue individuals of sexual maturity should also be prepared for the consequences of their sexual actions.

I argue, if a young adult is properly educated in the family and in the schools on matters of right and wrong the individual will have the ability to make responsible decisions in all areas. Children should be taught assertiveness skills in order to avoid unwanted sexual advances and be trained to effectively assert their limits and boundaries. Likewise, consensual sex among juveniles should not be addressed through the criminal justice system, but through other programs.

I do not like the idea of 30-year-olds having sex with 16 year olds. In reality, however, most teenage pregnancies are the result of much older fathers having sex with much younger mothers, and much of this sexual activity is consensual. The incidence of consensual sex among gay teenagers with older individuals is probably very high.

There is a growing trend to use sex as a weapon. However, if we make the argument for greater criminal responsibility at a younger age (where the young offender has victims), it is hard to make the argument these same individuals are victims when they engage in consensual sex with other individuals.

In the case of pure pedophiles who prey on prepubescent children the evidence is clear these individuals are pure predators. Many jurisdictions now have laws that incarcerate these individuals for life regardless of their sentence. Despite the harshness of such penalties, until there is a cure for this severe psychological disease there may be no other alternative.

I recently discussed the issue of pedophiles with an official of law enforcement who told me most pedophiles in prison are middle-aged men. I responded that it was probable pedophiles were of all ages, and that younger pedophiles are probably suspected less of engaging in this practice since they did not arouse as much suspicion. He tended to agree.

In fact, now that the Internet is being monitored heavily for pedophiles, there seems to be some support for my observation. In the most recent sting operation the suspects were as young as fifteen years of age. A recent murderer of a seven-year old child who was found to fantasize about pedophilia was only nineteen.

The penalties for possessing sexual images (whether real or digitally created) of prepubescent children include up to twenty years in prison, heavy fines, and forfeiture of property including homes. Even if the images have been erased from a computer, the individual with the computer can be charged with a felony.

These penalties are extremely frightening given the amount of spam mail a typical Internet user receives. Even the accidental entry into a web site containing pornographic images can leave records on a computer's hard drive.

Many porn stars and escorts receive numerous inquiries from children under eighteen about porn. Many of these children ask for pictures. Most porn stars and escorts will not knowingly talk on the computer with anyone under the age of eighteen. However, there are a number of vigilante groups who target adult web-site webmasters, porn stars, and escorts in order to entrap them into providing pornographic images. These vigilante groups then provide their information to law enforcement.

It is only a matter of time before unsuspecting individuals will be entrapped into either accidentally downloading child pornography or sending sexual images to individuals who are under age. Unfortunately, the laws are intolerant to any individual who engages in this activity, and the penalties are extremely severe. In a high percentage of cases where individuals have been arrested for having collections of sexually explicit images of prepubescent minors, the suspects have committed suicide before going to trial.

### *Addictions*

Many escorts and clients suffer from one or more addictions. The most common addictions are sexual addiction, alcohol addiction, and drug addiction. Typically, an addiction involves three elements:

- Constancy of the activity or use of the drug.
- Physiological or psychological changes in the person due to the activity or use of the drug.
- Significant distress or impairment in social occupational, or other important areas of functioning.

Addictions can be very stressful to people who are around the addict. Typically, an addict will pursue their addiction at the expense of others and have difficulty maintaining personal relationships.

Many addicts will look towards prostitution as either a way to have a pseudo intimate relationship with another person or as a means to support their addictive behavior. As one escort once said, "I'm an escort because it's the only addiction I have that pays for itself." There are even some escorts who allow their sexual addiction to interfere with their jobs.

Many escorts and clients have addictions to either drugs or alcohol. Many escorts have developed their addictions because of exposure to clients who have offered them drugs. In some cases, escorts have become addicts through their agents and have had to continue to work as an escort in order to pay off their drug debts.

There are several considerations for the client who has a drug or alcohol addiction:

- The client will be less likely to engage in safe sex.
- The client will be less vigilant in protecting his valuables.
- The client will is more likely to be hustled for tips (sometimes in the hundreds of dollars).
- The client is less safe from potential violence.

For the escort who is addicted to drugs or alcohol there are also several considerations in addition to the ones listed for the client:

- The escort will be unable to work.
- The escort may be unable to perform.
- The escort will be more likely to have mood swings.

Any type of addiction is certainly a sure way to strain personal relationships. Many escorts are in support groups to recover from their addictions, and do not take clients who ask if they "party". Historically, clients involved in drugs were considered good paying clients, but today many escorts will not take clients who are involved in drugs.

## Stress

A recent study concluded that prostitutes have a higher incidence and greater symptoms of post-traumatic stress than any other occupation including combat infantrymen. There are several reasons prostitutes may have more stressful lives than most people have.  First, lets take the example of escort who does not work the streets:

- Relationships are very difficult because of the nature of the escort's job.
- Family relationships may be strained, and the escort may have few friends because of their job.
- The escort is probably entirely self-reliant financially.
- Many escorts work seven days a week, twenty-four hours a day and may be sleep deprived.
- The escort may be financially insecure and cannot be assured of a regular income.
- The escort may have been sexually, physically, and emotionally abused as a child, and has not developed adaptive coping skills.
- The escort may be supporting a family.

For the prostitute who works the streets, the following stress factors can be added:

- The lack of a permanent location to live.
- Health issues.
- The need to work to pay for an addiction.
- Legal issues.

Perhaps it is the combination and the intensity of the stress factors that add up to severe stress.  Certainly, many escorts have seen psychologists at one time in their life.  Many of the top escorts have gone through years of therapy to resolve childhood issues.

### Stalkers

Stalking is an occupational hazard for any escort.  It is very rare for an escort to stalk a client.  Although, there are some escorts who will periodically contact with clients to build business or ask for favors.

Normally, an escort will take precautions against stalkers and know the signs of a potential stalker. If a client shows the signs of being a potential stalker it is best to stop the relationship immediately, and no longer see the client.

A client who stalks an escort can make life very difficult and will engage in many types of stalking activities:

- Make multiple phone calls to an escort.
- Make efforts to learn the escort's real name and address.
- Appear at the escort's place of employment.
- Make multiple calls to an escort's place of employment.
- Appear without notice at an escort's house.
- Attempt to make contact with an escort's friends or relatives.
- Threaten to blackmail the escort to the escort's employer, family, friends, or legal authorities.
- Cause damage to an escort's car or property.
- May threaten physical harm to an escort.

It only takes one stalker to make someone's life miserable. Fortunately, there are ways to identify potential stalkers at an early stage. An escort should look for the following signs:

- The first sign is when a potential client calls an escort, and in the first sentence says he needs discretion. A client who truly is concerned about discretion does not red flag the issue. Client's who state the need for discretion typically will expect someone to respect their limits and boundaries, but may not respect the limits and boundaries of others. This is not a sure sign of a potential stalker, but it is a red flag.
- A client who is persistent in getting personal information from an escort such as home phone number, place of employment, and place of residence is a potential stalker.
- A client who is looking for discounts, or expects services for free is a potential stalker. The usual line is "I thought we were moving past a professional relationship." A client may use this line after the first appointment.

- A client who controls conversations. Clients who attempt to control conversations may also try to control individuals in other ways.
- Any attempt by the client to control the escort's personal life.
- Any indication the client is collecting information on the escort from outside sources.
- A stalker will sometimes try to learn the personal tastes of an escort and buy them unsolicited gifts.

If an escort encounters any of these signs, there is a good chance the individual is a stalker. If a potential stalker is stopped early in the process there is a good chance the individual will stop the unwanted activities and move on to someone else. It is a big mistake to allow the situation to continue.

Stopping a stalker means to stop returning calls, do not accept them as a client, and to cut loose all attachments to them.

The client should also realize there are some escorts who are very good at using unwanted infatuation to their advantage. Some escorts are very good at manipulating clients to buy them expensive gifts or provide them with large amounts of cash before terminating the relationship. There are some clients who have had to declare bankruptcy due to the lavishness of their gifts to an escort.

### Antisocial Personality Disorder

Antisocial personality disorder is the current term for what was previously known as a psychopath or sociopath. There is heated debate over the precise definition of each of these terms, but for our purposes these terms mean the same thing.

Essentially, a psychopath is someone who does not respect the limits and boundaries of others and has no remorse or sense of guilt when inflicting harm on their victim. The harm a psychopath inflicts may involve theft, conning someone out of money or possessions, emotional abuse, or physical abuse. A very small number of psychopaths will resort to murder.

Prostitution attracts both clients and escorts who are psychopaths. It is very difficult for clients to tell if they are dealing with a psychopath because psychopath's tend to have very highly developed interpersonal skills associated with persons who are emotionally healthy. Also, psychopaths have the same skills possessed by very successful entrepreneurs. The difference between psychopaths and successful entrepreneurs is entrepreneurs have a conscience and respect limits and boundaries of others. Psychopaths are driven internally by a need to harm others.

In the extreme a psychopath has an internal need to murder people. This is a characteristic of less than 1% of all psychopaths. The psychopath who resorts to murder is oftentimes a serial killer or spree killer. There are examples of serial killers among prostitutes and clients.

The most notable serial killer of male prostitutes is John Wayne Gacy who picked up hustlers, took them back to his home, tortured them, sexually molested them, and strangled them. There are many more examples of serial killers of female prostitutes than of male prostitutes. Typically, the highest risk is to prostitutes who work the street.

The most notable male prostitute to kill clients is Andrew Cunanen. He was not considered a serial killer because of his different style. He is considered a spree killer because he went after people he knew, the killing spree was triggered by an emotional event, and he took his own life. Serial killers tend to kill strangers, kill to derive sexual satisfaction, and are captured alive. In the case of Andrew Cunanen he hunted down and killed former clients and lovers who he felt were responsible for his contraction of HIV (though there was no indication in the medical examiner's report he was HIV infected). Some of his victims have not been connected to him as clients, though there is some speculation there was a common thread to his killing spree.

A client or escort can also risk death even if they are not dealing with a psychopath. Some of the reported instances include:

- A client going into cardiac arrest and the escort not knowing how to revive the client and afraid to call an ambulance.

- Physically unsafe sexual practices including sadomasochism and autoerotic asphyxiation.
- Violence stemming from stalking.
- Failure to report a drug overdose.

Although these events are rare, these events are not unusual. If an escort encounters a situation where a client becomes non-responsive it is better to attempt CPR and to call 911. It will certainly be an awkward situation when the police arrive, but rest assured the police have seen everything. Escorts and massage therapists who have lost a client due to heart failure all feel a sense of responsibility for the death of a client for some time, but most are reassured by the fact everything possible was done to save the person's life.

The more common psychopathic tendencies encountered by escorts and clients involve physical violence, theft, and manipulation. There is no easy way for individuals to determine if they are dealing with a psychopath because psychopaths tend to be very charming. There are, however, a number of behavioral clues. If someone displays five or more of these clues then it a good sign the individual could be a psychopath. Here are some warning signs when dealing with an escort:

- An escort who either advertises or states on the telephone their rate "starts at". This is a sure sign the individual is a hustler.
- A client who states money is no object.
- An interest in the occult. Look for tattoos that suggest the occult such as skull and bones, dragons, and serpents.
- A sparkling personality.
- Sudden changes in personality ranging from pleasant, irritable and aggressive.
- Stories that appear unbelievable. Many psychopaths tell fantastic stories of their achievements beyond expectations.
- Repeated encounters with law enforcement.
- Frequent requests for money and evidence of financial irresponsibility.

- Frequent changes in address and telephone numbers.
- Missing items.
- Reckless behavior including unsafe sex, drug addiction, alcohol addiction, reckless driving, and the taking of unnecessary risks.
- Threats of violence towards individuals.
- Lack of possessions to be a successful escort such as a car, telephone and pager.
- Excessively opinionated, self-assured, or cocky.
- The repeated failure to return pages or calls.
- Early discharge from the armed forces.
- Bragging about their indifferent regard towards others.
- Repeated lying.
- Failure to honor financial obligations.
- The persistent inability to complete stated goals such as school.
- Lack of repeat customers.
- An escort who does not work well with other escorts.

One method to avoid contact with an escort with psychopathic tendencies is to always get a word of mouth referral. Unfortunately, most potential clients ignore warnings given by other escorts or agencies. Typically, if there is an escort with incredible looks; there is no stopping a potential client from pursuing them even with the prospect of physical violence.

Another method used to avoid escorts with psychopathic tendencies is to use an escort agency. Typically reputable escort agencies will ensure the return of stolen property and cooperate with law enforcement agencies if there is an act of violence. Escorts who work for an agency and engage in theft or violence are terminated immediately. Agencies that quote flat fees are more reputable than agencies that quote a base fee plus tip.

There are a number of good reasons for clients to understand the characteristics of an escort who is prone to psychopathic behavior. The risks to clients are:

- An escort getting their money up front and then leaving.
- Being hustled by an escort for far more money than the client expected to spend.
- Theft of valuables.
- Being pursued by an escort for loans, a place to live, or gifts.
- Accepting deposits and airline tickets and then not showing up for a travel appointment.
- The threat of blackmail.
- Physical violence.
- Murder.

Again, there are many clients who do not heed warnings. Escorts with psychopathic tendencies are very good at evading their target's defense systems. A good con artist preys on their target's good nature and sense of denial. Most victims of con artists do not believe any harm can come to them. Many victims exhibit psychopathic behavior themselves, and are genuinely surprised when the tables are turned on them.

Clients who exhibit psychopathic behaviors tend not to be violent. More often than not these clients restrict their activities to what would be considered petty theft or dishonesty. The risks for escorts are:

- Crank callers or persons calling for phone sex.
- Callers who make bogus appointments.
- Clients who like to have escorts come to the door and then reject them.
- Clients who do not pay or pay less than the agreed amount.
- Clients who try to get extra time or other services without paying.
- Clients who try to pay with bad checks.
- Clients who try to pay with credit cards that are stolen, or challenge the charge.
- Clients who try to get escorts to pay for plane tickets or other expenses with the promise of paying the amount back later.
- The stalking of an escort.
- The threat of blackmail to an escort's family or employer.

- Theft of money or valuables from an escort.

Although physical violence or murder of an escort is rare, physical violence or murder has occurred in many instances. A good rule of thumb is, once a client violates an escort's limits and boundaries the behavior will not stop. At that point, the escort should decline seeing the client in the future.

### Concluding Observations

Many people consider prostitutes mentally ill simply because of their profession. The sex industry does attract a lot of people who are less than mentally healthy. However, there are many people in the industry who have chosen their line of work and enjoy their line of work. Many of them take their physical and mental health very seriously.

There are many individuals who engage in prostitution to fulfill their fantasies, just as many clients hire a prostitute to fulfill their fantasies. The risks to being either an escort or a client should not be minimized, nor should the risks be magnified out of proportion. There are legitimate public safety issues that go hand in hand with prostitution. However, there is also a significant segment of the market that presents itself as a legitimate business enterprise and strives for honesty and integrity

# Chapter Thirteen

# Scams

A scam is a fraudulent or deceptive act or operation. A victim of a scam will generally lose something valuable to them such as their time, money or valuables. Nearly every escort and client who uses escorts on a regular basis has felt cheated at one time or another.

This section goes over the most common scams and how to avoid being a victim. Some people are very good at manipulating others, so there is no sure way to avoid being a victim of a scam.

Scams are not limited to the escort business. There are very few people who have not felt cheated at one time or another by a fast talking salesman, a car dealer, medical providers who take diagnostic tests without telling the patient the price, or airlines that do not fully disclose the penalties for cancellation of a ticket.

Scamming can be legally condoned as it is with airlines, medical providers, and cellular phone companies or with individuals where things are done on a handshake. In either case the victim feels duped into paying money for services not wanted or not received without their express intent. People who are self-employed also put considerable value on their time, and are especially sensitive when others steal their time.

Many of these issues were touched on the previous chapter in terms of how to identify someone who is displaying psychopathic behavior. This chapter is written in attempt to educate the reader on how to prevent being scammed.

## *Escort Scams*

Most clients who regularly use escorts report an escort at one time or another has scammed them. In some cases the experience has been so frightening the client stopped using escorts. In other cases, the client has developed precautions.

The best way to avoid being scammed by an escort is to either get a word of mouth referral from someone who has used the escort or to get a referral from another escort. High quality escorts tend to work together, and will accommodate a good client with referrals to other high quality escorts in their area or even around the country.

Another way to avoid being scammed is to use the services of a reputable agency. In the case of hustlers, it is always best to get a recommendation from a bartender or doorman.

The most commonly reported scams by escorts are:

- **Description misrepresentation.** If an escort has misrepresented themselves on the phone or in their advertising it is best to turn them away at the door.
- **An escort getting their money up front and then leaving, theft, and violence.** Clients should always ask the escorts they see if there are any escorts who generate client complaints. Unfortunately, most clients do not believe the word of mouth information given by escorts on other escorts. In reality, the top escorts have every incentive to provide factual and objective information on other escorts. First, the escort may work with other escorts on tandems. Second, 20-30% of a top escort's work comes from word of mouth referrals from other escorts. Finally, a top quality escort has

a genuine concern for the safety and well being of their clients.

- **Being hustled by an escort for far more money than the client expected to spend.** The biggest clue to whether or not a client will be hustled by an escort is if there advertisement reads "starting from" or the escort quotes their prices over the phone as "starting from". These escorts should be avoided.

- **Being pursued by an escort for loans, a place to live, or gifts.** There are some clients who take a genuine interest in escorts and provide them with loans, a place to live, or gifts. Many clients overspend on individuals with whom they are infatuated. Some escorts are especially good at manipulating clients for money or gifts. Some clients have gone bankrupt in the process. It is generally best for a client to budget for these expenditures, and have a cut off for spending at a certain point even if it means terminating the relationship with the escort.

- **Accepting airline tickets and deposits without showing up for a travel appointment.** Many of the top escorts spend most of their time traveling with clients. This can be a difficult experience for a client who is using an escort for the first time. An escort typically will require a deposit of between 20-50%, and the airline tickets to book a travel call. There are some escorts who will cash in the ticket, keep the deposit and not show up for an appointment. To avoid this problem the client can either deal with a reputable agency or get word of mouth referrals.

- **Straight escorts.** There are a number of escorts who are heterosexual who become escorts to victimize gay and bisexual clients. These escorts generate a high number of complaints from clients. Some clients fantasize about having sex with escorts who are straight, however client should be cautious of any escort who advertises as straight or bisexual.

There is a formula an escort uses to scam a client. The escort will build up the client's trust, manipulate the client for money, and then take the money without providing services. Oftentimes, the client gets scammed because of their unwillingness to take the advice of others or because the client feels he will not be subject to the same treatment of others. This is a fatal mistake. An escort with a bad reputation will attempt to scam every client.

Some clients make the mistake of setting unreasonable requirements on other escorts after they have had a bad experience with one escort. Typically, if an escort rejects the requirement, it is a good sign the client might be dealing with a high quality escort. High quality escorts have very strict rules on how they conduct business, and do not break those rules.

### Client Scams

An escort may encounter client scams. Typically, the types of scams inflicted on escorts are relatively petty, and are easily detectable. However, even well established escorts have been known to fall prey to the occasional con artist.

Typical cons used on escorts include:

- **Crank callers.** This is especially true for escorts who list their home phone numbers, cellular numbers or an 800 number pager. The prospective client is sometimes obvious and sometimes subtle in their approach. There are several signs someone is calling for phone sex:

  1. Heavy breathing is a good sign someone is masturbating at the other end of the line.
  2. If the prospective client starts the conversation by asking, "What are you into?"
  3. If the prospective client starts the conversation or at anytime during the conversations states a fantasy the client wants to experience.
  4. If the prospective client states he is coming into town but does not know when or where he will be staying.
  5. If the prospective client asks the escort to send them pictures.

6.  If the prospective client is vague about when he wants to set up an appointment.
7.  If the prospective client says money is no object.
8.  Some prospective clients are very good at making it sound as if a legitimate appointment is about to be set up and then hangs up abruptly in the middle of the conversation

Typically the way to effectively handle someone calling for phone sex is to not engage in phone sex. A well-seasoned escort will determine pretty quickly if a call is for phone sex, and will terminate the conversation by saying, "I need to go now, please call back when you are ready to make an appointment."

*   **Callers who make bogus appointments.** There are some people who get their kicks by making bogus appointments with escorts. Most escorts have several ways to detect the validity of an appointment:

1.  Escorts are suspicious of potential clients with young voices.
2.  Escorts check their caller identification system to ensure the number displayed on the system is the same number given for the appointment.
3.  Escorts typically will call back to confirm an appointment. If the registered name of the hotel guest is different from the name given over the phone the escort will cancel the appointment.
4.  Some escorts will not take appointments from people calling from pay phones or cellular phones.
5.  Escorts who provide their home number in their ads will program their phones not to accept calls from anonymous or unlisted numbers. About 90% of all calls from pay phones and anonymous numbers are crank callers.
6.  Some escorts will not travel to certain hotels or areas in a city known for crank callers.

7. Escorts will block out numbers from their phone system when the person is suspected of being a repeat crank caller.

8. Escorts are very good at remembering the sounds of voices. These escorts recognize the voices of individuals who repeatedly telephone for appointments and no show.

- **Clients who like to have escorts come to the door and then reject them.** There are some clients who get their kicks asking for escorts to come to their door to be rejected. There are escorts who misrepresent themselves on the phone and in their advertisements. In these cases it is appropriate to reject an escort. However, when the descriptions and pictures are accurate it is not understandable. It is very difficult to guard against this sort of ploy, but many escorts who work together share information on clients who play games with escorts.

- **Clients who do not pay or pay less than the agreed amount.** Typically an escort will ask for their money up front with a first time client. The top escorts will expect payment at the end of an appointment with repeat clients. An escort who is underpaid should smile, leave and never see the client again. Non payment is the number one reason why escorts get physically violent with clients. Non payment is a very rare occurrence.

- **Clients who try to get extra time or other services without paying.** Top quality escorts price themselves competitively based on the amount of time and types of services they provide. Clients who want extra time or services should expect to pay more. Escorts who build up their repeat clientele and increase their prices will typically drop the more demanding clients rather than raise their rates.

- **Clients who try to pay with bad checks.** With very rare exceptions an escort will not accept a personal check.

- **Clients who try to pay with stolen credit cards or challenge the charge.** There are very few escorts who accept credit cards. First, it is very expensive to qualify for and maintain a merchant account. Second, people who use credit cards for escorts oftentimes call their bank to challenge the charges. It is very difficult for an escort to challenge a charge back. Services that accept credit cards in the adult industry typically report charge backs that account for 20% or more of the services charged. High charge backs usually result in fines and penalties from the credit card issuer and may lead to revocation of the merchant account.

- **Clients who try to get escorts to pay for plane tickets or other expenses with the promise of paying the amount back later.** There are reports of escorts finding themselves stranded when they go on a travel call. This occurs when the escort does not have the client provide a ticket or a deposit.

- **The stalking of an escort.** There are many clients who use escorts as a way to enter into a relationship. These individuals generally have difficulty meeting people, are emotionally needy, and have a need to control others. When a client passes over the line of business and seeks a relationship other than friendship it can become a disastrous situation for an escort.

- **The threat of blackmail to an escort's family or employer.** This occurs very rarely, and is usually a sign of a stalker. There are other occasions when threats will be made against an escort when these threats are not warranted. In one case an escort was threatened by a client after a condom broke even though the escort was HIV negative and showed a copy of the test to the client. In cases such as this it is best to ignore the client, and hope he does not go through with his threats.

- **Theft of money or valuables from an escort.** This occurs very rarely, but it does happen. Escorts should take reasonable precautions to avoid the possible theft of money or valuables just as a client should take precautions.

### *Internet Scams*

The Internet is increasingly becoming the medium of choice for both clients and escorts. With every new medium there are new opportunities for con artists. The precautions on the Internet in some ways are similar to precautions a person would normally take, but there are some significant differences due to the nature of the medium.

The Internet has the following attributes that result in a different game being played by scammers:

- A person is relatively anonymous through the use of multiple identities on the Internet or by changing their identity frequently.
- A person can change their identity with relative ease.
- Addiction to the Internet means someone could be on the Internet for many hours each day. Many con artists use this time to hone their skills.
- Being logged on to the Internet means a person can have multiple conversations going on at the same time at little or no cost. Scammers who use the phone can only call one person at a time and may incur toll charges.
- It is very easy to provide false information in terms of descriptions, pictures, and location.

Typically, the scams against escorts are very similar to the ones previously described, but the methods used to deter a scammer are different from those used when running an advertisement in a publication.

The scams that are attempted by potential clients are:

- **Cyber sex.** This is when a person poses as a potential client and attempts to engage an escort in sexually oriented on-line conversations. The person may try to get an escort to call them or get the escort's phone number in order to engage in phone sex.
- **Cyber stalking.** This is when a person posing as a client repeatedly tries to engage an escort in cyber sex.
- **Picture hunting.** This is when a person poses as a client and is really collecting pictures.

More serious scams include trying to set up bogus
appointments, or trying to get the escort to make travel
arrangements to see the potential client.

There are various effective means for an escort to prevent
having their time wasted by scammers. These methods include:

- **Using the ignore function.** This allows the escort to block
  out on-line conversations from unwanted individuals.
- **Electronic logs of on-line conversations and e-mail.** This
  allows an escort to keep track of persons who have
  attempted to scam them in the past.
- **Multiple on-line screen names.** This allows escorts to
  uncover people who make a hobby out of harassing escorts.
- **Confirm appointments by telephone.** This prevents an
  escort from going out on phony appointments. The escort
  should also get a first and last name.
- **Do not advance money for a call.** No escort should go out
  on a travel call without the plane ticket and deposit.
- **Have a web page.** An escort should have a web page that
  provides a picture and detailed descriptive information.
  Potential clients should always be directed to the web page
  for descriptive information.
- **Report repeat harassers to the webmaster.** If an
  individual is sending offensive on-line communications or e-
  mails the individual should be reported to the webmaster.
  Typically, a person will get a first warning before the
  Internet provider terminates their service.

An escort can waste a considerable amount of time dealing
with people who are simply posing as clients. This is one reason
why many of the top escorts only work through agents, and other
well-established escorts rarely take new clients.

Since the first edition of this book a number of escorts and
escort agencies have compiled a blacklist of over 100 clients. I
have had nothing to do with the creation of this blacklist,
however, I have been accused of its creation. One client who has

provided invaluable information on what makes a bad client wrote me this letter:

*I write this memo not as a threat but more as information. As you are aware it has been brought to my notice that you are making libelous and slanderous statements about me. What I do, where I stay who I stay with is my affair and what you do is your affair. I do not say anything about you. However, my life obviously is a concern to you.*

*I wonder whether you are trying to do my family life harm or you just enjoy trying to harm me. I ask in the very nicest of ways to refrain from saying anything about me, good, bad or indifferent.*

*What you have said about me bouncing a check is totally incorrect. It never happened to you and if it happened to anyone else it is hearsay.*

*I don't bother you, never will. I would ask the same. Any threat, to me could be construed as blackmail and is a federal offense in this country.*

*So please let's leave each other alone. No more comments and life will just go on for both of us. I certainly wish you no harm. I request we respect each other's way of life, good or bad.*

*Sincerely,*
*Stuart*

The strategy being employed by Stuart is very similar to the strategies employed by most bullies. First, he has a national reputation for not paying escorts the agreed amount, for telephone stalking escorts, for being verbally abusive, and engaging in slightly sadomasochistic sexual activities. Second, he likes to make appointments with escorts around the country and no show them. In short, he is considered a pain in the ass client who likes to play mind games with people.

I do not keep records on clients who have contributed to this book. I do not have their phone numbers, and I do not keep track of their e-mail addresses. Stuart likes to give escorts his home phone number. Many escorts have commented that he receives some sort of sexual satisfaction when he gets someone upset, or when he is threatened, or when he risks discovery by his wife. My only regret of including this example in this book is that Stuart seems to enjoy public humiliation, and I hate to give satisfaction for no charge to anyone who has been so miserable to so many people.

My advice to Stuart, and others who do not liked being discussed, is they should think about cleaning up their act. Clients who treat escorts with respect do not get discussed in the escort community.

Although Stuart is my nominee for worst client, he does have some stiff competition for the title of worst client. Inasmuch as he does not present a physical danger to escorts I need to defer to another nominee for the distinction of worst client. I received this letter from someone who has extensively observed another client:

*I would have to say the DW of a wealthy suburb outside San Francisco makes Stuart look harmless. Not only is he under criminal investigation for raping, drugging and assaulting an escort, but he has a long track record of screwing over escorts.*

*His method of operation is to lure guys who are usually vulnerable, without resources, and around 20 years old to his home for an overnight or weekend stay. He pays for the incoming flight. He negotiates a sweet deal on the price with the understanding that his going to help with the necessities of life. He claims he was a former escort some 30 years ago and is now in his fifties. He tells his victims that because someone helped him, he feels obliged to return the favor. Once the victim is in the client's gated community, he usually promises a car, paid education, allowance, and separate bedroom.*

*The client then gets the victim to ship their entire worldly possessions to his home. Since most of them do not really have places of their own to start with, or any real roots, they gladly do so for the offer of getting out of the escort business and having all of their needs met.*

*Once the client has all of the victim's possessions the rules change. The lucky ones escape quickly. The unlucky ones don't. In his garage are the possessions of at least six escort he has lured to his home. Once he throws the victim out of the house he gets a restraining order against the victim.*

*The client is able to get away with this behavior because he is regarded as a respected businessman in the community. The escorts are not usually able to get any of their possessions returned, and usually leave with the clothes off their back.*

*A dear friend of mine, who was a victim of his three months ago, reported during his two weeks of hell he heard numerous calls on the answering machine from escorts begging to have their possessions returned.*

Why do crimes such as these continue? For the same reason serial murderers can avoid capture when their victims are prostitutes: Law enforcement does not understand the underground culture, and does not trust its members. The reason why serial killers, serial rapists, serial wife beaters get away with their actions is because they look and act so normal. They have jobs, they are friendly, and they are an established part of the community. They hide in plain sight. Their everyday normalcy is their mask of sanity.

In general, however, clients found through the Internet are higher quality than found through many other sources. Clients acquired through the use of the Internet typically have a higher income, higher education, and are fairly sophisticated in their buying habits.

A client is generally safer using an escort on the Internet than through advertisements for the same reason escorts get better clients. Escorts who use a computer also typically have a higher income, are more stable, have a higher education, and have better social skills. This means there is less of a chance for a client to be a victim of theft or violence.

There are, of course, exceptions to this rule of thumb. There are some very simple methods to avoid escorts with a bad reputation on the Internet.

- **Use escorts who have web pages.** First, choose escorts who have web pages over a long period of time, and regularly

answer their e-mail. This is a sign the escort has some
stability.

- **Evaluate the information.** The top escorts on the Internet
  provide the following information without fail: stage name,
  age, height, weight, hair color, eye color, penis size,
  versatility, body type, location available, a description of
  their personality, e-mail address, and pager number. This
  information is available on the escort's web page or the
  escort will gladly provide the information if it is not listed.
- **Use escorts who have pictures.** All good escorts market
  themselves effectively on the Internet. This includes being
  able to provide a recent photograph.
- **Check for references.** Most escorts are well known on the
  Internet. There are a number of places on the Internet where
  a client can ask about the reputation of a particular escort or
  ask for word of mouth referrals.

A client who follows these guidelines will generally have a
good experience with an escort. If a client has a bad experience
with an escort there are several ways to deal with the situation:

- Contact the web site that accepts advertising from the escort,
  and tell them what happened. Reputable web-sites will not
  accept advertising from escorts who steal from clients or are
  violent towards clients.
- There are several web-sites on the Internet where people post
  their bad experiences. Many of these web-sites allow people
  to post anonymously.

A potential client should avoid the following types of
escorts on the Internet:

- Escorts who are traveling through town unless they have an
  established web page.
- Escorts who advertise themselves as having attitude or say
  they are expensive but worth it.
- Escorts who say that the fee "starts from".

- Escorts who do not provide a physical description or picture.
- Escorts who do not have a pager number. Communications is very important to an escort, if they do not have a pager then they are fly by night. Escorts who do a lot of traveling have a nationwide pager.

There are some exceptions to the above rules. A lot of people on the Internet engage in escort work on a whim or to fulfill their fantasies. There are frequently some inexperienced escorts who will try it on a lark, or just to see if they can find work as an escort. So occasionally, there is a bargain to be found. The experienced client is well aware of an inexperienced escort and realizes there is very little risk with someone who is naïve and just getting into the business.

## *Agency Scams*

There are many reputable agencies, however there are also many agencies that engage in business practices that are perceived as dishonest or misleading. There has been a surprising growth in the number of escort agencies over the last several years. Former escorts start many of these agencies.

The most frequent complaints about agencies are:

- **Inaccurate descriptions.** Many agencies will lie about the physical descriptions of their escorts. The more reputable agencies will never oversell the appearance of an escort. Some agencies will use pictures of escorts who are not represented by the agency.
- **Agency fee plus tip.** Some agencies make their escorts work for tips. The escort will typically receive only a small fraction of the initial fee and will need to negotiate for a tip. The client is hustled for additional money before the escort will do anything, and the amount of the tip requested could be as much as one thousand dollars.
- **Constant phone calls during a session.** Sometimes an agency will call the hotel room every five minutes while an escort is in the room. Typically, the agency is attempting to

rush the session so the escort will come back to their office to make their drop. Reputable agencies will require the escort to call at the beginning of a session and at the end of a session.

- **Constant phone calls after a session.** Some agencies will call a client several times over a period of days after the client has seen an escort. This is an attempt to drum up additional business. Reputable agencies do not call clients; these agencies wait for the client to call them.
- **Sending over multiple guys.** Some agencies will send one escort after another over a period of an hour or longer until the client picks one. Reputable agencies will send the one escort who is requested. Some of the more exclusive agencies will refuse to send a second escort if the first one was rejected.

Agencies also attract more than their share of scammers. An experienced agency is well prepared for most of the annoying behaviors of potential clients. The top agencies have a profile of the ideal client, and pretty much stick to that profile in the selection of new clients. An inexperienced person on the phone at an agency will generally not pick up on a potential scammer.

Agencies have various methods to identify clients who are up to no good. Good agencies keep track of client's behaviors and may even share this information with other agencies around the country. In the case of good clients this is in order for them to receive good service as these clients travel around the country. In the case of bad clients it is to protect the agency from loss. A client who is dishonest will certainly lose their client confidentiality.

An agency is also subject to the problems of having dishonest models. Generally, agencies fire models dishonest to the agency. Most models engaged in dishonest practices are caught fairly quickly since agencies keep statistics on each of their models. Typically, a dishonest model will lose far more income through the lost business received from an agency than the business received by being dishonest with the agency.

The most common areas of dishonesty by a model are:

- Telling the agency a client was a "no go" when the model saw the client. Seeing a client behind an agency's back is considered dishonest and results in termination from most agencies.
- Seeing a client at a later time without going through the agency. Again, this is considered dishonest by the agency, and the agency will normally terminate the escort.
- No showing a client. An escort who "no shows" a client is generally terminated. This is considered the most serious infraction of any a model can commit.
- Client complaints. Most agencies listen very carefully to client complaints. Most agencies can tell very quickly the seriousness of a complaint.

The top agencies will no longer accept a client's calls if the client is found to be dishonest. The reasons for this are fairly simple:

- A reputable agency's income is primarily derived from repeat clients. It is not profitable to have a client who is engaging in activity that results in the firing of escorts. Good clients are generally easier to find than good escorts.
- The general rule of thumb is 20% of an agency's income comes from 80% of their clients. Troublemakers in this group detract from the ability to serve the 20% of the clients who generate 80% of the income for an agency. In other words, a reputable agency is generally more profitable when the agency terminates troublesome clients.
- Clients who break the rules are never profitable to an agency. First time clients who ask for exceptions to the house rules are always undesirable clients for an agency.

Most importantly, clients should realize that if they are dishonest to an agency they lose their client confidentiality. An agency will not threaten to expose a client's activities to their friends, family, or employer. The agency will, however, share information with other agencies and escorts in the area and possibly around the country. There are some clients who have developed a richly deserved national reputation for their dishonesty.

### What Happens In Disreputable Markets

Many markets can be considered competitive. However, when there are vigilant police efforts, a local culture that encourages the hustling of clients, a competitive agency environment, and local publications that have a blind eye to the activities of their advertisers, the result can be a dangerous situation.

First, a market can encourage the victimization of clients when the laws are structured in a way to require agencies to charge an agency fee, and requires the escort to work for tips. The logic to this method is that since the agency collects most of the fee, then the agency is not engaged in prostitution. The agency fee can range between $100 and $250 then the client is hustled for additional hundreds of dollars for the performance of additional services.

Second, since only escort agencies are licensed, they are the only ones that can advertise in the Yellow Pages. Individual escorts can advertise in other venues such as local publications and the Internet.

Although the FBI does not normally investigate escort agencies, let's assume one escort agency owner decides to take over the other escort agencies through organized crime. There is now a totally different ballgame. Federal laws are different from local laws. With all of the escort agencies under federal investigation, this frees up local law enforcement to concentrate on independent escorts.

Then, let's throw in a group of characters resembling the Three Stooges. First, there is an owner of a local publication who is a con artist, who likes males who are underage, who is running an unlicensed agency. Then, there is a young spoiled brat with a serious drug problem who gets people hooked on drugs, gets these guys to work for him, and decides he wants to be an amateur blackmailer of his clients. Then you have another publication owner who does not care that the escorts who advertise in his paper use fraudulent pictures or that those escorts rip off and are sometimes physically violent with clients. Of course, the first two stooges self-destruct (get busted or run out of town), and the third stooge sees his advertising drop from eight pages of advertisements to two pages of advertisements.

This leaves local law enforcement to clean up the rest of the town. However, there are three groups of escorts remaining. The first group has an established clientele and just stops taking new clients. Their business declines, but they can survive for six months to a year with their established clientele without advertising. The second group consists of escorts who do not have an established clientele and are relatively new to the escort business. These escorts are typically working their way through school, and have no particular interest in having a criminal record. They leave the business after the first time they are arrested.

This leaves a third group of escorts who are known to be dangerous to their clients. They do not have repeating clients because most clients do not like getting robbed or physically attacked a second time. However, since they are the only remaining escorts they now receive the bulk of the calls from new clients looking for escorts.

Law enforcement aggressively monitors the Internet, and repeatedly calls escorts who advertise in the local papers. If someone advertises for massage the police send a letter telling the advertiser to either print their license number or stop advertising or risk arrest. Law enforcement even poses as escorts on the Internet, and entraps individuals at neutral locations.

The choice for the client now becomes to use an agency and get hustled for hundreds of dollars, or to use an independent escort who may hustle them for hundreds of dollars and may become physically violent. Under this scenario someone will eventually get hurt or killed. Actually, more than a few clients have been hurt, robbed, or killed. Very little has been said in the local papers. The local gay paper has never reported on the victimization of a client or denied advertising to an escort who has been accused of violence.

This summarizes the current situation in Las Vegas. Although there is no other market that poses the degree of danger posed in the Las Vegas market, situations in local markets can change rapidly. It is better to be safe than sorry.

As one escort wrote to me:

> *As far as busts in the Vegas area, I'm not surprised at all. Las Vegas is the worst city in America for escorting. Anyone who has lived there knows. I certainly didn't enjoy getting arrested when I lived there. That is for sure.*

Although prostitution in Las Vegas appears to on the verge of being dealt several blows, it is fairly certain the result will not necessarily be a safer environment. At the present time, the danger and risk to the client has been significantly increased because the individuals who remain in the business will be more likely to see their clients as potential victims rather than a continuing part of their business.

### Concluding Comments

The male escort business is basically one of marketing and sales. The top people in the business have the same skills as a good real estate agent (and many real estate agents got their start as escorts). The top people in the business have the ability to determine the needs of the client and whether they will be able to meet the needs of the client very quickly. A good escort will also be able to determine if a client qualifies for their services very quickly.

Many clients do not realize an experienced escort picks up on every word, nuance, and tone of voice. An experienced escort listens to what a client says and picks up on what is not said. An experienced escort will pick up on whether a potential client is trying to control a conversation, is asking appropriate or inappropriate questions, and will have generally sized up the potential client in less than a minute. An experienced escort has had thousands of conversations with potential clients.    A potential client may well be making their first contact with an escort.  The potential client is generally at the disadvantage.

The good news is the top escorts will treat their clients with dignity and respect unless the escort is paid otherwise.  Likewise, the top escorts expect to be treated with dignity and respect unless the escort is paid otherwise.

# Appendixes

---

The purpose of these appendixes is to provide additional information on the male escort market and to provide additional sources for information. Using this information is at your own risk. There are many risks involved in providing services as a prostitute or in the procurement of a prostitute. These listings are only provided as a means to further understand the diversity, size and depth of the male prostitution market.

These resources are provided as a way for the reader to learn more about male prostitution or to observe the workings of the male prostitution market. Although escorts and clients can use these listings, researchers and law enforcement officials can also use them. As such, pursue these listings at your own risk. Again, this book is presented as a well-balanced and detailed study of the male prostitution market, and is not intended to promote illegal activity.

# Chapter Fourteen

# Analysis of the Top Markets

This section analyzes many markets around the country. The markets are divided into categories based on the diversity of male prostitution sources in the community. These ratings are based on the perceived number of male prostitutes, the range of available sources, the ease in procurement, and the range of types of prostitutes.

The research for this section includes review of local publications, a search on the Internet, interviews with clients, interviews with agencies, and interviews with escorts. Despite the amount of research, the ratings and descriptions are very subjective.

I expect to refine my methodology, and have many additional sources for the next edition. Reader feedback will be very important in expanding this section, and will be greatly appreciated.

The markets analyzed are divided into categories: most diverse, diverse, some diversity, limited selection, and very difficult. The definitions of these labels are:

**Most Diverse.** These are markets that are very competitive for escorts. There is an extreme range of services offered from a variety of sources. In these markets there are hustlers, strip clubs, agencies, advertised escorts, bathhouses or sex clubs, and a large number of escorts advertised on the Internet.

**Diverse.** These markets have all of the features of the most diverse markets, but there are fewer choices in each of these market segments.

**Some Selection.** These markets have advertised escorts, but there is limited selection. There are fewer market outlets than in a diverse market.

**Limited Selection.** These markets have some obvious outlets for finding male prostitutes, but the selection and opportunities are very limited.

**Very Difficult.** In these markets it will take some detective work to find any male prostitutes. Typically, the only choice is to find a hustler. The experience of a customer will be very hit and miss.

## *Most Diverse*

**Los Angeles**. This is the largest market in the United States for male prostitution. Being the center of the adult film industry it certainly attracts many of the top male escorts in the country. Sex is easy to find whether someone is looking for a sex club, bathhouse, hustler or escort. There is something for every pocket book and something for every desire.

**San Francisco**. This gay Mecca certainly has its share of available male prostitutes. From hustlers, to strippers, to agencies, and for a city with less than one million residents it offers great variety.

**New York**. The big apple may be cleaning its streets and reputations, but there are still some operations outside of the Disney domain. This may be the most expensive city in the country, but there is still a great variety. Although it has lost its famous hustler bar, there are still many other sources for male prostitutes.

**Washington, D.C.**  There is sex going on in the Nation's Capital.  The world's oldest profession is quite competitive with the world's second oldest profession.  Given the propensity for prying eyes to turn everything into a sex scandal, it certainly pays to go to a professional for sex in this town and there are many professionals from which to choose.

**Miami/Ft. Lauderdale.**  The South Beach gay culture is known for its vibrancy.  There is a definite slant towards Latin culture, but there is definitely something for everyone.  One escort once complained every party boy in South Beach works part time as an escort.  It is indeed a very competitive market.

## Diverse

**Las Vegas.**  Male prostitution is not family entertainment. It is known as an expensive market because of the local custom of having high agency fees and making the escort work for tips. There are very few hustlers in this market.  The best source is the local gay paper, and the Internet.

**Phoenix.**  This market has a thriving hustler and escort community.  There is one very reputable agency that controls the bulk of the market, and many independent escorts who have varying reputations.

**Chicago.**  The old hustler haunts may be gone, but there are still many sources for hustlers and escorts.  Given the Midwestern values of this town many of the escorts are well educated and professional.

**Philadelphia.**  Philadelphia is home to the most respected escort agency in the United States there are many ways to find escorts in this town.

**San Diego.**  This city known for its ideal weather is a very competitive market for escorts.  The supply certainly exceeds the demand in this town.

**Seattle.**  With the influx of emigrants from Los Angeles, it would not be surprising there is a thriving male escort market.  It is a very competitive market for escorts and the pricing is very reasonable.

**Palm Springs.** This destination resort attracts many escorts from Los Angeles. Although, many of the escorts may only be in residence during part of the year, there are many escorts and massage therapists who call Palm Springs home.

**New Orleans.** This town would not be able to use the slogan "Let the good times roll" if it did not have a thriving prostitution market. It is primarily a hustler market, but there are a number of established escorts. This market probably has the highest class of hustler in the United States.

**Honolulu.** Although this market seems to be very strict on prostitution it does have a couple long term established agencies, and several independent escorts. A couple clubs offer strippers, and it is nearly certain there are many available hustlers.

*Some Selection*

**Denver.** Given the size of this market it may be a surprise there is not a large selection. There is one agency that dominates the market, and this agency does not have the best reputation since its escorts hustle for tips. A number of independent escorts operate out of Denver, and since the bulk of the market is locals the pricing and reputability of these independents is virtually assured.

**Baltimore.** This town is called "charm city", and there is some charm to the available escorts in this town. It has perhaps one of the best strip clubs in the country though it is hit or miss as to whether the strippers are available for escort work.

**Dallas.** Texas has very strict laws against prostitution, and it is oftentimes difficult to even find male prostitutes in Texas. There is certainly demand since escorts around the country report clients from Texas consistently make the best clients. Texas clients are the nicest people and the biggest tippers. Dallas does not have a large selection given its size, but it does have some good choices.

**Boston.** Given all of the universities in the Boston area a client would think there would be a good assortment of male escorts. There are very few advertised escorts in Boston, however there is growing presence on the Internet.

**San Antonio**. This is perhaps the best-served market in Texas. There seem to be a number of hustler bars and strip clubs. There are even a fair number of escorts.

**Austin.** This university town has its share of escorts given its size. Like most cities in Texas there are very few advertised escorts, but there are at least a few escorts who can be found in various ways.

**St. Louis**. This is a good example where male escorts advertise in straight papers rather than the gay media. The reason for this is, in communities that are family orientated the clients of male escorts are predominately married. In these communities escorts tend to advertise in straight publications. These publications are weekly and free.

**Minneapolis.** There is reasonable availability through the normal methods of finding escorts.

**Detroit.** Again, there is a decent selection of independents and a couple of agencies. There are also strippers and escorts on the Internet.

**Tampa.** There is reasonable availability in this town. Due to the fact it has a lot of retirees and winter visitors it is certain the established escorts go for the repeat clients.

**Orlando.** This is an under-served market given the fact it is the number two-destination resort in the world. There are some advertised escorts, but the best selection seems to be through the Internet. Law enforcement seems to control this market very tightly.

**Key West.** Definitely a seasonal market, but it certainly attracts many of the escorts from Miami and around the country. There are certainly more than a few hustlers who can be found working in the local establishments. Many resort communities such as Key West and Provincetown tend to have a very large unadvertised male prostitution market.

### Limited Selection

**Houston.** For its size this is the most under-served market in the United States. There are no agencies, and very few advertised escorts.  There is a thriving hustler market, but only a few escorts who can be found on the Internet.

**Indianapolis**.  There are very few escorts in this market, but they are certainly there, just hard to find.  This market is closely controlled by law enforcement.

**Portland**.  There are lots of potential escorts they are just hard to find.  Since the local gay paper does not accept escort advertising it will take a little detective work, but anyone should be able to find an escort.

**Cleveland.**  It may be easier to find high quality escorts in Cincinnati or Columbus, but there is some selection.

**Pittsburgh**.  Limited supply, but there are some escorts who advertise.

**San Jose.**  Definitely a good selection, but it is best to take to the Internet.  After all, this is the home of Silicon Valley.

**Jacksonville.**  The West Coast of Florida seems to be under-served, but there are still escorts to be found, it just takes a little research.

**Nashville**.  There is some selection in this town and a small agency.

**Louisville**.  Best known as a town with good hustlers.  A client can always get good advice from a bartender.

**Charleston**.  The kindness of strangers is always appreciated in this town.  It is a small town where everyone talks, but there is some availability and a local bartender might be able to give a good referral.

**North Carolina**.  This home to Jesse Helms may be a bastion of conservatism, but it does not take a lot of detective work to find a date for the evening.  There is not a lot of selection, but the escorts seem to be uniformly scattered throughout the state.

**Cincinnati.**  There is no doubt any town that takes its artwork as seriously as this town would have a few escorts to satisfy prurient sexual interests in private.

**Columbus.**  A college town that seems to have a few guys working to pay their tuition.

*Very Difficult*

These are towns where it was very difficult to find any escorts or evidence of hustlers. It is almost certain male prostitutes exist in these markets, but they are very difficult to find. At best, many of these cities have the occasional hustler or the occasional escort who markets through the Internet. In some cases, male escorts can be found through escort services that primarily provide women.

In any case, even finding a male prostitute in these markets is very hit or miss, and may take considerable research.

Sacramento
Hartford
Providence
Des Moines
Wichita
Omaha
Albuquerque
Oklahoma City
Tulsa
Milwaukee
Memphis
Kansas City

# Chapter Fifteen

# Strippers

---

There are a number of different types of establishments that offer strippers. Some establishments offer strippers nightly, and others offer strippers only on occasion. It is best to call ahead of time to check the schedule for the featured performers.

There are also a number of different venues for strippers. Some establishments have totally nude strippers who put on a show and may masturbate or put on live sex shows. Other establishments may be totally nude. Most establishments will have strippers in g-strings or underwear.

Touching policies also vary depending on local laws, degree of enforcement and house rules. A stripper will typically be very polite about telling a customer what is allowed and not allowed. Customers should respect the rules since violation of the rules can mean the stripper is fired or the customer will be asked to leave.

Not all strippers are available for escort work. Many strippers will deny they are available for escort work if they are asked directly. Strippers will deny they do escort work because most establishments discourage solicitation on premises and will fire a stripper caught soliciting. There are other establishments that will turn a blind eye and even allow the exchange of services to occur on premises.

There are several methods to develop the trust of a stripper who you are interested in as an escort:

- Tip well. Good tippers always get a stripper's attention. Strippers like to see their repeat customers.
- Be discrete. Develop a conversation when the stripper is not performing. Bring up the subject of escort work discretely.
- Offer to talk somewhere else. Many strippers will not talk about escort work on premises, however they may talk out in the parking after their show or give a customer their pager number.

## Alabama
### Mobile
B-Bob's, 6157 Airport Blvd. #201, 334-341-0102
## Arizona
### Phoenix
Cruisin Central, 1011 N. Central Ave., 602-253-3376
The Park, 3002 N. 24$^{th}$ St., 602-957-6055
Three-O-Seven Lounge, 222 E. Roosevelt, 602-252-0001
Winks, 5707 N. 7th Street, 602-265-9002
## Arkansas
### Little Rock
Five-O-One at Backstreet, 1021 Jessie Rd., 501-664-2744
## California
### Buena Park
Ozz Supper Club, 6231 Manchester, 714-522-1542
### Los Angeles
Hunter's, 7511 Santa Monica Blvd., 213-850-9428
Numbers, 8737 Santa Monica Blvd., 310-652-7700
Detour, 1087 Manzanita St., 213-669-9472
Club Tempo, 5520 Santa Monica Blvd., 213-466-1094
Spotlight Club, 1601 N. Cahuenga Blvd., 213-467-2425
Caper Room, 2445 Market St., Inglewood, 310-671-7323
Gold Coast, 8228 Santa Monica Blvd., 213-656-4879

**Pomona**
Robbie's, 390 College Plaza East, 909-620-4371
**Riverside**
V.I.P. Club, 3673 Merrill Ave., 909-784-2370
**San Diego**
Club Montage, 2028 Hancock St., 619-294-9590
Rick's San Diego, 1051 University, 619-497-4588
**San Francisco**
The Nob Hill Adult Theatre, 729 Bush St., 415-781-9468
Endup, 401 6th St., 415-357-0827
QT, 1312 Polk St., 415-885-1114
N Touch, 1548 Polk St., 415-441-8413
Campus Theatre, 220 Jones, 415-673-3384
Asia SF, 201 9th St., 415-255-2742
Esta Noche, 3079 16th St., 415-861-5757
Tea Room Theatre, 145 Eddy St., 415-885-9887
**Stockton**
Club Paradise,10100 N. Lower Sacramento Rd., 209-477-4724
**Colorado**
**Boulder**
The Yard, 2690 28th St. Unit C, 303-443-1987
**Connecticut**
**Danbury**
Triangles Café, 66 Sugar Hollow Rd., 203-798-6996
**Hartford**
Chez Est, 458 Wethersfield Ave., 860-525-3243
**Delaware**
**Dover**
Rumours Restaurant & Night Club, 2206 N. DuPont Hwy.
        302-678-8805
**Wilmington**
The Eight Fourteen, 814 Shipley St., 302-657-5730
**District of Columbia**
**Washington**
La Cage Aux Follies, 18 O St. SE. 202-554-3615
Ozone, 1214 18th St. NW. 202-293-0303
Wet & Edge, 56 L St. SE, 202-488-1200
Ziegfeld's & Secrets Complex, 1345 Half St. SE, 202-554-5141

# Florida

## Cocoa Beach
Wanna Be's, 231 Minuteman Causeway, 407-868-1898

## Daytona Beach
Barracks & Officers Club Complex, 952 Orange Ave., 904-254-3464

## Ft. Lauderdale
Saint, 1000 W. State Rd. 84, 954-525-7883
Johnny's, 1116 W. Broward Blvd., 954-522-5931
Omni, 1421 E. Oakland Park Blvd., 954-565-5151

## Ft. Myers
Bottom Line, 3090 Evans Ave., 941-337-7292

## Gainesville
Univeristy Club, 18 E. University Ave., 352-378-6814

## Gulfport
Sharp A's, 4918 Gulfport Blvd. So., 813-327-4897

## Jacksonville
Bourbon Street, 10957 Atlantic Blvd., 904-642-7506

## Key West
Numbers, 1029 Truman Ave., 305-296-0333
Epoch, 623 Duval St., 305-296-8522
One Saloon, 524 Duval St., 305-296-8118

## Lakeland
Roy's Green Parrot, 1030 E. Main St., 941-683-6021

## Miami Beach
Boardwalk, 17008 Collins Ave. N., 305-354-8617
Westend, 942 Lincloln Rd., 305-538-WEST
Patio Lounge, 5249 SW 8$^{th}$ St., 305-445-6301
Warsaw Ballroom, 1450 Collins Ave., 305-940-9887
Sugar's, 17060 W. Dixie Highway, 305-940-9887
Ozone, 6620 Red Rd., 305-667-2885

## Orlando
Wylde's, 3400 S. Orange Blossom Tr., 407-843-6334
Club Quiet, 5244 W. Colonial Dr., 407-297-3992
Roman's, 3400 S. Orange Blossom Trail, 407-422-6826

## Sarasota
Bumber's Nightclub, 1927 Ringling Blvd., 941-951-0335

## Pensacola

Red Garter, Main St. at Palofox, 850-433-9292
### Port Richie
BT's 7737 Grand Blvd., 813-841-7900
### St. Petersburg
Fourteen Seventy West, 325 Main St., 813-736-5483
### Tampa
Angel's, 4502 S. Dale Mabry Hwy., 813-831-9980
Annex, 2408 Kennedy Blvd. W, 813-254-4188
Metropolis, 3447 W. Kennedy Blvd., 813-871-2410
### West Palm Beach
H G Rooster's, 823 Belvedere Rd., 561-832-9119
Heart Breaker, 2677 Forest Hill Blvd. Lake Shore Plaza 561-966-1590
## Georgia
### Atlanta
The Metro, 1080 Peachtree St. NE, 404-874-9869
Heretic Complex, 2069 Cheshire Bridge Rd., 404-325-3061
Guys & Dolls, 2788 E. Ponce de Leon, 404-377-2956
Swinging Richards, 1715 Northside Dr., 404-355-6787
### Augusta
Way Station, 1632 Walton Way, 706-733-2603
B & D's West Spot, 2822 Dan's Bridge Rd., 706-793-5111
### Savannah
Felicia's, 416 W. Liberty St., 912-238-4788
## Hawaii
### Waikiki
Fusion, 2260 Kuhio Ave., 808-924-2422
Angles Waikiki, 2256 Kuhio 2nd Floor, 808-926-9766
Venus, 1349 Kapiolani Ave., 808-955-2640
## Illinois
### Chicago
Lucky Horseshoe Lounge, 3169 N. Halstead, 773-404-3169
Numbers, 6406 N. Clark, 773-743-5772
Man's Country, 5017 N. Clark, 773-878-2069
Glee Club, 1543 N. Kingsbury, 312-243-2075
### Forest Park
Ultimate Oz, 7301 W. Roosevelt, 708-771-4459
### Rock Island

JR'S, 325 20th St., 309-786-9411
**Indiana**
　　　**Bloomington**
Bullwinkle's, 201 S. College, 812-334-3232
　　　**Evansville**
Scottie's Bar, 2207 S. Kentucky Ave., 812-425-3270
　　　**Ft. Wayne**
After Dark, 231 Pearl St., 219-424-6130
　　　**Indianapolis**
Unicorn Club, 122 W. 13h St., 317-262-9195
Metro, 707 Massachusetts Ave., 317-639-6022
　　　**South Bend**
Starz, 1505 Kendal, 219-288-7827
**Iowa**
　　　**Davenport**
Club Marquette, 313 20$^{th}$ St., 309-788-7389
　　　**Waterloo**
The Bar, 903 Sycamore, 319-232-0543
**Kansas**
　　　**Wichita**
Metro, Central & Waco, 316-262-8130
**Kentucky**
　　　**Louisville**
The Teddy Bear, 1148 Garvin Place, 502-589-2619
**Louisiana**
　　　**Baton Rouge**
George's Place, 860 St. Louis St., 504-387-9798
　　　**New Orleans**
MRB, 515 St. Philip, 504-524-2558
TT's, 820 N. Rampart, 504-523-9521
The Corner Pocket, 940 St. Louis, 504-568-9829
Mother Bob's, 542 Rampart, 504-593-2558
Oz, 800 Bourbon St., 504-593-9491
　　　**Shreveport**
Central Station, 1025 Marshall St., 318-222-2216
**Maine**
　　　**Bangor**
Spectrum, 190 Harlow St., 207-942-3000

**Ogunquit**
The Club, 13 Main St., 207-646-6655
**Portland**
Underground, 3 Spring St., 207-773-3315
**Maryland**
**Baltimore**
Club Atlantis, 615 Fallsway, 410-727-9099
**Hagerstown**
Headquarters, 41 North Potomac, 301-797-1553
**Massachusetts**
**Boston**
Paradise, 180 Massachusetts Ave., 617-864-4130
**New Bedford**
Puzzles Lounge, 428 N. Front St., 508-991-2306
Le Place, 20 Kenyon St., 508-992-8156
**Provincetown**
Student Union, 9-11 Carver St., 508-487-3490
**Springfield**
David's Nightclub, 397 Dwight St., 413-734-0566
**Michigan**
**Battle Creek**
Partners, 910 North Ave., 616-964-7276
**Belleville**
Granny's Place, 9800 Haggerty, 313-699-8862
**Detroit**
Off Broadway East, 12215 Harper Ave., 313-521-0920
Gigi's, 16920 W. Warren Ave., 313-584-6525
Club Gold Coast, 2971 E. 7 Mile Rd., 313-366-6135
Club Innuendo, I15 and Nevada, 313-892-1444
**Flint**
State Bar, 2512 S. Dort Hwy., 810-767-7050
Club Triangle, 2101 S. Dort Hwy., 810-767-7550
**Grand Rapids**
City Limits, 67 S. Division Ave., 616-454-8003
**Kalamazoo**
Brothers, 209 Stockbridge, 616-345-1960
**Lansing**
Club Paradise, 224 S. Washington Sq., 517-484-2399

### Mt. Clemens
Mirage, 27 N. Walnut, 810-954-1919
### Port Huron
Seekers, 3301 24th St., 810-985-9349
### Saginaw
Bambi's, 1742 E. Genesee, 517-752-9179
### Traverse City
Side Traxx, 520 Franklin, 616-935-1666
## Minnesota
### Minneapolis
Gay 90's Happy Hour, 408 Hennepin Ave., 612-333-7755
## Mississippi
### Columbus
Columbus Connection, 107 Front St., 601-545-2714
### Meridian
Crossroads, Hwy 59 South, 601-655-8415
## Missouri
### Columbia
Styxx, 3111 Old Hwy 63 S., 573-443-0281
### Kansas City
Cabaret, 5024 Main St., 816-753-6504
### St. Joseph
Club 705, 705 Edmond, 816-364-9748
### St. Louis
Faces, 130 4th St., E. St. Louis, IL, 618-271-7410
## Nebraska
### Lincoln
Q, 226 S. 9th St., 402-475-2269
Panic, 200 S. 18th St., 402-435-8764
### Omaha
Max & Stosh's Saloon, 1417 Jackson, 402-346-4110
## Nevada
### Las Vegas
Gipsy, 4605 Paradise Rd., 702-731-1919
Flex, 4371 W. Charleston Blvd., 702-385-FLEX
## New Jersey
### Asbury Park
Down the Street, 230 Cookman Ave., 908-988-2163

**Jefferson**
Yacht Club, 5190 Berkshire Valley Rd., 973-697-9780
**River Edge**
Feathers, 77 Kinderkamack Rd., 201-342-6410
**New Mexico**
**Albuquerque**
Foxes Lounge, 8521 Central Ave. NE,    505-255-3060
Pulse, 4100 Central Ave. SE, 505-275-1616
**New York**
**Binghamton**
Risky Business, 201 State St., 607-722-2299
Chances, 256 Main St., 607-770-7516
**Brooklyn**
Spectrum, 802 64th St., 718-238-8213
**Buffalo**
Underground, 274 Delaware Ave., 716-855-1040
**Long Island**
Bunk House, 192 Montauk Hwy., 516-567-2865
**New York City**
Julius, 159 W. 10th St., 212-929-9672
The Web, 40 E. 58th St., 212-308-1546
The Works, 428 Columbus Ave., 212-799-7365
Candle Bar, 309 Amsterdam Ave., 212-874-9155
Stella's, 266 W. 47th St., 212-575-1680
Gaiety Theatre, 201 W. 46th St., 212-221-8868
The Roxy, 515 W. 18th St., 212-645-5156
King, 579 Sixth Ave., 212-366-5464
Splash, 50 W. 17th St., 212-691-0073
Champs, 17 W. 19th St., 212-633-1717
The Break, 232 8th Ave., 212-627-0072
Axis, 17 W. 19th St., 212-633-1717
Tunnel Bar, 116 First Ave., 212-777-9232
Two Potato, 143 Christopher St., 212-255-0286
The Roxy, 515 W. 18th St., 212-645-5156
Twirl, 208 W. 23rd St.,
Circles, 1134 1st Ave., 212-588-0360
Tool Box, 1742 2nd Ave., 212-348-1288
**White Plains**

Club 202, 202 Westchester Ave., 914-761-3100
### Queens
El Bar, 63-14 Roosevelt, 718-651-4145
Magic Touch, 73-13 37$^{th}$ Rd., 718-429-8605
### Upper Nyack
Barz, 327 Rte 9 W, 914-353-4444
## North Carolina
### Charlotte
Oleen's, 1831 South Blvd., 704-373-9604
Chasers, 3217 The Plaza, 704-339-0500
Masquerade, 3018 The Plama, 704-344-1770
Three Hundred Stonewall, 300 E. Stonewall St., 704-347-4200
### Fayetteville
Spektrum, 107 Swain St., 910-868-4279
### Greensboro
The Palms, 413 N. Eugene St., 910-272-6307
Warehouse 29, 1011 Arnold St., 910-333-9333
### Hickory
Club Cabaret, 101 N. Center St., 704-322-8103
### Wilmington
Mickey Ratz, 1155 Front St., 910-251-1289
### Winston-Salem
Bourbon Street, 916 Burke St., 910-724-4644
## Ohio
### Akron
Interbelt, 70 N. Howard St., 330-253-5700
### Cincinatti
Cincinnati Dock, 603 W. Pete Rose Way, 513-241-5623
### Cleveland
Aunt Charlie's The Cage, 9506 Detroit, 216-651-0727
The Grid, 1281 W. 9th St., 216-623-0113
### Columbus
Garrett's Saloon, 1071 Parsons Ave., 614-449-2351
### Dayton
Jessie's Celebrity, 850 N. Main, 937-223-2582
DJ's, 237 N. Main St., 937-223-7340
### Lima
Somewhere In Time, 804 W. North St., 419-227-7288

**Lorain**
The Serpent, 2223 Broadway, 440-245-6319
**Springfield**
Chances, 1912-1914 Edwards Ave., 513-324-0383
**Oklahoma**
**Oklahoma City**
Copa, 2200 NW 39th Expressway, 405-525-0730
**Tulsa**
Concessions, 3340 S. Peoria, 918-744-0896
**Oregon**
**Portland**
Silverado, 1217 SW Stark, 503-224-4493
**Pennsylvania**
**Harrisburg**
Stallion, 706 N. 3rd St., 717-232-3060
**New Hope**
Cartwheel Club, 437 York Rd., 215-862-0880
**Philadelphia**
Key West, 207 S. Juniper, 215-545-1578
**Pittsburgh**
Pegasus Lounge, 818 Liberty Ave., 412-281-2131
**Scranton**
Buzz, 131 N. Washington Ave., 717-969-2899
**Rhode Island**
**Providence**
Yukon Trading Co., 124 Snow St., 401-274-6620
**South Carolina**
**Charleston**
Déjà vu 2, 445 Savannah Highway, 803-556-5588
**Columbia**
Metropolis, 1800 Blanding, 803-799-8727
Downtown, 1109 Assembly, 803-771-0121
**Greenville**
Club 621, 621 Airport Rd., 864-234-6767
**Spartanburg**
Cheyenne Cattlemen's Club, 995 Asheville Hwy. 864-573-7304
**Tennessee**
**Knoxville**

Electric Barroom, 1213 Western Ave.,    423-525-6724
   **Nashville**
Chute Complex, 2535 Franklin Rd., 615-297-4571
**Texas**
   **Austin**
Oilcan Harry's, 211 W 4, 512-320-8823
Charlie's, 1301 Lavaca Ave., 512-474-6481
   **Beaumont**
Copa, 304 Orleans St., 409-832-4206
Crockett St. Station, 497 Crockett St., 409-833-3989
   **Corpus Christi**
U B U Club, 511 Star St., 512-882-9693
Zodiac, 4125 Gollihar, 512-853-4077
   **Dallas**
Metro Club, 2204 Elm, 214-742-2101
Crews Inn, 3215 N. Fitzhugh, 214-526-9510
Village Station, 3911 Cedar Springs, 214-380-3808
Zippers, 3333 N. Fitzhugh Ave., 214-526-9519
Midtowne Spa, 2509 Pacific, 214-821-8989
Kolors, 2525 Wycliff, 214-520-2525
Brick, 4117 Maple Ave., 214-521-2024
JR's Bar & Grill, 3923 Cedar Springs, 214-380-3808
   **Denison**
Good Time Lounge, 2520 N. Hwy 91 N, 903-463-9944
   **El Paso**
Whatever Lounge, 701 E. Paisano, 915-533-0215
New Old Plantation, 219 S. Ochoa St.,    915-533-6055
San Antonio Mining Co., 800E. San Antonio St.,915-533-9516
   **Fort Worth**
Magnolia Station, 1851 W. Division, 817-332-0415
   **Galveston**
Kon Tiki, 315 Tremont, 409-763-6264
   **Houston**
Rich's, 2401 San Jacinto, 713-759-9606
Midtowne Spa, 3100 Fannin St., 713-522-2379
Incognito, 2524 McKinney, 713-237-9431
QT, 534 Westminister, 713-529-8813
JR's, 808 Pacific, 713-521-2519

Gentry, 2303 Richmond, 713-520-1861
EJ's, 2517 Ralph, 713-527-9071
Santa Fe Bar & Patio, 804 Pacific, 713-521-2519
### McAllen
PBD Lounge, 2908 Ware Rd., 210-682-8019
### San Antonio
Woody's, 826 San Pedro, 210-271-9663
Twenty Fifteen Place, 2015 San Pedro, 210-733-3365
Pegasus, 1402 N. Main St., 210-299-4222
Sparks, 8011 Webbles Dr., 210-653-9941
Metropolis, 309 W. Market, 210-527-1707
## Utah
### Salt Lake City
Bricks, 579 W. 2nd St., 801-328-0255
## Virginia
### Norfolk
Garage, 731 Granby St., 757-623-6303
Private Eyes, 249 W. York St., 757-533-9290
## West Virginia
### Huntington
Beehive, 1121 7th Ave., 304-696-9858
### Morgantown
Class Act, 355 High St., 304-292-2010
## Wisconsin
### Eau Claire
Wolfe's Den, 302 E. Madison St., 715-832-9237
### Milwaukee
Club 219, 219 S. 2nd St., 414-271-3732
La Cage & Dance Dance Dance, 801 S. 2nd St., 414-383-8330
C'est La Vie, 231 S. 2nd St., 414-291-9600
### Superior
JT Bar & Grill, 1506 N. 3$^{rd}$, 715-394-2580

# Chapter Sixteen

# Places to Find Sex

This chapter is comprised of a listing of bathhouses and sex clubs. These establishments are classified based on the following definitions:

**Bathhouses**. Bathhouses are places that generally have private rooms, gym facilities, showers, swimming pools, Jacuzzi's, steam rooms, and saunas. To enter a bathhouse a customer needs to show a driver's license or passport and sign a waiver. A customer will be asked whether a locker or a room is preferred. A room is preferable since it offers a degree of privacy.

Customers will be asked if they want to store their valuables. This is highly recommended. A customer will be provided with a towel, key to the room or locker, key to the lock box, and be provided with condoms (and sometimes lubricant). A customer will be required to only wear a towel when walking around the club.

The cost to enter a bathhouse typically ranges from $15 to $25 depending on the day of the week, time of day, specials, and whether the customer prefers a room or a locker. Some of the private rooms can be quite luxurious. It is advisable to bring a toiletry kit, any toys, a blanket, and a pillow in a gym bag. Although the customer may not be able to sleep with the heavy beat of disco in most of these facilities, it is always nice to be as comfortable as possible.

Bathhouses are considered private clubs. Customers from out of state may not be required to buy a membership card and the customer can buy a one-day membership card. Membership cards are usually good for six months.

**Sex Clubs**. Sex clubs are different from bathhouses because sex clubs do not have amenities. Typically, sex clubs are clothing optional, but most people choose to wear clothes. There generally is a place to store valuables. There are generally no showers or private rooms. Sex clubs allow varying degrees of sexual activity.

In previous printings I had listed adult bookstores and adult theatres. A few of these places are listed under establishments with strippers, however, for the most part **www.cruisingforsex.com**, and various gay travel guides have much more up to date listings than this book could ever have. I recommend that readers interested in the sexual activities that occur in various locations throughout the world consult **www.cruisingforsex.com**. I have included my definitions of adult bookstores and adult theatres below:

**Adult Bookstores.** Adult bookstores are known for their video arcades. The degree of sexual activity that occurs in these places depends on local laws and the enforcement of those laws, the amount of privacy afforded in the video booths, the management, and the individuals on duty. Sex in adult bookstores has its dangers including surveillance by video camera, monitoring by local law enforcement and theft by hustlers.

**Adult Theatres.** Adult theatres have big screens. These establishments also tend to have video arcades. Many of these establishments attract hustlers, both male and female. These establishments have many of the same characteristics as adult bookstores in terms of the sexual activity that occurs on premises. These establishments have the same risks as adult bookstores.

**Arizona**
    **Phoenix**
        **Bathhouse**
Chute, 1440 E. Indian School Rd., 602-271-9011
Flex Complex, 1517 S. Black Canyon, 602-271-9011
**California**
    **Berkeley**
        **Bathhouse**
Steamworks, 2107 4th St., 510-845-8992
    **Cathedral City**
        **Bathhouse**
Club Palm Springs, 68449 Perez Rd., 619-324-8588
        **Sex Club**
The Gravel Pit, 68774 Summit, 760-324-9771
    **Chico**
        **Sex Club**
Cowboys, 477 E. 9th St., 916-345-8073
    **Hollywood**
        **Bathhouse**
Coral Sands, 1730 N. Western Ave., 213-467-5141
Hollywood Spa, 1650 N. Ivar Ave., 213-463-5169
        **Sex Club**
The Zone, 1037 Sycamore Ave., 213-464-8881
    **Los Angeles**
        **Bathhouse**
Flex Complex, 4424 Melrose Ave., 213-663-5858
Midtowne Spa, 615 Koler St., 213-680-1838
        **Sex Club**
Basic Plumbing, 1924 Hyperion Ave., 213-953-6731
Explode, 5140 Washington Blvd., 213-934-7919
Exxile, 1800 Hyperion Ave., 213-661-9417
MB Club, 4550 Melrose, 213-669-9899
Night Hawk, 1064 Myra Ave., 213-662-4726
    **North Hollywood**
        **Bathhouse**

North Hollywood Spa, 5636 Vineland Ave., 818-760-6969
### San Diego
### Bathhouse
Club San Diego, 3955 4th Ave., 619-295-0850
Mustang Spa, 2200 University Ave., 619-297-1661
Vulcan Steam & Sauna, 805 West Cedar St., 619-238-1980
### Sex Club
Dave's Club, 4969 Santa Monica Ave., 619-297-1661
### San Francisco
### Sex Club
Blow Buddies, 933 Harrison St., 415-863-4323
Castro Party, 633 Castro St., 415-863-6358
Eros, 2051 Market St., 415-864-3767
Mack, 317 10th St., 415-558-8300
Power Exchange Mainstation, 74 Otis, 415-487-9944 (also has a
straight sex club at the same location).
### San Jose
### Bathhouse
The Watergarden, 1010 The Alameda, 408-275-1215
### Van Nuys
### Bathhouse
Roman Holiday, 14435 Victory Blvd., 818-780-1320
### Wilmington
### Sex Club
Club 1350, 510 W. Anaheim, 310-830-4784
## Colorado
### Denver
### Bathhouse
Denver Swim Club, 6923 E. Colfax, 303-321-9399
Midtowne Spa, 2935 Zuni St., 303-458-8902
### Sex Club
Community Country Club, 2151 Lawrence St., 303-297-2601
## District of Columbia
### Washington
### Bathhouse
Club Washington, 21 'O' St. SE, 202-488-7317
Crew Club, 1321 14th St. NW, 202-319-1333
### Sex Club

GHC (The Gloryhole), 24 'O' St. SE, 202-863-2770
## Florida
### Ft. Lauderdale
#### Bathhouse
Club Fort Lauderdale, 400 W. Broward Blvd., 954-525-3344
Clubhouse II, 2650 E. Oakland Park Blvd., 954-566-6750
### Jacksonville
#### Bathhouse
Club Jacksonville, 1939 Hedricks, 904-398-7451
### Miami
#### Bathhouse
Beach Head, 1510 Alton Rd.
Club Miami, 2991 Coral Way, 305-448-2214
### Orlando
#### Bathhouse
Club Orlando Athletic Ventures, 450 E. Compton, 407-425-5005
New Image Fitness Center, 3400 S. Orange Blossom Trail, 407-420-9890
Parliament House Motel, 410 N. Orange Blossom Trail, 407-425-7571
### Tampa
#### Bathhouse
Club Tampa, 215 N. 11th St., 813-223-5181
### Wilton Manors
#### Sex Club
Thinkers, 2929 NE 6th Ave.
## Georgia
### Atlanta
#### Bathhouse
Flex, 76 4th St., 404-815-0456
### Augusta
#### Bathhouse
Parliament House, 1250 Gordon Highway, 706-722-1155
## Hawaii
### Honolulu
#### Bathhouse
Koko Pacific, 2139 Kuhio Ave. Waikiki, 808-923-1852
Max's Gym, 444 Hobron Lane, 808-951-8332

### Sex Club
P-10-A, 444 Hobron Lane, 3rd Floor
## Illinois
### Chicago
#### Bathhouse
Man's Country, 5017 N. Clark St., 773-878-2069
Man's World, 4740 N. Clark St., 773-728-0400
Unicorn Club, 3246 N. Halsted St., 773-929-6080
## Indiana
### Indianapolis
#### Bathhouse
Club Indianapolis, 620 N. Capitol Ave., 317-635-5796
The Works, 4120 N. Keystone Ave., 317-547-9210
## Louisiana
### New Orleans
#### Bathhouse
Midtowne Spa, 700 Baronne St., 504-566-1442
The Club New Orleans, 515 Toulouse St., 504-581-2402
## Massachusetts
### Boston
#### Bathhouse
Safari Club, 90 Wareham St., 617-292-0011
## Michigan
### Centerline
#### Bathhouse
Tranquility Spa, 24420 Van Dyke
### Detroit
#### Bathhouse
TNT Health Club, 13333 W. 8 Mile Rd., 313-341-5322
### Grand Rapids
#### Bathhouse
Diplomat Health Club, 2324 S. Division Ave., 616-452-3754
## Minnesota
### Duluth
#### Sex Club
Duluth Family Sauna, 18 N. 1st Ave. E., 218-726-1388
## Missouri
### Kansas City

**Bathhouse**
1823 Club, 1823 Wyandotte
### St. Louis
**Bathhouse**
Club St. Louis, 2625 Samuel Shepard Dr., 314-533-3666
### Nevada
#### Las Vegas
**Bathhouse**
Apollo Spa & Health Club, 953 E. Sahara Ave., 702-650-9191
#### Reno
**Bathhouse**
Steve's, 1030 West Second St., 702-323-8770
### New York
#### Buffalo
**Bathhouse**
New Morgan Sauna, 655 Main St., 716-852-2153
#### Flushing
**Bathhouse**
Northern Men's Sauna, 3365 Fairington St., 718-359-9817
#### New York City
**Bathhouse**
82nd Street Club, 40-33 82nd St.
East Side Club, 227 E. 56th St., 212-753-2222
Mt. Morris Baths, 1944 Madison Ave., 212-534-9004
The Circle Club, 17 West 60th St.
Wall St. Sauna, 1 Maiden Lane, 212-233-8900
Westside Club, 27 W. 20th St., 212-691-2798
**Sex Club**
J's/The Hangout, 675 Hudson St., 212-242-9292
Manhole, 28 9th Ave., 212-647-1726
S. L. A. G., 257 W. 29th St., 212-465-2506
The Toolbox, 1742 Second Ave.
Triangle Event, 10 West 18th St.
Vault, 28 10th Ave., 212-255-6758
#### Rochester
**Bathhouse**
Rochester Sap & Body Clubs, 109 Liberty Pole Way, 716-454-1074

**Ohio**
### Akron
#### Bathhouse
Akron Steam & Sauna, 41 S. Case, 330-784-0777
Club Akron, 1339 E. Market Street, 330-784-0309
### Cleveland
#### Bathhouse
Flex, 1293 W. 9th, 216-696-0595
The Club Cleveland, 1448 W. 32nd St., 216-961-2727
### Toledo
#### Bathhouse
Diplomat Health Club, 1313 N. Summitt St., 419-255-3700
**Oregon**
### Portland
#### Bathhouse
Club Portland, 303 SW 12th Ave., 503-227-9992
Olympic Steam Bath-Downtown, 509 SW 4th Ave., 503-227-5718
**Pennsylvania**
### Philadelphia
#### Bathhouse
Chancellor Athletic Club, 200 S. Camac St., 215-545-4098
Club Body Center, 120 S. 13th St., 215-735-9568
### Pittsburgh
#### Bathhouse
Arena Health Club Baths, 5888 Ellsworth Ave., 412-471-8548
**Rhode Island**
### Providence
#### Bathhouse
Club Providence, 257 Weybosset St., 401-274-6620
### Warwick
#### Adult Bookstore
Video Expo, 2318 Post Rd., 401-739-3080
**Texas**
### Austin
#### Bathhouse
ACI, 500 Chicon, 512-472-1443
Midtowne Spa, 5815 Airport Blvd., 512-302-9696

### Dallas
#### Bathhouse
Club Dallas, 2616 Swiss, 214-821-1990
Midtowne Spa, 2509 Pacific, 214-821-8989
#### Sex Club
Brotherhood, Maple and Oak Lawn Ave.
### Houston
#### Bathhouse
Club Houston, 2205 Fannin, 713-659-4998
Midtowne Spa, 3100 Fannin, 713-522-379
### San Antonio
#### Bathhouse
Alternative Clubs Inc., 827 E. Elmira St., 210-223-2177
Executive Spa, 703 Ave. 'B', 210-225-8807
## Utah
### Salt Lake City
#### Bathhouse
14th St. Gym, 1414 W. 200 S., 801-363-2023
## Washington
### Seattle
#### Bathhouse
Club Seattle, 1520 Summit Ave., 206-329-2334
South End Steam Baths, 115-1/2 1st Ave., 206-223-9091
#### Sex Club
Basic Plumbing, 1104 Pike St., 206-682-8441
Club Z, 1117 Pike St., 206-622-9958
Seattle Jacks, 1115 Pike St.

# Chapter Seventeen

# Publications

---

This section has a listing of the most commonly referred to publications for escort listings. There are a few publications listed that either do not accept advertising from escorts or restrict advertising to licensed massage therapists. In most localities there will be very few or no listings for escorts due to local laws. However, these publications may list massage therapists, establishments with strippers, bars with hustlers, bathhouses, sex clubs, and adult bookstores.

Travelers to an area can usually write them ahead of time to get a copy of the publication. It is advisable to send the publication a few dollars to cover postage and handling. Some individuals call these publications and ask them about the availability of escorts in the area. Even if the publication does not carry escort advertisements, many of these publications are helpful if the person called is not otherwise busy.

Many of these publications now have Internet web pages that contain most if not all of the advertisements in the publication.

A person can generally find these publications at most gay establishments or even on the street in heavy traffic areas in newspaper racks.  When people call any establishment found in a publication, they should always state where they heard about the establishment.  Some escorts and agencies will not take clients who do not tell them which advertisement a client read.

Other good sources for information are local straight publications available for free either in stores or on the street in newspaper racks.  A person can also look in the yellow pages under adult entertainers, escorts, and massage therapists. Information can be gathered from gay book stores, gay and lesbian community centers, and by calling gay bars.  A good escort will build up as many word of mouth referral sources as possible.

## Atlanta

Southern Voice
1095 Zonolite Rd. Suite, Atlanta, GA  30306
404-876-1819

Etcetera Magazine
151 Renaissance Parkway, Atlanta, GA  30308
404-888-0063

## Baltimore

Baltimore Gay Paper
PO Box 22575, Baltimore, MD  21203
410-837-7748

Alternative
PO Box 2351, Baltimore, MD  21203
410-235-3401

City Paper
812 Park Ave., Baltimore, MD  21201
410-523-2300

**Boston**
  In Newsweekly
  544 Tremont, Boston, MA  02116
  617-426-8246
**Charlotte**
  Q Notes
  PO Box 221841, Charlotte, NC  28222
  704-531-9888
**Chicago**
  Gay Chicago
  3121 North Broadway 2$^{nd}$ Floor, Chicago, IL  60657
  312-327-7271
**Cleveland**
  Gay People's
  PO Box 5426, Cleveland, OH  44101
  216-631-8646
**Columbus**
  Stonewall
  1160 North High St.,  Columbus, OH  43201
  614-299-7764
**Denver**
  Out Front
  244 Washington St., Denver, CO  80203
  303-778-7900
**Detroit**
  Cruise Magazine
  660 Livernois Ave., Ferndale, MI  48220
  248-545-9040
**Florida**
  Contax
  901 Northeast 79th St., Miami, FL  33138
  305-757-6333

## Hawaii
Dakine
2410 Cleghorn St. #2302, Honolulu, HA  96815
808-923-7378

Odyssey
1750 Kalakaua Ave. Suite 3247, Honolulu, HI  96826
808-955-5959

## Houston
Houston Voice
811 Westheimer Suite 105, Houston, TX  77006
713-529-8490

OutSmart
3406 Audubon Place, Houston, TX  77006
713-520-7237

## IN/KY/OH
Word
501 Madison Ave.  Suite
Indianapolis, IN  46225
317-725-8840

## Indiana
Out & About Indiana
133 W. Market St. #105, Indianapolis, IN  46204
317-923-8550

## Jacksonville
The Last Word
P.O. Box 60582, Jacksonville, FL  32236
904-384-6514

## Kansas City
Current News
809 W. 39th St. Suite 1, Kansas City, MO  64111

816-753-4300

**Laguna Beach**
The Blade
PO Box 1538, Laguna Beach, CA  92652
714-494-4898

**Las Vegas**
The Las Vegas Bugle/Out
714 E. Sahara, Las Vegas, NV  89104
702-369-9325

**Los Angeles**
The Frontier
PO Box 46367, West Hollywood, CA  90046
213-848-2222

IN Los Angeles
7985 Santa Monica Blvd.  #109, West Hollywood, CA  90046
213-848-2200

FAB
6399 Wilshire Blvd. Suite 200, Los Angeles, CA  90048
213-655-5716

Nightlife
1800 N. Highland Ave. Suite 604, Hollywood, CA  90028
323-462-5400

The Next LA Magazine
7985 Santa Monica Blvd., Suite 207
West Hollywood, CA  90046
323-656-8118

4Front
7985 Santa Monica Blvd. #69, West Hollywood, CA  90046
323-650-7772

Edge
6434 Santa Monica Blvd., Los Angeles, CA  90038
213-962-6994

New Times Los Angeles
1950 Sawtelle Blvd.  Suite 200, Los Angeles, CA  90025
310-477-0403

## Miami
Scoop
2205 Wilton Dr., Ft. Lauderdale, FL  33305
954-561-9707

Hot Spots
5100 N.E. Twelfth Ave. Ft. Lauderdale, FL 33334
954-928-1862

## Minneappolis
XL Magazine
2344 Nicollet Ave. Suite 130, Minneapolis, MN  55404
612-871-2237

## National
Bound & Gagged
PO Box 2048, New York, NY  10116
212-736-6869

Unzipped
PO Box 4356, Los Angeles, CA  90078
213-468-1900

## New Orleans
Ambush
828-A Bourbon St., New Orleans, LA  70116
504-522-8049

Eclipse
PO Box 52079, New Orleans, LA  52079
504-944-6722

**New York**
HX
230 W. 17th St. 8th Fl, New York, NY  10011
212-352-3535

Next
121 Varick St. 3$^{rd}$ Floor, New York, NY  10013
212-627-0165

The Village Voice
36 Cooper Square, New York, NY  10003
212-475-5555

New York Blade
242 W. 30$^{th}$ St. 4$^{th}$ Floor, New York, NY  10001
212-268-2069

**Orlando**
Watermark
PO Box 5336555, Orlando, FL  32853
407-481-2243

**Palm Springs**
The Bottom Line/Pulp
1243 N. Gene Autrey Trail, Palm Springs, CA  92262
760-323-0552

**Philadelphia**
Philadelphia Gay
505 South 4th Street, Philadelphia, PA  19147
215-625-8501

AuCourant

2124 South Street, Philadelphia, PA  19146
215-790-1179
**Phoenix**
X-Factor\Echo Magazine
POB 16630, Phoenix, AZ  85011
602-266-0550
**Pittsburgh**
Out
747 South Ave., Pittsburgh, PA  15221
412-243-3350
**Portland**
Just Out
PO Box 14400, Portland, OR  97293
503-236-1252
**Raleigh**
The Front Page/Carolina Pulse
PO Box 27928, Raleigh, NC  27611
919-829-0181
**Sacramento**
Sacramento News & Review
1015 20$^{th}$ St., Sacramento, CA  95814
916-498-1234

OutWord
709 28$^{th}$ St., Sacramento, CA  95816
916-498-8445

**San Diego**
Update
POB 33148, San Diego, CA  92163
619-299-0500

South Coast Insider

501 Washington St. #644, San Diego, CA 92103
619-542-0353

Gay & Lesbian Times
3911 Normal Street, San Diego, CA 92103
619-299-6397

### San Francisco
Bay Area Reporter
395 Ninth Street, San Francisco, CA 94103
415-861-5019

SF Frontiers
2370 Market St. 2nd Floor, San Francisco, CA 94114
415-781-4333

The San Francisco Bay Guardian
520 Hampshire, San Francisco, CA 94110
415-255-7600

SF Weekly
185 Berry Suite 3800, San Francisco, CA 94107
415-541-0700

SF Bay Times
3410 19th St., San Francisco, CA 94110
415-626-0260

### Seattle
Seattle Gay News
PO Box 22007, Seattle, WA 98122
206-324-4297

### South Carolina
Unison

PO Box 8024, Columbia, SC  29202
803-771-0804

## St. Louis
News Telegraph
PO Box 14229-A, St. Louis, MO  63178
314-664-6411

## Tampa
Encounter
1222 South Dale Mabry Hwy. Suite 913, Tampa, FL  33629
813-877-7913

## Texas
Texas Triangle
4001-Cedar Springs, Dallas, TX  75219
214-599-0155

Texas This Week
3300 Regan Ave., Dallas, TX  75219
214-521-0622

## Virginia
Shout
PO Box 21201, Roanoke, VA  24018
540-989-1579

## Washington DC
The Washington Blade
1408 U Street NW, Washington, DC  20009
202-234-5400

Metro Weekly
1012 14th St. NW, Washington, DC  20005
202-638-6830

## Wichita
The Liberty Press
PO Box 16315, Wichita, KS  67216

316-262-8289
**Wisconsin**
In-Step
1661 North Water Street Suite 411, Milwaukee, WI 53202
414-278-7840

# Chapter Eighteen

# Male Escort Agencies

---

This chapter has a listing of male escort agencies in the United States. In some localities there may not be an escort agency that specializes in male escorts. Many escort agencies that market female escorts also handle male escorts. Typically, escort agencies will not have a wide selection, but they will accommodate a good client.

There are many escort agencies that do not have good reputations. Some escort agencies misrepresent their models. Some escort agencies only quote the agency fee, and all services performed are for tips. The reader is advised not to use the firms that engage in these practices.

Many agencies now have web pages with pictures and descriptions of their available models. The maintenance of these web pages varies considerably.

Many agencies are reluctant to take new clients, and may have very few models available at the last minute. It is best for first time clients to call an agency several days ahead of time to find out about their policies. A first time client should call early in the day or the day before to make an appointment.

**Arizona**
> Phoenix

Christopher & Friends          602-391-0441
> Perhaps one of the most reputable agencies in the United

States.
**Australia**
> **Sydney**

Knight Call                    61-(2)9368-0511
This agency is included because they advertise from time to time
in the United States.
**California**
> **Long Beach**

Fantasies R Us                 714-636-4513
> **Los Angeles**

Red Dragon Escorts             210-836-3846
Crème de la Crème              213-656-7680
Rated as the best escort agency in Los Angeles.
Excelsior Escort Service       310-281-5780
Rated as the most reputable escort agency in Southern
California.
> **Orange County**

Man to Man                     714-480-0772
> **Palm Springs**

Elite Escorts                  760-322-9506
> **San Diego**

Man to Man                     619-563-0666
> **San Francisco**

Boys 2 Men                     800-666-6933
Rated the best agency in San Francisco.
**Delaware**
Premier                        215-765-6665
**District of Columbia**
> **Washington**

The Capital Men                202-554-9837
Tops Agency                    202-319-0100
This agency is rated as the best agency in Washington, D.C.
The Raymond Agency             301-468-3525
The Agency                     202-829-0121

A well regarded agency in Washington, D.C.

| | |
|---|---|
| Boystown Crew | 202-332-0031 |

**Florida**

### Central Florida

| | |
|---|---|
| Boys | 941-610-2697 |

### Miami

| | |
|---|---|
| Secrets Escorts | 305-379-0920 |
| St. Tropez Escorts | 305-669-2115 |
| Gorgeous Guys | 305-535-1400 |

### Tampa

| | |
|---|---|
| Studz | 813-535-8839 |

**Georgia**

### Atlanta

| | |
|---|---|
| Sachi | 404-872-2758 |
| Executive Models | 404-875-1927 |

**Hawaii**

### Honolulu

| | |
|---|---|
| Gavin & Co. | 808-599-1900 |
| Daaks | 808-926-2242 |

**Illinois**

### Chicago

| | |
|---|---|
| Male Call | 310-805-5402 |
| Chicago Men | 312-740-1400 |
| Champs Playmates | 773-296-0006 |
| US Studs | 773-381-3775 |
| Chicago Guys | 312-848-3868 |
| The Gentlemen | 312-664-6353 |

**Indiana**

### Indianapolis

| | |
|---|---|
| Man Handlers | 317-255-8624 |

**Massachusetts**

### Boston

| | |
|---|---|
| Dream Crew | 800-249-8249 |
| Bodyworks | 617-269-0089 |

**Michigan**

### Detroit

| | |
|---|---|
| Hardbodies | 313-434-4644 |
| Men4Men | 800-401-7679 |

**National**

| | |
|---|---|
| Male Model Listing | 1-900-740-8665 |
| Massage Hot Line | 1-900-844-7828 |

These are nationally advertised phone lines that provide free ads to escorts and massage therapists. The prospective client can listen to the ads for $2.99 per minute.

**New Jersey**

| | |
|---|---|
| Stud Escorts | 973-471-7794 |
| Premier | 215-765-6665 |

**New York**

### New York City

| | |
|---|---|
| Fresh Faces | 917-749-4443 |
| Chelsea Guys | 212-533-5600 |

This agency is rated the best in New York City, and also provides national services.

| | |
|---|---|
| College Guys | 212-751-4280 |
| Man to Man | 212-243-6320 |
| The A List | 212-243-3842 |
| WOW | 212-219-1186 |
| Fantasy Men | 212-388-1500 |

**North Carolina**

| | |
|---|---|
| College Boy Escorts | 919-507-1884 |

### Charlotte

| | |
|---|---|
| Tiffany Escorts | 704-820-9415 |

### Greensboro

| | |
|---|---|
| Adam's Escorts | 910-574-1524 |

### NC/SC/VA

| | |
|---|---|
| Frat Boys | 919-856-1212 |

### Triangle Area

| | |
|---|---|
| Triangle Escorts | 919-899-0291 |

**Ohio**

### Cincinnati

| | |
|---|---|
| Man Dates | 513-258-8571 |

**Pennsylvania**

### Philadelphia

| | |
|---|---|
| Elite Escorts | 215-574-1076 |
| Princeton Men | 215-732-4111 |

Premier                              215-765-6665
Premier is the most highly regarded escort agency in the United
States.
**Tennessee**
      **Nashville**
Menz Escorts                         615-331-8275
This is the most highly rated male escort agency in Nashville.
**Texas**
      **Dallas**
Male to Male                         972-960-8882
Physiques Models                     972-842-2816

# Chapter Nineteen

# Internet Addresses

The Internet is rapidly becoming the medium of choice for the top escorts and agencies. The easiest way to find male escorts on the Internet is to do either a profile or web page search query by using the words "male" and "escort".

There are several things to keep in mind when searching the Internet for escorts. First, many escorts are not terribly stable in the business, and do not maintain their profiles or web pages. Second, this is not the best way to reach an escort at the last minute. Third, advertisers of escorts come and go very quickly for a number of reasons.

While revising this listing I made three observations. First, many of the more amateur web sites have disappeared. Second, web site addresses change with some frequency. Third, the more professional web sites have expanded dramatically in just a few months. Among the sites expanding at a rapid rate are various escort web rings and the largest web site advertising escorts (http://www.escorts4you.com). Typically, the escorts who are a part of either of these web sites are more professional in the way they operate their business.

There are two web-sites that stand out in their contributions to the professionalism of the escort industry.  First, **www.escorts4you.com** takes client complaints seriously and will not allow any escort to advertise on their site if they receive repeated client complaints.  Second, the Excelsior Escort Agency servicing Southern California maintains a database of clients who are a danger or a threat to escorts.  Both of these entities are making a valuable contribution to the safety of both clients and sex industry workers.

There are very few web pages that are well maintained and many web pages do not update link changes.  Accessibility to a web page can difficult due to Internet traffic and whether the service provider places a usage limit on a web page.  However, many of the escort agencies and escorts are of the highest quality.

Here is a listing of popular web pages.  The listings are divided into advertisers, escort agencies, individuals, and link pages.  I have included a few interesting web site listings at the end.

## Advertisers

**http://www.bbmen.com**
A web site dedicated to body builders and their admirers.
**http://www.GlobalEscorts.com**
A new web site covers the international market.  This site has grown considerably since it was last visited.
**http://www.sf-exotics.com**
A number of escorts working in the San Francisco Bay area.
**http://www.sandiegoaccess.com/escorts/escorts1.htm**
A nice listing of escorts available in San Diego.
**http://www.martinryter.com**
A good selection of Los Angeles escorts.  Has a number of porn stars featured.
**http://www.quest-online.com**

Some ads for guys available in Wisconsin.
**http://www.remingtons.com**
Although an advertisement for a Toronto strip club, many of their dancers are rumored to be available as escorts.
**http://www.escort-massage-ads.com**
Some international ads.
**http://www.mansclub.com**
Lists a number of escorts around the country.
**http://www.man-sex.com**
A pay site that has a number of ads for escorts.
**http://www.rising-sun.com**
Provides first rate information on several countries in Europe, and a few listings in the United States.
**http://www.perfectmen.com**
A good assortment in New York and California, with a number of others scattered around the country.
**http://www.gayglobal.com/escort/index.html**
A good assortment of escorts in the San Francisco area.
**http://www.rentboy.com**
A good selection of escorts from around the country. Good selection for New York City.
**http://www.mastervu.com**
Features a number of model listings for New York, San Francisco, and Los Angeles.
**http://www.pantsdown.com**
Lists male and female escorts and escort agencies.
**http://www.frontiersweb.com**
California newspaper that lists all of their in-line escort and massage ads on-line.
**http://www.areagay.com**
An on-line emporium with some escort ads.
**http://www.escorts4you.com**
The largest advertising site on the Internet for male escorts around the country. Many good pictures. Features many of the top escorts in the country.
**http://www.accesstoronto.com**
A listing of male and female escorts in Toronto, Canada.

**http://www.streetlife.com**

A pay site that lists escorts.

**http://www.gayamerica.com/escorts**

A web site that features New Orleans escorts.

**http://www.escorts-london.co.uk/topsites/**

A listing of the top 100 male and female escort site in the world.

**Agencies**

**http://www.theagencydc.com**

An escort agency in Washington, DC.

**http://www.ravenevents.com**

A Toronto male escort agency web page.

**http://www.rdescorts.com**

Los Angeles escort agency.

**http://www.professionalescorts.com**

A Los Angeles agency.

**http://www.bostonescorts.com**

An agency serving Boston.

**http://www.londonmen.com**

A London escort agency.

**http://www.rdescorts.com**

A long established Los Angeles agency.

**http://www.tops69.com**

An escort agency in DC.  Rated as the best agency in Washington, DC.

**http://www.premierescorts.com**

A good listing for the most respected male escort agencies in the United States.  They are located in Philadelphia.

**http://www.hardbodiesny.com**

A good web site for an escort agency in New York.

**http://www.activemedia.net/knights/**

An agency serving Orlando and Tampa.  This agency is rapidly listing escorts around the country.

**http://www.asgardescorts.co.uk/home.htm**

An excellent web site listing London escorts.

**http://www.peoplemale.com**

The web site for an Amsterdam agency. One of the best agency web-sites.

**http://www.seattleescorts.com**

A seattle agency.

**http://www.streetlife.com**

This is a pay site, but offers a unique and broad assortment of escort of color. For a number of clients, this is their favorite web- site.

**http://sfboyz4rent.com**

This is a San Francisco agency that also offers services in other cities.

**http://207.149.42.146**

This is the web-site for one of the best Los Angeles agencies. This agency is rated as the most reputable agency in Southern California. They can be reached at **XcelsiorLA@aol.com** or at 310-281-5780.

**Independent Escorts**

.

**http://www.latinoboy.com**

Hot Puerto Rican escort in San Francisco.

**http://members.aol.com/i4hireaz**

An independent Phoenix based escort.

**http://www.alecpowers.com**

One of the most popular porn stars on the market.

**http://www.classactmt.com**

A New York based and Yale educated Latino escort.

**http://biz.gaynet.net/M4Hire**

An independent escort in Denver.

**http://member.aol.com/NiceEscort/pubpage.htm**

Perhaps the most well known escort in Cleveland.

**http://www.geocities.com/HotSprings/8456/escort.htm**

An asian escort in Nottingham, England.

**http://www.geocities.com/hotsprings/spa/9698**

An independent escort in London.

**http://members.aol.com/bbescort**

A bodybuilder escort in Los Angeles.

**http://members.aol.com/PvtShow/3.html**
John Ramsey is considered one of the top male escorts in the United States. He is first class in everything he does.
**http://www.mrcolorado.com/mike.htm**
A competitive bodybuilder in Colorado.
**http://www.cyberbellion.com/mitch.htm**
An independent escort in San Francisco.
**http://www.sexyman.com**
Atlanta escort who was probably the first escort to exploit the Internet to any degree.
**http://www.bodydesign.com**
A Los Angeles escort.
**http://www.mattadams.com**
He's retired, but the page is still there.
**http://www.willclarkusa.com**
A very well done web page by one of the top escorts.
**http://www.ChadConners.net**
Porn star and independent escort in Los Angeles.
**http://www.chance-caldwell.com**
One of the top porn stars and a well respected escort.
**http://www.dfwmale.com**
A selection of escorts in Dallas.
**http://www.malekey.com/mark-wolff**
A bodybuilder who does not have the best reputation, but has many good clients.
**http://www.jonramsey.com**
Another address for the top independent escort in the United States.
**http://www.hotndc.com**
An independent escort in Washington, D.C.

**http://www.musclesex.com**
Independent bodybuilder escort.
**http://www.maxgrand.com**
The web site for another of the top escorts.
**http://www.perfectmen.com/njescort/home.htm**
A very detailed home page for a New Jersey escort who is also on the list of the top escorts.
**http://members.xoom.com/maksvienna**

An escort in Vienna, Austria.
**http://www.esc4men.com/frames.htm**
An independent escort in central London, England. He seems to be very friendly and good at marketing.
**http://members.aol.com/spoilaboy**
A good example of what to avoid. This web site earns my vote for the worst escort web site.
**http://members.aol.com/hotop4hire/frame.htm**
This is the web site for one of the best escorts in Los Angeles.
**http://freetown.com/suburbs/PecanHill/1095**
An escort in Tampa.
**http://www.cole-tucker.com**
Certainly one of the most talked about web sites of a porn star. Cole is definitely first class in anything he does, and his web site shows it.
**http://www.acme-atlanta.com/adult/finest**
An escort in Atlanta.
**http://members.aol.com/topsfstud**
The web page for a very high quality escort in San Francisco.

### Link Pages and Interesting Web Sites

**http://www.gaynation.net**
Many links to escort web pages.

**http://www.gayscape.com**
Lots of links to top quality escort web pages.
**http://www.gay1000.com**
A ranking of the top gay sites on the Internet.
**http://www.adonisweb.com**
Lots of good links.
**http://www.cruisingforsex.com**
This is an online worldwide listing on how to locate the cruisy areas. This is definitely an incredible site.
**http://atkol.com**
Lots of good links and gossip on escorts.
**http://www.radvideo.com/Radnews/forums.html**

A good gossip page on the porn stars.

**http://www.ManNet.com**

Lots of very good links provided by Butch Harris.

**http://www.queery.com**

Search engine for gay sites.

**http://www.queerplanet.com**

Web site devoted to Atlanta.

**http://www.QueerLINKS.com**

Limited links to male escort sites.

**http://www.escorts4you.com/webring/**

The most complete listing of escort sites on the web. This web ring connects almost 100 web sites at this time. It has doubled in size in the last six months. Many of the web sites participating in this ring are among the top escorts in the country, and many of the others are just a notch below the top escorts.

**http://www.gaystuff.com**

Links to many web pages.

**http://www.gaysf.com**

Lots of links to sex sites in San Francisco.

**http://homepages.skylink.net/~blake77/GLV.htm**

A group of free male escorts who provide gang bang services for women.

**http://www.realm-of-shade.com/meretrix**

A web site devoted to providing educational resources on prostitution.

**http://www.muscleservice.com**

A web site devoted to devotees of bodybuilders. Many of the individuals on this site do escort work.

**http://www.onelist.com/subscribe.cgi/EscortMale**

This is a subscription only mailing list. Members of this mailing list must be working escorts. After signing up for this mailing list an escort must send e-mail to the moderator listing their credentials. The e-mail should be addressed to cris@manfourman.com.

**http://www.escortlinks.com**

This is an eclectic listing of escort links.

**http://www.masseur.net**

A web-site listing massage therapists around the country. This web-site was created by a massage therapist who wanted to promote professional advertising for massage therapists. This site is open to all gay-friendly men who practice massage, energy work, or other related bodywork modalities.

**http://www.masseur.net/ring.htm**

Web rings are perhaps the most effective means for anyone to advertise and for clients to find good information. Almost every field has someone who sponsors a main web-site as well as a web-ring that links home pages.

# Chapter Twenty

# Highly Recommended Escorts

There are many high quality escorts who deserve mention. Their names have been collected from a number of sources and the only information is provided from public sources such as magazines, newspapers, and the Internet.

Although there are a number of escorts with less than desirable reputations, it was decided not to give them print space. Many clients typically work on a high level of denial, and despite warnings clients will continue to pursue someone they are infatuated with regardless of the possible dangers.

There are no pictures in this section because this would require getting model releases and copies of identification from every model listed. This is an overwhelming task when dealing with models. Instead, I decided to stick with information available in the public domain.

Many escorts move, come in or out of the business, or change their phone numbers frequently. As such, the contact information will change. Where possible I have included a pager number, web address and where the escort normally advertises.

If you feel there is an outstanding escort who deserves mention in a future edition then you can feel free to send me a letter with your experience, and a copy of any advertising or reference a web page.

Models were selected for this section based on their professionalism and reports of client satisfaction. In many cases I have had contact with the escort, but in many cases I only know of them by their reputation. I have added a few escorts who are relatively obscure because I was impressed with their professionalism. There is a very wide selection, and based on the client comments there is very little risk a client would be disappointed.

The final cut was based on both my objective and subjective feelings about the individual. Some have displayed erratic behavior in the past due to drugs, however, after much soul searching I decided to include them because of their commitment to staying clean and sober.

This listing tends to be biased towards the muscular escort because these are the most popular types of escort and the most talked about type of escort. I have added a few non-muscular escorts to provide some variety to the list.

As with top escorts, these escorts are very difficult to book since many of them travel over 50% of the time. Some of these escorts only work part of the year, and take long breaks to travel or relax. Some of them are difficult to contact. Many of these escorts see very few clients or do not accept very many new clients. As such, a prospective client may need to convince these escorts to accept them as a client.

As for the list, I received this comment from one client:

*I've seen several of the escorts you mention, and you are right on target about each one.*

A comment from another client was:

*Until this past weekend I had only had sex with one woman, my wife. I had long fantasized about men, but had never acted on it. A few months ago, the thought of hiring an escort occurred to me.*

*I did quite a bit of research and decided on one of the individuals listed in your book. I have to say that all of the things you say about individual escorts in your book are understated. He was tremendously kind and understanding, and he made me feel incredibly important and special.*

I received this note from one of the escorts listed:

*The best result of your book will be a well-informed clientele who treat escorts with respect and vice versa. I have already noticed the people who have called me after reading your book seem to have taken your advice to heart, and do not make the mistakes common to many clients.*

As far as the top ten, here are my picks in no particular order:

Tony Cummings (Tampa).   Southern charm all the way around.  One of the most disarming people I have ever met.

Cole Tucker (Boston).   Who else could be involved in an international scandal and handle the situation with pure class. This guy is one of a kind.  At the age of 44 he won three porn awards.  Essentially, in the real man category he is the sexiest of everything.

Jon Ramsey (Boston).   Always mentioned as one of the best.

Damon Wolf.  This is definitely a class act.  One of the nicest people I know.

Alec Powers.   This dizzy blond has probably been photographed and filmed more than almost any porn star.  He may seem dizzy, but underneath he is very shrewd.

Nick (New York).  He uses the term "class act" in his screen name.  There is no mistake in his use of the term.

Kevin Williams (San Diego).  At 29ish he pretty much has the life time achievement award for being an escort and porn star.  He is extremely charming and fun.

Kurt Rosser (Canada).  I don't know what it is about this guy, but he certainly seems to make people melt in his hands.

Mike Maxx (District of Columbia).  A disarming individual who is good at everything he does.

Kirk (San Francisco).  This is my discretionary choice based on my hunches.  Everyone else on this list is muscular.  Here is someone who has a young and cute personality.

Here are my picks for the top escorts in the United States:

## California
### Los Angeles

- **Ted Matthews.**  This is one of Los Angeles' most popular escorts.    He advertises in Frontiers, UnZipped and **www.perfectmen.com**.    He is dark and handsome, and apparently a personality to match.  His pager number is 213-812-8010 or he may be contacted at 323-654-2630.  His e-mail address is **hotop4hire@aol.com**.
- **Chad Conners.**    This muscular blonde porn star has many fans and apparently a good personality.  He advertises in the Frontiers, UnZipped and has his own web page at **www.chadconners.net**.
- **Tommy Cruise.**  This relatively new porn star is an ex-marine with a nice tight body.   He is relatively new to escorting and has some learning to do, but he shows a lot of promise.  He advertises in the Frontiers, and can be paged at 213-218-3328     or     he     may     be     e-mailed     at tommycruise@loop.com.
- **Chance Caldwell.**   This porn superstar from the Czech Republic is known to be one of the nicest guys around.  At 6'1" and 220 pounds he has the ideal look for many clients.  His rates are also very reasonable considering the demand for his services.  He advertises in the Frontier, UnZipped, and on several web-sites on the Internet.  His pager number is listed as 213-878-3497.
- **Casey Morgan.**  Another relatively new porn star.  He is entertaining and intelligent, and a good example of an escort who is a well kept secret.  He is 5'7" and 135 pounds, but has a very tight body, and a great attitude.  He can be contacted at **prnstar68@aol.com**.

- **Brian.** One of the few massage therapists listed in this section, but is known for his clients with special needs for discretion. Even he does not know who his clients are, and they keep coming back. He is very reasonably priced and has a great attitude. He can be reached at 213-549-1210.
- **Marco Rossi.** Another one of the L.A. muscle guys. He is very popular and oftentimes advertises in Frontiers and Unzipped.
- **Will Clark.** This long time favorite travels between New York and Los Angeles and helps to raise a lot of money for charity. His web page is **www.willclarkusa.com**, and his e-mail address is **willclark@aol.com**.
- **Max Grand.** This bodybuilder and porn star has a very large following. He can be reached at 310-298-3951.
- **Rich Raines.** The talk of Los Angeles. He advertises in the Frontiers and can paged at 213-397-6704.
- **Don.** Another very popular body builder at six foot and 235 pounds. He calls Los Angeles home but is also available in Chicago, Miami, Dallas, and Houston. The best method to reach him is through his web page at **http://members.aol.com/bbescort** or at 310-262-1000 or at **bbescort@aol.com**.
- **John.** Here is another choice for massage in Los Angeles. He is older and muscular, and has reasonable rates. He can be reached at **hardlamasg@aol.com** or 213-448-6303.
- **Brian.** This is a different Brian than the massage Brian. He has an excellent reputation and can be reached at **awsm4hire1@aol.com**. Clients have written to say he is everything his screen name says. His website is http://www.pantsdown.com/escorts/awsm.html.

## San Diego

- **Ryan Wagner.** This very popular porn star is very charming, and a lot of fun by all accounts. He is based in San Diego, but travels extensively. He can be reached at **RJWagner@aol.com**.

- **Kevin Williams.** This elusive porn legend is based in San Diego, but is primarily only available for travel clients. He is the stereotypical tall, blond and muscular Adonis with the all-American look. He can be reached through desertagnt@aol.com.
- **Reed Parker.** This 29 year-old escort is 5'10" and 160 pounds. This escort is reported to be reliable and sweet. He can be reached through e-mail at info@mindspring.com

## San Francisco

- **Tom Katt**. Currently in the Bay Area, but known to be in Los Angeles from time to time. He oftentimes advertises in the Frontiers. His pager number is 1-800-605-9605. He is definitely is known to be hard to reach.
- **Kirk**. This 25 year-old looks younger. He is very much kid at heart, and has a definite preference for older gentleman. He is disarming and cute. Well read and educated he is the ideal travel companion. He can be reached at **SFEscort25@aol.com** or at 415-207-1780.
- **Tom Howard**. A very popular escort in San Francisco. He advertises in the Bay Area Reporter. His pager number is 415-270-7896.
- **Jake**. One client describes this 6' and 170 pound escort as very sexy and very sweet. He can be reached at 415-679-1864 or e-mailed at topsfstud@aol.com.
- **Gavin**. Clients describe him as being very satisfying. He is 29 years old, 6' and 180 pounds. He can be reached at 415-902-9041 or e-mailed at **biggmann9@aol.com**.
- **Jim**. This tall, lean, and personable Asian top has been around for about ten years. Some things just improve with age. He can be reached at 415-267-1817.

## District of Columbia, Washington

- **Bryan.** Perhaps the most popular escort in Washington, D.C. He is reputed to be very sexy, very good at massage, and a super nice guy. He can be reached through his web site at **www.hotndc.com** or through e-mail at **hotndc@aol.com**.

- **Mark.** For those that like them tall, this is a good choice. He is 6'8" and 215 pounds. He can be reached at **dcstallion@aol.com** or at 888-556-9967.
- **Mike Maxx.** This bodybuilder gets nothing but praise. His web-site is **www.mikemaxx.com**. He can be reached at mrmikemaxx@aol.com..

## Florida

### Ft. Lauderdale

- **Bo.** If you are looking for southern charm this is the guy for you. He advertises in HotSpots Magazine as a handsome Alabama boy ready to relieve you of your tensions. He has no attitude and has a striking friendly look. He can be reached at **KinkXXX@aol.com** or at 954-460-6461.

### Miami

- **Chad Champion**. This six foot, 200 pound muscular blonde has the boy next door looks and attitude. He generally advertises in Hot Spots magazine. He can be reached by e-mail at **chad4rent@aol.com** or paged at 305-870-8300.
- **Jim Bentley**. This very popular escort is rumored to be in Miami, Los Angeles and San Francisco at various times. As with any of the top escorts he may advertise infrequently if at all.

### Tampa

- **Tony Cummings.** This sweet Southerner is extremely charming and very sensual. He can be reached at **tonycummings@hotmail.com**.

- **Chris Duffy (Bull Stanton).** This versatile 6'1" and 275 pound bodybuilder is an all time favorite of many clients. He advertises no attitude. Clients report he is prompt, courteous, reliable, and very professional. He can be reached at 727-336-8919 or e-mailed at **duffythebb@aol.com**.

## Hawaii, The Big Island

- **Matthew.** For the adventurous and the hardy there is no better experience than this kayaking tour and massage combination. Of course, before you go to Hawaii you might want to pick up his book The Rainbow Handbook to Hawaii. He can be reached at **MrLinkk@aol.com** or at 808-328-8406.

## Illinois, Chicago

- **KC.** This popular bodybuilder is rarely available for appointments. His clients describe him as awesome and extremely courteous. He is 5'9" and 235 pounds of ripped muscle. He can only be reached by e-mail at **soloflexkc@aol.com**.
- **Alan.** This slim smooth guy is considered one of the best in Chicago. His web site is **www.chicagoguy.com**. He can be reached at **wntcash@aol.com** or by phone at 773-665-4924.

## Louisiana, New Orleans

- **Todd.** This 21 year-old escort in New Orleans is 6' and 155 pounds. He can be reached at 504-524-5998 or at nolaescort@aol.com.

## Massachusetts, Boston

- **Cole Tucker.** Living proof some things get better with age. This 40 something model is very popular with clients of all ages that are looking for a real man. He can be reached through his web page at **www.cole-tucker.com**. His e-mail address is tuckerlive@aol.com.

- **Jon Ramsey**. Without any doubt, Jon is one of the top recommended escorts in the United States. He is 5'8", 175 pounds and in his late twenties. This escort consistently rates the highest in terms of professionalism and quality in every respect. He is typically available in Boston and New York. He can be reached through his web-site at **www.jonramsey.com**.

### Missouri, St. Louis

- **Tyler Kennedy**. This escort was formerly located in New York City, but has relocated back to St. Louis. He is a long time advertiser in Unzipped, and is definitely a nice guy. He can be reached at 314-960-7501.

### Nevada, Las Vegas

- **Damon Wolf**. Definitely one of the top escorts in the country he rarely advertises, and is primarily booked by travel clients. He sometimes advertises in Unzipped, and his pager number is 702-251-6896.
- **Alec Powers**. This popular blonde porn star seems to be everyone's dream date. He can be seen at his web site **www.alecpowers.com**.
- **Jay.** One of the few massage therapists on this list. He has been in the business a long time and has no signs of slowing down. He advertises in UnZipped magazine. He can be reached at 702-792-6632.
- **Jim.** This construction worker dude is as well known for his incredible personality as he is known for his heavy equipment. He can be reached at studdnutts@aol.com or at 702-378-5768.
- **Mario.** This Italian transplant is known for his infectious personality. He advertises on escorts4you and can be reached at mario3674@aol.com or 702-222-9589.

- **Greg Rockwell.** This porn star with the gymnast body has been in the business for a long time, and is still in his twenties. He can be reached at 1-800-796-6878.

### New Jersey

**Aaron Lawrence.** Aaron is a very talented individual. This young slender escort can be reached at 908-561-3412 or e-mailed at njescort@aol.com.

### New York, New York City

- **Dann.** This good-natured Australian attracts more New York City visitors than the Statue of Liberty. He is known for his great body and wonderful personality. He advertises in UnZipped and lists his number as 917-851-5250.
- **Nick.** This young latin escort apparently has a lot of happy clients. He can be reached through his web site **www.classactmt.com** or by paging him at 917-284-9865.
- **Mike.** This 5'10" and 175 pound escort is very popular. He can be reached through e-mail at mike4hire@aol.com or he advertises in UnZipped magazine.
- **JJ.** When size matters there is only one choice. I am oftentimes asked who is the escort with the largest penis. At over 13 documented inches this is your choice. He can be reached at **JonahNYnLA@mindspring.com** or at 212-563-4986.
- **Brandon.** This very popular escort advertises at hot, muscular, 26 years old, 6 foot, and 185 pounds. He advertises in Next and Hx magazines and can be reached at 917-782-7084.
- **Scott Matthews.** This blond porn star has a wonderful homepage at **www.nycguy.com**. Don't be intimidated by his classy marketing, he is a super nice guy. He can be reached at 917-701-7274 or at scottmatthews@nycguy.com.

### Utah, Salt Lake City

- **Jordan West.** This popular escort and porn star is definitely the all-American boy. He does not see very many clients, but when he does see a client they are very satisfied. He can reached at jordanwest@prodigy.net.

## Texas

### Austin

- **Austin.** This escort is highly recommended by clients. He is considered affectionate and cuddly. He advertises in Unzipped and can be reached at **travelboy1@aol.com** or at 1-800-910-6452.

### Dallas

- **Ty O'Brien.** This all-American type has a good following in Dallas. He can be seen at **www.dfwmale.com** or contacted at **maledfw@aol.com**.
- **Kohl.** Charming and fun are two ways to describe this escort according to clients. He is 5'9" and 165 pounds. He can be reached at **escortkohl@aol.com** or 214-219-1559. His web page is www.escortkohl.com.

### San Antonio

- **Karl Thomas.** This popular porn star is pretty much retired, but still sees an occasional travel client. Travel appointments are arranged through **desertagnt@aol.com**.

## Canada

- **Kurt Rosser.** This real man escort is based in Calgary, but travels quite a bit. He is a body builder and very much into the outdoors. He can be reached at flex4hire@aol.com.

# Chapter Twenty-One

# Reader Feedback

This book is a result of thousands of interviews and encounters with individuals in the sex industry over more than twenty years. I want to expand the book in the next edition to include the following:

- A review of international markets.
- Letters from escorts, clients, participants in the male sex industry, and other observers of the male sex industry.
- Refinement of my observations based on the experiences of others.
- Reader comments on their experiences with establishments listed in the appendixes.
- Anything else interesting or relevant.

Letters or information on how to order this book may be sent to:

The Insider's Guide
4640 Paradise Road

Suite 15-123
Las Vegas, NV  89109

I can be reached by e-mail at:

Bestofvgs@aol.com

You do not need to provide your name or any other
information.  Letters will be published without attribution unless
otherwise instructed.  All letters will be become the property of
the Insider's Guide.

"I was pleased to see that I was doing a lot of things right, but also saw some of the things I was doing wrong.  I look forward to seeing my hobby grow.  Thanks for giving the pointers and support I really needed right about now."
*New escort response from reading the book*

"You are absolutely correct about your observations, of the porn industry."
*Male Adult Film Star*

I received a copy of Hustler, Escorts, and Porn Stars in today's mail.  Up to that point, I had been pretty industrious, but the next three hours were given over to pure pleasure.  You tell a good story with some interesting details and some useful information, included.
*Escort Client*

I found your book to be illuminating, insightful, amusing, and entertaining.
*Escort Client*

# Order Form

To order an additional copy of Hustlers, Escorts and Porn Stars, The Insider's Guide to Male Prostitution in America please send $16.95 to:

Insider's Guide
4640 Paradise Rd.
Suite 15-123
Las Vegas, NV  89109

Name: _____
Address: _____
City: _____ State: _____ Zip: _____

Credit Card: Amex  Visa Mastercard
Credit Card Number: _____
Expiration Date: _____
Signature: _____

Credit card orders are processed by Get Booked. For bookstore ordering, bulk orders or other inquiries we may be reached at (702) 435-0970 or e-mailed at bestofvgs@aol.com.

"Never before has a book been published that demystifies, destigmatizes, and legitimizes the male sex industry and prostitution such as this one does. This book reads as a "how to" or "user's guide" to male prostitution, but is interesting social commentary for anyone who may be interested in the subject. I would strongly recommend it as an adjunct text in any field of gay studies. Adams outlines the various forms of male prostitution, including massage therapy, street hustling, elite escorts, body builders, leather, and the porn industry."
*Orange County Blade*

"The shadowy world of the male sex industry has always been a source of speculation and fascination in our culture. With his new book, Hustlers, Escorts, and Porn Stars, The Insider's Guide to Male Prostitution in America, author Matt Adams dispels the myths and superstitions of the subject and presents only the cold, hard facts."
*Out Front Colorado*

# Order Form

To order an additional copy of Hustlers, Escorts and Porn Stars, The Insider's Guide to Male Prostitution in America please send $16.95 to:

Insider's Guide
4640 Paradise Rd.
Suite 15-123
Las Vegas, NV  89109

Name: _____

Address: _____

City: _____ State: _____ Zip: _____

Credit Card: Amex  Visa Mastercard

Credit Card Number: _____

Expiration Date: _____

Signature: _____

Credit card orders are processed by Get Booked. For bookstore ordering, bulk orders or other inquiries we may be reached at (702) 435-0970 or e-mailed at bestofvgs@aol

"This book is an unabashed, unadulterated, uncensored look at a world that many guys out there don't want to believe, or acknowledge that it exists. After reading this book, you'll undeniably know what hustling is all about in every way, shape, form, and position."
*Mickey Skee, author Best of Gay Adult Video, Companion Press*

"Hustlers, Escorts, and Porn Stars is the only handbook you'll ever need to travel into the underbelly of the male sex trade. Whether you are buying, selling, or just doing research, author Matt Adams brings a strange honor and dignity into the world of male prostitution. Propelled by twenty years of experience the author brushes aside the moral disputation, and attacks the subject from the inside out. Travel this taboo highway, and enjoy the ride into the world of the male prostitute."
*Peter Scott, Adult Film Star Superagent*